CONTROVERSY
OF ZION

By THE SAME AUTHOR

Le Prince et le Prophète	Jerusalem 1966
The Prince and the Prophet	Helsinki 1979
	Jerusalem 1979
Périple africain	Jerusalem 1969
Pour l'amour de Sion	Jerusalem 1970
Le Sionisme de Dieu	Paris 1970
	Jerusalem 1972
Lettre de Jérusalem à une demoiselle maoïste	Paris 1972
Jésus et la Communauté nazaréenne (Doctoral thesis)	Jerusalem 1974
Sur tes murailles Jérusalem	Jerusalem 1976
Moïse (Honoured by the Académie Française)	Paris 1977
Moses	Hambourg 1977
Compagnon de la Parousie	Jerusalem 1978
L'Apocalypse a déjà commencé	Neuchatel 1980
Qui a tué Jésus?	Neuchatel 1981
Scandaleux Jésus	Neuchatel 1984

CONTROVERSY OF ZION

A Biblical view of the history and meaning of Zion

CLAUDE DUVERNOY

Translated from French by:
Johanan Eldad

New Leaf Press

P.O. BOX 311, GREEN FOREST, AR 72638

New Leaf Press Edition
1987

Typesetting: A.G.A.P.E. Graphics and Printing
Berryville, Arkansas

Library of Congress: 86-63886
ISBN: 0-89221-144-X

CONTENTS

FOREWORD: Dr. David Flusser   7
FOREWORD: David Allen Lewis   9

PART ONE: From The Origins to the Prophets

I   The Vision of History in Antiquity   12

II   The Biblical Concept of History   16

III   Zionism in the Hebrew Bible   23

IV   The Dialectics of Exile and Return in Israel's Prophetic Writings   44

V   General Conclusion   69

PART TWO: From Jesus to Herzl

I   The Zionist Climate at the Time of Jesus   74
The Jewish Diaspora. The messianic hope in Israel. Jesus and the messianic mystery. The temptation of the crown. The great temptation in Jerusalem. The messianic misunderstanding. The zionist vision of Jesus. The messianic birth-pangs.

II   The Apostle Paul's Zionism   92

III   The Church and Israel   96

IV   Zionism before Theodor Herzl   109
In the Talmud. In the prayer-book of the Synagogue. In the Psalms of Ascent. In the Passover Haggadah. The false hopes. Forgotten Jerusalem. The zionist Rabbis.

V   The Zionist Significance of Israel's Martyrdom   133

**PART THREE: The Resurrection of Israel or
The Beginning of the Messianic Era**

I   The Zionist Turning Point of Contemporary History   140
The Balfour Declaration. The betrayal. The White Paper of 1939 The birth-pangs, 1948. The Sinai campaign, 1956. The Six-Day War, 1967. The Yom Kippur war and its consequences, 1973. The hard way towards Redemption.

II   The Spiritual Crisis in Israel   166

III   Prophetical Aspects of the State of Israel   177
      The ingathering of the Exiles. The renaissance of the Hebrew
      language. The communal life. The revival of the Negev. The
      biblical revival. The aid to the new nations.

IV   The Church in the Israeli Nation   198

V   The Eschatological Significance of Israel   203
      The beginning of sufferings. The Gospel preached to the world.
      The Abomination on Temple Mount. Cosmic troubles and the
      messianic Parousia.

VI   A Definition of Zionist Theology   215

FOREWORD
By Dr. David Flusser

"The Controversy of Zion" seems to me a highly important work, in particular for the non-Jewish reader. It has repeatedly been said that there can be no free dialogue between Christians and Jews unless the Christians understand how the Jew himself experiences his Judaism.

The author makes it very clear that the idea of the Jewish people's return to the Holy Land has always been at the heart of authentic Jewish thought. It should be kept in mind that the majority of contemporary Jews, throughout the world, have linked their fate to that of Zion with stronger bonds than ever before since the destruction of the Temple. For the Return is no longer an eschatological dream, but historical reality.

The brilliant pages in Claude Duvernoy's book devoted to the Hebrew Bible and the New Testament alike show that the idea of Return is a central motif of the biblical writings. Today these texts speak for themselves, but let us not forget that for centuries Christian theological tradition used to regard these prophecies as religious utterances which had become invalid in the wake of the appearance of Jesus. This tradition still has its adherents, but is becoming increasingly indefensible.

Isn't it, indeed, a conspicuous fact that this new approach to the Bible (characterized by its respect for the received text) coincides with the resurrection of the Jewish people in its Land?

The author stresses that the Return to Zion was already announced by the prophets of the First Temple period, and that this "Zionist" hope was not extinguished after the Babylonian but, on the contrary, was very much alive during the inter-testamental era, as is attested by the following fragments from the 13th chapter of the Book of Tobit:

> And He will scourge us for our iniquities, and will have mercy again, and will gather us out of all nations, among whom He has scattered us... O Jerusalem, the Holy City, He will scourge thee for thy children's work, and will have mercy again on the sons of the righteous.
> Give praise to the Lord, for He is good; and praise the everlasting King, that His tabernacle may be builded again with joy, and let Him make joyful there in thee those that are captive, and love in thee for ever those that are miserable.
> Many nations shall come from far to the name of the Lord God with gifts in their hands, even gifts to the King of Heaven; all generations shall praise thee with great joy, and the name of Jerusalem shall be exalted for ever and ever...

We see that the hope of Return is an indissoluble part of the universalist message in the wisdom literature and the prohetical writings alike.

It is well known by which mortal dangers Israel and Judaism were threatened under the reign of Antiochus Epiphanes, but not many are aware of the real nature of the Maccabean expectations. It may therefore be useful to quote a fragment from the Second Book of Maccabees, where Judah addresses the Jews of Egypt in the following words:

> Whereas we then are about to celebrate the Purification of the temple, we have written unto you, and ye shall do well, if ye keep the same days. We hope also that the God, who delivered all his people, and gave them all a heritage, and the kingdom, and the priesthood, and the sanctuary, as He promised in the Torah will shortly have mercy upon us, and gather us together out of every land under heaven into the Holy Land: for He hath delivered us out of great troubles, and hath purified the Temple.
>
> (2:16–18)

In addition to these fragments from the Book of Tobit and the second Book of Maccabees (which are both included in the canon of the Catholic Church), we follow the example of the author of this book and quote from the words of Jesus as well, to show that his hopes were the same as those of the fathers: that God will one day gather the Jews together *from their dispersion among the nations:*

> And they shall come from the east, and from the west, and from the north, and the south, and shall sit down in the Kingdom of God."
>
> (Luke 13:29)

The author also calls attention to Jesus' prophecy, likewise mentioned by Luke (21:24), concerning the fulfillment of "the times of the Gentiles," when Jerusalem will be returned to the heritage of Israel.

With Albert Schweitzer and the author of this book we are convinced that Jesus' eschatological expectations were exactly those of the biblical prophets.

Without dwelling at length on the arguments and elaborations of Claude Duvernoy, I wish to emphasize that every theologian should comprehend that nothing in the New Testament contradicts the Divine promises to Israel in the Hebrew Bible. To be sure, no man knows "of that day and that hour."

Let us be grateful to the author, himself a Christian theologian, for having so passionately and rightfully elucidated that the recent developments in the Middle East affirm the faith and hope of Israel. Let us hope that the beliefs and expectations of the Christians be equally fortified by them, for all that unfolds before our eyes is no less in conformity with the prophetical message of the New Testament.

Professor David Flusser
The Hebrew University of Jerusalem

FOREWORD
By Dr. David Allen Lewis

All the world's heavy artillery seems to be trained on the tiny nation of Israel. Zechariah's prognostication that Jerusalem would be a "cup of trembling" was never more appropriate than in our time. The People's Republic of China has the largest population of all the nations in the world, yet receives only a fraction of the media coverage that is directed upon Israel with its miniscule population of less than four million souls. Further, Israel represents less than one percent of the land mass of the entire Middle East, yet commands a lion's share of the world's attention.

What curious phenomenon is it that promotes such bias and slanted reporting in the secular and even much of the religious press when it comes to discussion of Israel and the Jewish people? What is going on in our world? What produces the great *Controversy of Zion?* And controversy there is. Whether one agrees with anything else Duvernoy says, one must agree that this is one of the great and distressing issues of our times. Is the *Controversy of Zion* an apocalyptic sign as the author indicates or merely a bothersome thorn in the flesh of humanity?

In a day when strange "new wave theologies" are sweeping through the churches, this clarion call to biblical truth comes as needed illumination of the timeless truths of scripture. Indeed, those who are carelessly embracing theological anti-semitism in the form of the doctrine of replacement, indicating that since the church has taken the place of Israel that God has no more purpose for the Jewish people, will find in these pages a strong challenge to re-assess some of these digressions from scripture being promulgated in high places in the church world.

Jewish people who want to understand the point of view held by those Christians who accept the authority of the Bible will benefit from reading the *Controversy of Zion.* The widespread use of this book will promote yet another step forward in ongoing Jewish-Christian dialogue and understanding.

Seldom is a book of this importance brought to the Christian public. The publishing industry is surely appealing to the least common denominator of Christian values when the current four "best selling" books are "Christian" romance novels! They will pass from the scene, forgotten, but the *Controversy of Zion* will be around for a long time.

Duvernoy carries you through the Bible's major stream of history relating to Zion, the Jewish People and the Land of Israel. The scope of this book is truly staggering. His claim that the message of Zion is a theology of history is well proven.

Supporters of Israel are frequently accused of overlooking her faults. Not so with Duvernoy! As the maxim is true, "faithful are the wounds of a friend," here it is exemplified. The author speaks to us not only the calling and glory of Israel, but also what he perceives to be some of her present flaws. But this is couched in the language of hope for tomorrow and never with despair or a sense of bitter rejection.

The *Controversy of Zion* could well become a standard textbook for the Christian who supports Israel, not because she is perfect, but for the sake of the Word of God; yes for the sake of the Almighty Himself.

Some may take issue with the author's political slant or his eschatological views, but this in itself is an answer to those who think that only people from a certain political camp or from a certain prophetic tradition could support Israel.

I enthusiastically endorse this work and encourage its distribution and use. Every Bible College and Seminary should incorporate it into its required textbook list. Classes on Jewish-Christian matters can profitably study this text.

The concept of Zion is first and foremost a Biblical, not a political, concept. Most simply defined, it is the idea that God who owns the whole earth can sovereignly grant any portion of it to whomsoever He wills. He has given the land of Israel to the descendants of Jacob for all of time. The Jewish people have returned to the land of their fathers as a direct fulfillment of God's will and Word. Duvernoy points out that the return is in stages: first the physical return, the national restoration, and then the full spiritual recovery in the messianic age (Ezekiel 36-39). That the Bible is absolutely unerring in it's accuracy should be a comfort to the Christian who claims the Bible as his text for all of life's issues.

If the modern day children of Israel, after the Holocaust, have returned to the land with a certain bitterness of spirit, even hardness of heart and even unbelief (and this certainly is true of only a portion of the populace of the land), this should not come as any surprise to the student of God's Word — for that is exactly the way the prophets said it would be.

Along with many rabbis and Jewish leaders we look for the day of the spiritual renewal that is coming to Israel, so remarkable in its effect that the prophet Zechariah says that God will "remove iniquity from the land in one day." Since that has certainly not been fulfilled historically we look then for its eschatological fulfillment. We lift our voices with the rabbis who are crying out the slogan "We want Moshiach *NOW!*"

David Allen Lewis
President: Christians United For Israel

PART ONE

FROM THE ORIGINS
TO THE PROPHETS

"The sun rises at thy will, the water of the rivers — we drink it when thou willst, the air of heaven — we breathe it when thou speakest."

(Herodotus, on Pharaoh)

"I set fire to their artfully built houses and made the smoke thereof rise up as in a storm, covering the face of heaven."

(Sargon II, Chronicles)

"Plato emphasizes that it is the master's interest to treat his slave well. He regards the slave as a simple brute, but this brute may not revolt against his condition of servility, for according to his philosophy it is the result of an inequality which is in the nature of things. He admits therefore that 'the brute' should be treated well, but specifies: 'For our sake, rather than for his own...'"
"War, according to Aristotle, is the hunt for human beings, who, though born to obey, refuse to submit."

(André Bonnard: *Civilisation grecque*, I,
pp. 137, 145.
La Guilde du Livre, Lausanne)

"And what great nation is there, that hath statutes and ordinances so righteous as all these laws, which I set before you this day?

(Deuteronomy 4:8)

11

I

THE VISION OF HISTORY IN ANTIQUITY

Zionism, when approached from the biblical angle, reveals a specific vision of history. When it is regarded under its political aspect alone — which is nearly always the case — it is reduced to a mere contingency of history and, to the historian, to nothing but a meagre chapter in the multiple and contradictory events which have convulsed the entire Middle East since the 19th century.

Zionism rests entirely on the specific, Jewish concept of history and has, from the onset, been a logical link in the chain of what is known as sacred history. Theologians have never accorded to the word 'sacred' the meaning of 'perfect', but have understood it in its strict sense of 'set apart', which is something different altogether. It is precisely because Israel is a people 'set apart' that its history is different from that of other nations. Every honest historian realizes this and knows that he faces a historical enigma when encountering Israel's past. Hence, the modest place always assigned to Jewish history in the handbooks of general history. When one considers the tremendous role of the books ascribed to Moses in the sociological context of their time, one can only be amazed about the silence surrounding them. Indeed, one is inclined to speak of a conspiracy of silence. For was it not Israel which, through the mouth of Moses, was the first in history to call for social justice, equality and brotherly love? The first to advance the concept of one Creator-God who works in the world not in order to amuse himself or to play with human beings, as in all cosmogonies of Antiquity, but for man's happiness and his ultimate salvation?

It is evident that such a message implies a very distinct concept of history which is neither imperialistic nor fatalistic or absurd. But what Moses and the prophets really offered the world was not just a certain concept, but rather a *theology of history*, unlike anything advanced by Israel's powerful neighbors, the giants of whose exploits and power Antiquity resounds.

Let us therefore briefly review the historical concepts that were current in ancient Egypt, Sumer, Athens and Rome.

EGYPT

Endless lists of kings and great men; marvellous monuments erected for the glory of the Pharaohs; 'revised and corrected' accounts of the sovereign's great military victories — these are the sources for a study of this chapter of history.

The theological myths introduce us to a court of rival and cruel gods, similar to all other courts of this type, but with one specifically Egyptian feature: animal images. Pharaoh is the incarnation of the divine and his will can never be disputed. He makes and shapes history at will. Adversities and defeats are not recorded by his scribes (who do not deserve the title of historian), but his conquests, the razed cities, the massacred and enslaved populations vie with each other for a place on the bas-reliefs, steles, pillars and stones of ancient Egypt.

History had, consequently, no meaning. Even the Egyptian language had no equivalent for our word 'history'. After all, the Egyptians were the natives of an isolated country surrounded by seas and deserts; their daily life depended on the whims and fancies of a father-river who turned this country into one great and fantastic avenue of teeming mankind. Such a geographical situation left little room for a philosophy of history, which was already ruled out by the worship of a divine Pharaoh. What we do find here is downright fatalism and absolute imperialism incessantly nourished by the pride of the Pharaohs and sustained and encouraged by a multitude of court-priests who were themselves little inclined to accord a meaning to the future beyond the static present.

Past, present and future merge in the deified person of the sovereign. Death alone stirs the imagination and stimulates spiritual life, and thus becomes the real substitute of the future.

SUMER

Mesopotamia introduced an ethical element into history by demanding that every man, including the sovereign himself, live in harmony with the laws of the universe and the gods. Peace and success depend therefore on faithful observance of the ritual, while catastrophes and defeats are the automatic consequences of a serious disrupture of the cosmic harmony. This cosmic relationship could have given an entirely new meaning to history, if it had expressed itself in terms of a *Creator–Earth*. But as in Egypt and, for that matter, everywhere else except in Israel, the divine world is conceived as an analogy of the world of man; the many gods are engaged in endless wars, usually at the expense of man.

The real heartbeat of what might be called Sumerian history is the past. Man must behave in such a manner that the Flood will not recur. But since he can never be sure of the laws which reign the universe, nor of the caprices of the gods, his vision of the future is inevitably fatalistic and pessimistic. As in Egypt imperialism triumphs, drawing its inspiration and power from the mythical ancestor Gilgamesh who may perhaps be identified with the Nimrod of Genesis, the first empire-builder and maker of history.

Unlike in Egypt, however, in Sumer the king is not the incarnation of the divine, but rather the mediator between man and the powers of the universe. In this sense he is accountable and, to a certain degree, a redeemer. But nothing could prevent the destruction of Nineveh or the fall of Babylon; and thus the absurdity of history is revealed. History becomes the frozen — albeit happy — past. It is reduced to the nostalgic memory of a Golden Age which will never return.

ATHENS

Herodotus, the inventor of the term 'history', assigned to the historian a unique task, namely to ferret out the past systematically. He went to Egypt where he met the priests of Thebes. Like his predecessor Hecate he was deeply impressed with the three hundred and forty-five aristocratic generations of Egypt.

There is no doubt that it was characteristic of the Greek historians to accord a tragic note to history: the Golden Age belongs to the past and the subsequent conquests and victories were not worth the blood that was shed. Plato counters this introduction of the tragic with his myth of the *perfect king* who is also the wise legislator, and this move represents the great attempt of Antiquity to assign to history a meaning beyond the tragic and absurd. The premature death of Alexander the Great spoiled the beautiful dream of the Greeks (which Rome subsequently tried to arrogate to itself with the sword and fire of its legions).

Even though the Greek historians had, in general, shaken off the yoke which the gods and the mysterious laws of the universe imposed on their Egyptian and Sumerian colleagues, they still had to wrestle with human nature which drove them to ever new struggles the bitterness of which was never entirely alleviated by victory. "There have always been wars and there will always be wars," is doubtless an adage of Greek pessimism. But the Greek historian wrestled no less with the inexorable absurdity of death which cuts down a man like Alexander when he is about to establish a regime of universal peace and brotherhood on earth (as in heaven?)

Thus Greek history is like a wheel which cannot be halted by anything, but rolls on forever along the same highways and over the same blood-stained cities, further and further away from the Golden Age, that is lost forever.

ROME

Where Alexander could not succeed Rome was triumphant; it became master of the world, but cared little for Plato's ideal of the philosopher-king. Its atmosphere is imbued with cynicism and the desire to enjoy the fruits of victory here and now. History is consequently elevated to the level of a science charged with the sole task of gathering the past events in order to derive from them the maximum inspiration and comfort for the present and its vicissitudes. In this sense the Roman concept of history concurs with that of ancient Egypt. The glory and power of Caesar must for ever be engraved in stone, in gigantic edifices. It is the legions which make history and which, before long, will make and unmake the Emperors. The wheel rolls along the network of Roman roads which covers the world. May it roll along as long as possible! Who knows? By rolling thus along the Roman highway, proclaim the magicians, the astrologers and the sybils, the wheel of history will, perhaps, one day return to the Golden Age of the days of yore... Thus they accord a meaning to life, for it is unthinkable that this Empire, built for eternity, will ever collapse...

The imperialistic vision of history became thus triumphant in Rome, but together with it the anguished feeling of man that death is not the only risk he runs, not the only danger which undermines his structure of pride and power. In its decline Rome despairs by and large of its ability to find a satisfactory meaning in history.

However, a small people within this Empire had for a moment raised its voice to proclaim that history does have a meaning, that the Golden Age, far from being a frozen memory of the past, is man's destiny towards which he marches forward. This new message did not come through easily from the obscure city lost in the mountains of Judea. The Jewish sense of history had no room for Caesar, nor for the gods of Rome and was therefore not likely to stir the imagination of the legionaries. Before long the Roman eagles were hoisted on the ruins of Jerusalem, the plough drew its Roman furrows in which, as in Carthage, salt was sown so that this most rebellious of cities would never again rise from its ashes...

Such was Rome's encounter with Jerusalem, more than once. That Jerusalem will never dare again to proclaim the truth to Rome!

Such is — and such will always be — the response of the nations, in their imperialistic self-delusion, to this people which is the sole holder of history's keys. In their gross ineptitude to decipher the writ of history the nations conspire persistently to ban this people from history, this very people which holds the keys to history's vaults, and this very city, Jerusalem the capital, which is history's magnetic center. No wonder that it is said in the Psalms that the Master of history laughs...

II

THE BIBLICAL CONCEPT OF HISTORY

History has an origin, bereshit, it has a direction, just as the ripening of the tree is directed towards the fruit... Biblical metaphysics, like Bergsonian thought, is a philosophy of the germ. It is not mathematical, but rather biological... The Scriptures are metaphysics and theology in the form of a historical narrative...

Claude Tresmontan, *Essai sur la pensée hebraique*, pp. 35, 45, 70)
Editions du Cerf, Paris 1956

The ancient cosmogonies tell us of the beginning of history — or in other words, the story of creation — in obscure terms. The gods are themselves the prey of primeval chaos and divided among each other; it is clear that from such stories no historical sense can develop.

The opening chapters of Genesis, on the other hand, breathe such a majesty, such a sense of victory over chaos, such a harmony of will of ancient narratives, we can only be captivated and admit: indeed, these page are inspired by a spirit entirely different from the human imagination, however poetical the latter often may be. It is obvious that a clear and unique concept of history is at the root of these first pages of the Hebrew Bible.

Since all things came into being through the word of the one and only Creator, one Will directs history and no cosmic or other intervention will be able to withstand it. Nor will it be human beings who shape history, neither the Pharaohs, nor the Caesars of this world, but their designs must be in harmony with the will of the Creator. Finally — and this finds unequivocal expression in the first chapter of Genesis — man is placed in the center of creation to dominate it and to be happy in it. From the beginning man was placed in a face-to-face relationship, in a dialogue with his Maker. He is known, beloved. He is protected, even in his revolt Adam does not die (as has been wrongly understood) in his shame. This is revealed in the beautiful story of the garments with which God covers him when, after the Fall, he suddenly becomes aware of his nakedness. Even Cain in his crime is not destroyed by God, but "marked" to be safe-guarded against vengeance and arbitrary punishment. True, Adam's fall puts the Golden Age of Eden behind man, but God lets it be known to the rebel, to the criminal, that the game is nevertheless not over, although an unbridgeable gap henceforth separates creation and Creator, and the paradisiac dialogue becomes extremely difficult.

But the dialogue is nevertheless maintained, whatever may happen. It is maintained with the generation of the Flood as with the generation of Sodom and Gomorrah. Adam and Eve, in the mysterious promise of ultimate victory over the serpent, Noah and his family in the midst of the Flood, Abraham and Lot in the cataclysm of the Dead Sea — they are all witnesses and beacons of a history that is guided from Above and is neither imperialistic, nor obscure or absurd. God does not want man to vanish from the face of the earth and with him his work and civilization. God wants man to regain the conditions of the Garden of Eden and, if need be, He will even force him towards salvation.

Such is the situation, such is the historical concept of the Hebrew Bible, long before the Jewish people makes it appearance, against the will of the nations, on the stage of history.

SOME PROBLEMS POSED BY THE ELECTION
OF ISRAEL

From the secular point of view, or more precisely, from the point of view of the Egyptians and the Canaanites, the pretentions of the Jewish people since its appearance on the stage of history seem to justify strong reservations and even objections.

After all, Egypt, too, claimed to be 'elected', if only because of the divine nature of its Pharaoh, and so did a fair number of other, more or less theophorous nations, nations which had proved their 'election' by their conquests, their wealth and culture. Why then should this YHVH, of whom nobody had ever heard, impose his authority on the nations with more right than other gods who had a more brilliant and established history? Moreover, these Jews, led by the mysterious Moses, a renegade of the pharaonic court, were nothing but a bunch of mutinous slaves. Had it ever before been seen for slaves who had broken their bonds to claim national, let alone cultural independence? Could this be anything but ludicrous in the eyes of the aristocrats and priests of Memphis and Thebes?

First outrage: these Jewish slaves demanded for themselves a place under the sun, a place in history.

And what about the land of Canaan? Did not its very name indicate that it belonged to a people which had also passed the test? It is true that in those days people were not sentimental about political and imperialistic conquests. The law of the strongest was then already common law. But the point is that it was a band of slaves, the personal property of Pharaoh, mutinous slaves and therefore twice criminals, who suddenly appeared before the walls of Jericho!

Second outrage: these Jewish slaves seized a fertile country inhabited by its legitimate population.

But even if we admit their right to revolt and allow that the law of the strongests applies to this people as well, even if we accept military conquest by such an unconventional strategy — what about their outrageous religious pretentions? Who had ever heard of a comparable scandal? At the most, some room may be allocated to this God of Israel, provided he keeps quiet in his own corner (a little lightning from time to time on Mount Sinai, maybe, but nothing more...). Isn't it enough to admit that these mutinous slaves are entitled to worship their tribal god? Isn't that sufficiently magnanimous?

But the more one gives in to this contemptible Israel, the more it demands. It even wants to impose its god on the whole world, foolishly claiming that he is the only one and that all other deities are but witless, man-made idols. How can one get along with such a people, let alone support it? Wouldn't it be much more expedient to join forces and declare war on it, to destroy it once and for all?

Third outrage: the God of Israel is proclaimed the only One.

In such or similar words might the Egyptians and Canaanites have expressed their legitimate point of view...

How, on the other hand, was the biblical point of view put into words? Or, in other words, how did the Creator Himself, as the sole Master of history, tell the nations why He had chosen the Jewish people? With these two statements:

> The Lord did not set His love upon you, nor choose you, because ye were more in number than any people — for ye were the fewest of all peoples — *but because the Lord loved you?*

and

> Praise the Lord! Proclaim His name! *Declare His doings among the peoples...*

The explanation of Deuteronomy (7:7–8) and the solemn call of Isaiah (12:4) are God's response to the indignation of the nations. If it consisted only of the first part — 'because I love you' — it would be a poor argument merely suited to arouse the hostility of the nations even more. 'Favorites' have never an odor of sanctity about them, neither in the family circle, nor in the classroom or anywhere else. On this point the Bible is very explicit: Israel is not the 'little favored one', but the first-born who is charged with a heavy responsibility towards his brothers and sisters. True, he is beloved, particularly beloved, but never at the expense of others. He is especially precious to the Father, *because* of the others, *because* of his special ministry among the others.

Against Egypt and Babylon Israel could obviously never claim the right of the strongest. Even against Canaan it could not do so, for the military experience and power of the Canaanites were infinitely superior to those of these Jewish tribes who had no training worth speaking of.

But in the midst of a world that was at the mercy of its idols and their barbarous cults, in the midst of a society corrupted by slavery of every type, Israel received the commandment to proclaim the existence and the Will of the God of love, truth and *justice*. The least one can say is that this commandment is certainly not a sinecure and the Jewish people would subsequently have reason enough to appreciate this. If the idols are the work of man, their priests and all who depend on them, will know how to defend this unenlightened system.

Before long, however, some of Israel's neighbors came to realize that this people was indeed not like others. In one of the most difficult chapters of the Hebrew Bible we find proof of this awareness. When the Jewish people, under the leadership of Moses, had left the desert of Sinai behind them, they were preceded by ominous and contradictory rumors of the miraculous circumstances of their exodus from Egypt and their victory over Pharaoh's armies. Balak, the king of Moab, had heard of the crushing defeat of the kings of the Amorites and Basan. As a member of an alliance against Israel he was hardly in a position to allow Moses free passage through his country, but he feared, he had a foreboding, that his turn to be defeated had come. He therefore sought to employ the services of Balaam, the most famous diviner of the period. His messenger to Balaam, on the borders of the Euphrates, entreated him as follows:

> Come now therefore, I pray thee, curse me this people... for I know that he whom thou blessed is blessed, and he whom thou cursest is cursed.
>
> (Numbers 22:6)

Initially Balaam refused, for a divine oracle had revealed to him that this Jewish people was under the special protection of their God. Or perhaps, in a subtle manner, he tried to blackmail king Balak. The latter sends indeed a second, more important delegation with more and richer gifts, and this time Balaam starts on his way riding his famous she-ass...

On a high place, from where the Moabite dignitaries, together with the king and Balaam, overlook the plain where Israel has put up its temporary encampment, the diviner speaks these words:

> How shall I curse, whom God hath not cursed? And how shall I execrate, whom the Lord hath not execrated? Far from the hills I behold him: Lo, it is a people that shall dwell alone, And shall not be reckoned among the nations...
>
> (Numbers 23:8–10)

The deceived and infuriated king demands a second oracle, of which the following words are particularly striking, coming as they do from the mouth of the most famous diviner of a period which teemed with sooth-sayers:

> For these is no enchantment against Jacob. Neither is there any divination against Israel...

Balak, in his desperation, then prays Balaam to grant him at least this: if you cannot curse this accursed people, please, do not bless it! But this

19

'fuehrer' has no luck, for he is compelled to listen to these words:

> How goodly are thy tents, o Jacob Thy dwellings, o Israel! As
> valleys stretched out, As gardens by the river-side As aloes
> planted by the Lord... Blessed be every one that blesseth thee
> And cursed be every one that curseth thee.
>
> (Numbers 24:5, 6, 9)

To the indignation of the deceived king the diviner then delivers a final blow by disclosing the future destiny of Israel. For the first time the famous House of David is mentioned, whose scion shall one day in the history of the nations fulfill the Will of the Creator and, as we have said before, lead the world towards salvation.

> The saying of Balaam, the son of Beor... The saying of him who
> heareth the words of God, And knoweth the knowledge of the
> Most High... I see him, but not nigh; There shall step forth a star
> out of Jacob, And a sceptre shall rise out of Israel...
>
> (Numbers 24:15–17)

The diviner seems to know the history of the twelve Jewish tribes quite well and his parable is, in fact, merely a paraphrase of Jacob's blessing of Judah:

> The sceptre shall not depart from Judah, Nor the ruler's staff
> from between his feet Until He shall come to Whom it
> belongeth... and unto Him shall the obedience of the people be.

Thus, all through these difficult chapters 23 and 24 of the Book of Numbers, with their story of the frustration of one of the many 'fuehrers' of history who tried to liquidate the Jewish people, Israel's place in history and its role among the nations are clearly defined. On the one hand the Jewish people shall, nolens volens, always remain 'apart' in the midst of the nations — that is it will never be able to assimilate — and on the other it is rewarded with its awesome and unique elections: to be a light unto the nations, a light whose source is in the very nature of the Creator. Only this explicit mission can explain the mystery of Israel's history and survival. If the God of Israel had given His people the Land of Canaan merely for love's sake, He would have been but one among the many deities of the period, a mere pretext for a classic imperialistic policy of conquest and national pride. All the idols of ancient history, up to the time of the Roman Empire, were the 'protectors' of the worst undertakings of the princes, and the 'guarantees' for their military, economic and — secondarily — cultural accomplishments. If one God of Sinai had merely been an invention and an asset of the Jewish priests and princes and as such the justification of Israel's power and conquests, He would surely have been buried, along with his fellow-deities, in the handbooks of ancient history and in museums; and the Jewish people would certainly have vanished in the haze of history as so many other, much more powerful peoples. Nor would it have occurred to anybody that there is a land which was promised to

Israel. But this Promised Land does exist, and is the earthly dwelling place of the Jewish people from where, for better for worse, it has propagated the knowledge of the Creator and Master of History among the nations of the world and in particular throughout the Roman Empire. Zion was not given to Israel for sentimental reasons, but first and foremost because out of this City must go forth the light of redemption into the darkness of idolatry and totalitarianism.

God uses human channels to guide history towards salvation, for it is to human beings that He addresses Himself. Indeed, Israel was not the first of God's 'experiments'. Adam and Eve in the Garden of Eden — who were not the first living creatures, but the first who were *conscious of God's existence* — were the first through whom the Holy Will of God was revealed in history. They were followed by the antediluvian patriarchs, among whom Enoch deserves special regard. Then came Noah and his family. They were the first 'elected' — and they were not Jews! But individuals alone cannot prepare the world for God's pedagogy. What is needed is a community, a people, which cannot be wiped out by anything or anyone, but will never cease walking with God, literally hand in hand with Him, through revolts and debacles, even through apostasy. This is why this mysterious — and to historians unfathomable — people has not vanished. For He cannot vanish who has extended His hand to this people since the first adventure with a man named Abram, since this first Zionist adventure...

AN ATTEMPT AT A BIBLICAL DEFINITION
OF HISTORY

Let us begin by stressing what, from the biblical point of view, history cannot be.

It cannot be eternal renewal as, for example, in the Greek concept of a historical cycle. The ancient and depressing dictum: 'There have always been wars, and there will always be wars,' has no place in biblical wisdom. The succession of empires, revolutions and catastrophes is not arbitrary.

It cannot be chaotic and absurd. It has a beginning in which its 'meaning' becomes manifest. It has a point of break-through.

It is not delivered into the hands of man, of the politicians, so that they may lead it either towards a new Golden Age or to its destruction in an ultimate universal conflagration. They cannot lead it (or lead it back) to a Golden Age, for the sanguinary history of millenarianism has sufficiently demonstrated that the heart of man is irreparably corrupt, that he cannot redeem himself. Nor can they lead it towards utter destruction, even though human nature and contemporary history tend to make us think otherwise, for God has not endowed man with absolute power, but has set him certain limits.

History cannot be reduced to what is called high politics, nor is man's final destiny in the hands of international organizations. Such organizations

21

are merely the stage, never the wings, never the great wheelworks which run the human drama.

There is a policy of God, a policy whose historical progress is only rarely visible to the human eye. This policy uses those who boast to be the craftsmen and masters of history. It pursues a well-defined goal, which is not the establishment merely of some universal government, for this can ultimately only be a new empire doomed to decadency, but the renewal of original harmony, of happiness for all mankind: the restoration of the dialogue which unites man with his Creator in a relationship of absolute trust and perfect knowledge. In other words, the establishment of what man has always yearned for since the days of Nimrod and the Tower of Babel, namely mastery of the universe, not to satisfy the pride of the strongest or bring about the suppression of the weakest, but for the joy of all.

This policy of God has its ambassador: Israel. A strange policy, to be sure, which frequently pursues its goals against the will and sometimes even without the knowledge of this equally strange ambassador. It is obvious that the Church's role in the world is different, beyond the political conflicts. It has never been able to become a nation, or a group of nations (although it has wanted to and, to a considerable extent, still wants to). Israel, however, is the nation par excellence. The Church propagates the knowledge of God among the Gentiles. In this sense it has taken the missionary torch from the hands of Israel. At a certain point of history Israel has recovered its national independence. And, as in biblical times, the Promised Land and its capital city Jerusalem have regained their position as the center of attraction (and conflict). When, at the 'D-Day' of history 'all the nations' shall 'go up to Jerusalem,' this will occur because it is here, according to the prophetic vision, that our prehistory will be fulfilled. And is not our time the last and gravest convulsion of a cruel prehistory? It is here that at last history will begin, a history worthy of its name, of peace and justice.

Thus it may be said, from the biblical perspective, that history is guided by the Creator *in spite of* man and in spite of the politicians. The policy of the Kingdom of God circles around the resettlement of Israel in its Promised Land. Jerusalem, its capital, is its heart and magnetic centre, for all nations shall be united here in brotherly love, assembled around their common Lord and Messiah, the Viceroy of the Kingdom of God on earth as in heaven.

III

ZIONISM IN THE HEBREW BIBLE

Who am I, O lord God, and what is my house, that Thou hast brought me thus far? And this was yet a small thing in Thine eyes, O Lord God. But Thou hast spoken also of Thy servant's house for a great while to come, and this too after the manner of great men. O Lord God, what can David say more unto Thee? ... And who is like Thy people, like Israel, whom God went to redeem unto Himself for a people and to make Him a name, and to do for Thy land great things and tremendous...?

Prayer of King David
II Samuel 7:18–23

In this chapter we intend to show that what is known as Zionism is not the essentially political movement which made its appearance on the stage of history towards the end of the 19th century. For if it were merely this, Zionism would be reduced to but one of the many contemporary movements of national awakening in the Middle East.

The first Zionist in history was named Abraham and his personal adventure marks the beginning of Jewish history which is itself one tremendous Zionist epic, full of human drama. In fact, it is a dialectical process of Exile and Return.

After Abraham and his circle, after Moses and the conquest of Canaan, the Prophets were to develop a comprehensive concept of history which we call Zionism, but which might as well be characterized as a theology of history.

ABRAHAM

A man named Abram, a product of Sumerian civilization, doubtless the most advanced of antiquity, one day embarked on a journey which was not a pleasure trip, nor a scientific or commericial exploration. Abram broke with his bright and comfortable world to become an emigrant. Why? For business or family reasons? Because he yearned for new horizons? No — in these highly religious surroundings Abram had encountered a God who did not resemble the deities of the city or the empire. He entered into a dialogue with the Creator, the Master of History. It was this renewal of the dialogue of Eden in Abram's life, which has made him the central figure of every monotheistic religion, which had made him Abraham, the father of many nations, the father of the faithful and the friend of God,

23

as he is called in the Hebrew Bible — the only man on whom this extraordinary title has been conferred. For in harmony with God the patriarch designed a new history, just as he gave birth to a new people which was never to be "like the others."

These were the first marching orders Abraham received from his God:

> Get thee out of thy country and from thy kindred and from thy father's house unto the land that I will show thee.
>
> (Genesis 12:1)

Note the insistence: "thy country, thy kindred, thy dwelling place and that of your ancestors." A departure with no return, a total uprooting is indeed, a radical disregard of all sentimental, patriotic and family ties.

These marching orders were immediately followed by the well-known promise to which the children of Abraham, throughout their tragic history, have clung so fiercely and sometimes so desperately; a promise which, once and for all, spelled out a theology which the Hebrew Bible alone among all the sacred books of mankind of propounds:

> I will make of thee *a great nation* and I will bless thee and make thy name great; and be thou a blessing. And I will bless them that bless thee and him that curseth thee will I curse; and in thee shall *all the nations* of the earth be blessed.
>
> (Genesis 12:2–3)

Such are the essentials of the new history, but with the following emphasis:

> ...all the land which thou seest to thee will I give it and to thy seed *forever*
>
> (Genesis 13:15)

In harmony with his Creator, Abraham was to bring forth a people which, like himself, would be set apart for the service of God. From this first promise — which was subsequently reaffirmed to Abraham's descendants — did not introduce into history a new form of nationalism but, to the contrary, a universal spiritual mission. Not the conquest of the nations by Jewish armies is the aim of history, but the happiness of man, the resumption of the paradisiac dialogue and original harmony, for the sake of all nations lost in the darkness of idolatry. The aim of history is the reconciliation of creation with its one benevolent Creator, so that at the culmination of history all peoples will greet and recognize each other as brothers, equally loved, equally blessed, equally united in perfect cognition of God, in joy shared by the entire universe. Because a new policy, a new guidance of human history has been proclaimed. This policy, linked to the fate of a particular people, has found a terrestrial seat, a capital, as it were, from where its guidelines are issued, from where this message of hope and salvation goes out unto all nations.

This is the meaning of this new land of Canaan and of its occupation by Abraham. This policy is forever linked to this people and this land,

24

even through all the tragedies that have visited them. And which people has been tried more than the people of Israel, which land has been more mishandled than the Land of Israel? We can never take the Divine promise too literally:

> All the land... will I give to thy seed *forever*

This, it seems to us, is the soundest foundation of every "Zionist" claim that has been made throughout history. That the politicians of our time contemptuously shrug off this evocation, is easy enough to understand. But that the theologians of the Church ignore it, or do not take it seriously is a very serious matter. *Let us make it clear from the outset: this book was written with the purpose of combatting this mentality.* We shall have reason to return to this subject.

For many years Abraham lived by these promises alone. Canaan was given to him and the gift was frequently reaffirmed by the Lord, but nevertheless he remained a stranger in the land until his last day, so much so that when Sarah died at Hebron, he had to enter into long negotiations with the sons of Heth for the right to buy a family tomb!

> ...Abraham came to mourn for Sarah and to weep for her. And Abraham rose up from before his dead and spoke unto the children of Heth, saying: *I am a stranger and a sojourner with you.* Give me a possession of a burying place with you, that I may bury my death out of my sight.
>
> (Genesis 23:2–4)

Such was the position of the man to whom Canaan had been offered, fifty years after his immigration... He truly deserved the title of father of the faithful!

One day he asked God for a token, different from the visions in which he used to converse freely with his Creator. In accordance with the usage of the time, a "blood" contract (covenant) was concluded between the two parties under such strange circumstances that I must cite the pertinent biblical text before commenting on it:

> And He said unto him: Take me a heifer of three years old, and a she-goat of three years old, and a ram of three years old, and a turtle dove, and a young pigeon. And he toke him all these, and divided them in the midst, and laid each half over against the other; but the birds divided he not.
> And the birds of prey came down upon the carcasses, and Abram drove them away.
> And it came to pass, that, when the sun was going down, a deep sleep fell upon Abram, and lo, a dread, even a great darkness, fell upon him.
> And He said unto Abram: Know of a surety that thy seed shall be a stranger in a land that is not theirs and shall serve them; and they shall afflict them four hundred years... and in the fourth generation they shall come back hither...
>
> (Genesis 15:9–13)

In this very concrete manner, not only with mere "beautiful promises", God committed Himself for ever to Abraham and his descendants. It was the practice of the time for two parties to enter into an alliance by such a sacrifice, by passing between the pieces of the animals and through their blood. Verse 17 of the same chapter of Genesis indeed shows us the Creator passing between the pieces as "a smoking furnace and a flaming torch."

But the deep trance into which Abraham sank, and the birds of prey attempting to despoil the sacrifice — and thereby to annul the Divine contract for the Promised Land — were the forebodings of the difficulties which were, in the course of history, to obstruct the consummation of this extraordinary contract. One of these obstacles was the first "exile" in Egypt, which was here predicted by the Lord Himself.

In the course of the centuries the Promised Land would indeed frequently be like these carcasses: left to the sand and mismanaged and exploited by occupying powers, while many nations, these "birds of prey," came down upon it whenever the Jewish people wanted to reclaim and revive it.

The biblical narrative immediately continues with a description of the borders of the land promised to Israel:

> Unto thy seed have I given this land, from the river of Egypt unto the great river, the Euphrates; the Kenite, and the Kenizite, and the Kadmonite, and the Hittite, and the Perizite, and the Rephaim, and the Canaanite, and the Girgashite and the Jebusite.
>
> (Genesis 15:18–21)

These tribes and populations inhabited at the time not only Palestine proper, but the whole vast region that was centuries later, at the zenith of his power, to become the territory of Solomon's kingdom.

Even though the Patriarch remained until his death, the respected guest of the tribes of Canaan and all the neighboring countries, he lived with the assurance that one day his descendants would possess this vast territory. Henceforth he knew its exact borders. He also knew that neither catastrophes, nor exile would ever be able to annul the unique contract that bore the signature of the Master of History, the Lord of all nations' destiny. There is no reason to doubt that this is what Isaac and Jacob were told by him, nor that the latter, the first to bear the name of Israel, passed it on to the twelve tribes of the Chosen people.

When God changed Abram's name into Abraham (when he was ninety-nine years old), He reaffirmed His contract with him in the following words:

> ...thou shalt be the father of a multitude of nations. ...I will establish My covenant between Me and thee and thy seed after thee... *for an everlasting covenant*... And I will give unto thee, and to thy seed after thee, the land of thy sojournings... *for an everlasting possession*...

These are the biblical foundations of Zionism, whether the Zionists acknowledge it or not. For although the Hebrew Bible has become the Holy Writ of all monotheistic religions, it has remained in the first place the great handbook of the history of the people of Israel.

But the fact that it is much more than a mere record of Israel's history and that God appears in it at every turn, is ignored by the historians who can see Israel only as a historical phenomenon, and are, most of the time, careful to avoid the thorny question of the inspired nature of the biblical writings. This aspect of the mystery of Israel they prefer to leave to the theologians, and the entire problem is consequently distorted and the whole vision obscured or even obliterated. But such is the case and it cannot be helped. This is perhaps the reason why the Jewish people is different from others, puzzling and even irritating to every historian — its book of history does not resemble that of any other nation.

Abraham will for ever remain the first campaigner for God's policy on earth, and the contract he signed with the sole Master of History, without anyone's knowledge or consent, will forever be the true charter of Israel's independence.

ISAAC

Abraham waited for twenty-five years for the birth of the son on whom in fact all the Lord's promises were built. When his birth was eventually to take place his aged mother Sarah could not help laughing:

> God hath made laughter for me; everyone that heareth will laugh on account of me.
>
> (Genesis 21:6)

But it was she herself who had laughed and derided Abraham when he told her the startling news. Let us beware of saying: He laughs longest who laughs last, for it is not Sarah's laughter, nor the mockery of her neighbors which resounds in this story, but the laughter of God Himself.

> And the Lord said unto Abraham: Shall I of a surety bear a child, who am old? Is anything too hard for the Lord?
>
> (Genesis 18:13–14)

When from the human point of view the dice seem to have been cast, amidst doubt and sardonic grins, the will of the Creator becomes triumphantly manifest. Whenever the hope of Israel reaches its nadir and all circumstances conspire against its chances of survival, precisely then does its deliverance become apparent. Isaac's whole life story is an illustration thereof. He was born under circumstances that can only be regarded as miraculous, he escaped at the last moment from being sacrificed by his father. Like Abraham, he never took actual possession of the country, but remained a stranger, even without the indubitable respect in which his father was held by the Canaanites. To be sure, he too heard the promise affirmed:

> ...I will be with thee, and will bless thee for unto thee, and unto thy seed, I will give all these lands and I will establish the oath which I swore unto Abraham thy father.
>
> (Genesis 26:31)

But this is all. There came even a moment in his life that he was pursued by Abimelech, the king of the Philistines. And nonetheless, Isaac was neither a conqueror, nor a warrior; on the contrary, his activities merely aimed at developing the country's fertility and resources: he was indeed a prodigious "digger of wells" throughout the land of Canaan. Instead of being rewarded he was accused of imperialistic designs and his wells were filled with sand. Even then there were obviously already pashas who were not interested in the prosperity of the country, nor in good neighborly relations between the children of Abraham and their own oppressed subjects...

Isaac's peaceful band of Zionism was even less acceptable to his adversaries than the militant Zionism of Moses and Joshua was to *their* enemies. In other words, it was the failure of this Zionist pacifism which led to the rise of militant Zionism. We shall see that Moses himself had no other choice.

Faced with the hostility of the "League" of his days, Isaac had nothing but the Divine Promises to cling to, and all he could do was to pass them on to his son, ironically enough against his own paternal wishes, for only the mother discerned that Jacob was the chosen one. But eventually, old, peace-loving Isaac bestowed without complaint, without equivocation, his last blessing on him who would soon be called Israel and who would be forced to flee from Esau's wrath:

> (God Almighty) give thee the blessing of Abraham, to thee, and to thy seed with thee, that thou mayest inherit the land of thy sojournings which God gave unto Abraham.
>
> (Genesis 28:4)

Three generations had succeeded each other in this Promised Land, but the lot of Abraham's children was still that of less and less tolerated strangers. Actually, the situation had even deteriorated: whereas Abraham had been a feared and respected Patriarch, Isaac, himself pursued by the local pashas, witnessed how his son Jacob, the undeniable trustee of the Promise, was forced to take to flight. Not from the Philistines, but from the ire of his own brother. In such a state of mind Isaac gave up the ghost to his Maker, but nevertheless in faith, a faith worthy of that of the Father of the Faithful. And for the time being this was all God demanded from His chosen one.

JACOB

Of all biblical figures no-one has been more controversial and, to say the least, less understood by the theologians of the Church than this grandson of Abraham. It is not surprising, though not always evident to the Christian observer, that it was the people of Israel who would have to suffer, from their origins until these days of national resurrection, as a result of this fundamental and time-honored misunderstanding.

Jacob's character and the dramatic dimensions of this misunderstanding more than deserve a somewhat lengthy discussion.

It has become fashionable to vilify Jacob as an "imposter" or, in popular language, a "shyster." And from here to regarding the entire Jewish people as a nation of more or less dangerous shysters is but a step, which the world has blithely taken, encouraged by an allegedly "Christian civilization."

If Jacob was a liar and a thief, than it follows that his historical pretension deserve to be valued as almost entirely irrelevant. This would be particularly true of his right to the land of Abraham which Israel, throughout the ages, has claimed with such grim determination. Jacob's Zionism would then be reduced to an ideology of imposters, and as such would, of course, in no way have any serious bearing on biblical promises.

Let us therefore have a close look at this Jacob who called himself Israel. Or rather, for the sake of brevity, let us first have a look at the first-born, at Esau.

That Esau was a capable hunter and an excellent cook is attested by the biblical writings, and it is not these qualities that should be questioned. What should be questioned is whether there is more to Esau's character than these qualities. The famous prerogtives of the birthright must be judged by other criteria than the not less famous lentil pottage. It is much too simplistic to reduce this right to the title to the paternal possessions (although this would be helpful to stress once again Jacob's "sordid interests").

But let us be serious and recall that the primogeniture, aside from all other considerations, placed on the first-born the sacred duty of taking upon himself the tasks assigned to the trustee of the divine promise, tasks of a priestly, sacrificial and — I do not hesitate to say so — missionary nature. It is clear that Esau scoffed at this duty — which was certainly not an easy one considering the sociological and religious context of the period.

The Genesis narrative of the bowl of lentils concludes with a little phrase which the Christian exegetes seem to have gladly forgotten. This little phrase is actually God's judgement of the two brothers. God does *not* say: "Jacob, behaving as a wicked brother by exploiting the distess of the unfortunate Esau and robbing him of Isaac's riches, brought upon himself Our just and eternal wrath..."

No, the biblical judgment is:

So Esau despised his birthright.

(Genesis 25:34)

In other words: Isaac's first-born, the natural heir of the Divine Promise destined to lead the nations towards their salvation, banished his Maker

29

from his existence. The case has been judged by a higher tribunal than the Areopagus of the theologians...

But let us return to Jacob and admit right away that he was in no way a "little saint," for the simple reason that there are no such people in the Bible. There are in the Bible human beings who are *set apart* for the advancement of the Kingdom of God on earth as in heaven. No one, and Rebecca less than anybody else, could dispute that Jacob, from his early childhood, had been mysteriously set apart. For Rebecca had discerned what good, old Isaac was unable to see: that Esau was not the elected one.

Jacob himself had an intimation of this, but even if he had not had such forebodings his long and thorough acquaintance with his brother's character would have convinced him.

Jacob, who — we repeat — was not a little saint, passionately desired to be the ambassador of the Lord, for the sake of his family and the world, and to bring forth a nation of ambassadors. He was aware of the formidable adventure this entailed. Esau knew this too, and that is precisely why he preferred the creature comforts! Both were familiar with the absurd adventure on which their grandfather Abraham had embarked at God's command, and with his total uprooting, and certainly with those terrible fifteen minutes in the life of their father Isaac when he had lain on the expiatory altar, bound by his father's hands...

"It was nevertheless worth it," young Jacob said to himself. And that is why God loved him, this Israel in search, who was willing to stake everything in order to be God's partner in this strange adventure for the sake of the Kingdom of justice. This is why God reassured his chosen one, after his flight, in these classic words:

> I am the Lord, the God of thy fathers. The land whereon thy liest, to thee will I give it and to thy seed... And in thee and thy seed shall all the families of the earth be blessed.
>
> (Genesis 28:13)

In this same vision of the ladder Jacob was comforted in his first exile by a new promise:

> Behold, I am with thee and will keep thee whithersoever thy goest and will bring thee back into this land.

Unlike the other divinities of the time who were confined to their own territory and whose favors could not be experienced beyond its borders, the God of Abraham, Isaac and Jacob is not confined to the land which He has given them for ever. From the onset the Lord revealed Himself to Jacob as a universal God, entirely different from all local deities. Exile does not negate His Presence. As a matter of fact, this specific Exile turned out to be a haven of refuge where Jacob was forged, but did not take permanent roots. The Return was ensured but only God knew its hour. It came at the right moment: when "the family" began to frown on him and to envy his considerable wealth, exactly then the marching orders were given:

> Return unto the land of thy fathers and to thy kindred, and I will be with thee.
>
> (Genesis 31:3)

Threatened by an even greater danger: Esau and his four hundred men who had made up their mind to wipe from the face of the earth this man who pretended to be the Chosen One.

The same exegetes who, to say the least, do not hold Jacob to be a saint, are nevertheless willing to regard his struggle at the ford of the Jabbok as his "conversion." Only from then on, they contend, did he become somehow respectable and worthy of a place in the gallery of the great biblical figures. We, however, cannot see that Jacob-of-the-Jabbok is in any way different from Jacob-of-the-lentils...

When do we ever see him bewail and reject his past and implore for forgiveness? When do we ever see him as a humble penitent? At the moment of certain defeat, faced with one mightier than himself, faced with death — for how could a man survive this terrible night — at this hour he cried out:

> I will not let thee go except thou bless me.   (Genesis 32:26)

Is this the cry of a humble penitent? It is the cry of Israel at the acme of its trial. For the blessing is more important to him than life. He had rather die in the face of God, in the love of God, than "save his skin" and deny his past. This is what God loves in Jacob: that he takes Him seriously. It does not mean that God closes His eyes to the less savory traits of his character. God knows him well because, as Peguy has said, He has made him Himself.

However this may be, this baptism in the darkness — which left Jacob-Israel crippled — is the epitome of Jewish history. How else can we understand this extraordinary statement:

> Thou hast striven with God and with men, and hast prevailed!
>
> (Genesis 32:28)

To be the Chosen People is in no way easy, as the Bible itself acknowledges: "It is a fearful thing to fall into the hands of the living God" (Hebrews 10:31). Israel has always known this. Is not its history one long succession of abandonment and betrayal, of last-moment rescue and never failing forgivingness? But God is never abandoned entirely, the betrayal is never absolute; there always remains a faithful rest which keeps the flame of Sinai burning through study and observance of God's Word.

If Israel somehow prevails in its struggles with God, it is because His mercy exceeds His other attributes. It is also because God keeps His promises to the Fathers and honors the contract He signed in Abraham's blood and sealed anew in Jacob-Israel's dislocated hip.

Israel's struggles with men — an essential aspect of the mystery of Election — are not in the first place a reflection of its own resistance to

God's mercy, but rather of the nations' deep-rooted inaptitude to accept the Jewish people and, above all, the message of this people of priests, witnesses and ambassadors to the world of the Master of history.

Jacob-Israel died in Egypt, surrounded by his family, bathing in the glory of Joseph the viceroy. But this glory did not turn the Patriarch's head; his last thoughts, his last wishes were focused on the Promised Land where his ancestors and his wife Rachel were laid to rest. He died in exile, but the fact that it was an illustrious exile could not eliminate the secret bitterness of the Patriarchs: only in hope they possessed their country and entrusted it to their children.

When Jacob left his country for the second time, it was for the sole reason of finding Joseph, his favored son whom he had believed to be dead for many years. Evidently he had his doubts at the time of departure, for the Bible tells us that God "endorsed" this journey to Egypt:

> Fear not to go down into Egypt; for I will there make of thee a great nation: I will go down with thee into Egypt: and I will also surely bring thee up again:
>
> (Genesis 46:3–4)

On the other hand, Joseph should be told of the promise, so that the glory of Egypt would not bedazzle him and Egypt not become his children's fatherland. As a kind of introduction to his great farewell speech and his blessing of the tribes, Jacob-Israel therefore declared:

> God Almighty said unto me: ...Behold, I will make thee fruitful, and multiply thee, and I will make of thee a multitude of people: and will give this land to thy seed after thee for an everlasting possession.
>
> (Genesis 48:4)

And to ensure that Joseph would understand him properly he added:

> Behold, I die: but God will be with you, and bring you back unto the land of your fathers.
>
> (Genesis 48:21)

Jacob's utterances on his deathbed concerning the destiny of the twelve tribes "in the end of days" were not only prophecies, but also Divine commandments. Joseph could undeniably have given the sign for return. Whether he considered staying in Egypt, where he was the viceroy, more profitable than colonization of the promised land, or whether he waited for official orders from Above, we do not know, but it is a fact that he died in Egypt, like his father before him. And like his father, he gathered his family around him and told them:

> I die, but God will surely remember you and bring you up out of this land unto the land which He swore to Abraham, to Isaac, and to Jacob... God will surely remember you and ye shall carry up my bones from hence.
>
> (Genesis 50:24–25)

From hence... on these somewhat disillusioned undertones the Book of Genesis, the Book of Beginnings, ends. Coming from Pharaoh's deputy they were of particular significance and to Egyptian ears they must almost have sounded as sacrilege. At the zenith of his glory Joseph was undeniably still a stranger in Egypt. Undeniably it has always been difficult for Israel to die in exile without feeling a stranger. It has always been difficult for this people, certainly in the hour of death, to forget the far-away vistas of the Promised Land...

Four generations of patriarchs, four centuries, had passed since God called Abraham. Four centuries of promises had left Israel in this paradoxal situation: none of its sons did actually live in the Promised Land! The bones of Abraham and Sara, Isaac, Rebecca and Rachel were waiting for the mummified bodies of Jacob and Joseph..., waiting whether they decide to return, these Children of Israel, these guests of honor of their father, the viceroy of alluring Egypt... How many still remained in Canaan to remember Abram the Chaldaean? Hadn't they already forgotten peace-loving Isaac? And how many would, tomorrow, remember Jacob-Israel?

It is obvious that at the time of Joseph's death the historical pretentions of Israel were rather shaky and with every year that passed tended to vanish altogether. Only the promise of God, whom no one in Canaan or elsewhere knew, remained.

It is on this hazard that all of Jewish history rests and that the election is fulfilled. History balances on this ludicrously narrow fulcrum.

MOSES AND THE FIRST ZIONIST EPOS

It is not at all certain that the Children of Jacob-Israel had forgotten the Promised Land during their long sojourn in Egypt. However, a simple phrase in the first verses of Exodus, the words of the new Pharaoh "who had not known Joseph," gives us an interesting clue:

> Behold, the people of the Children of Israel are too many and too mighty for us. Come, let us deal wisely with them, lest they multiply, and it come to pass, that, when there befalleth us any war, they also join themselves unto our enemies, and get them up out of the land.
>
> (Exodus 1:9–10)

The hope to return to the Land of the Fathers was doubtless still alive in the hearts of a selected few, notwithstanding the attractions of life in exile. It may be assumed that from the day that Jacob's sons entered the country where Joseph still "reigned," they followed the example of their illustrious brother and installed themselves pretty soon in various positions and levels of command. The new Pharaoh, in his hatred of Israel, nevertheless realized before long that a mass exodus of the Jews would undermine the entire Egyptian economy. He decided therefore cunningly to make them his selected slaves as soon as the key positions could be taken over by "pure" Egyptians. He was prepared to use all possible means to prevent the exodus of the Jews. Israel had to be trapped and subsequently, when his fantastic projects would be completed, scientifically liquidated.

As an echo to Pharaoh's perfidious designs the laughter of God, whose Will is so often expressed in "the weak and foolish things of the world," resounded once again in Israel's history. For what is the instrument He choses to obstruct the designs of the "Hitler" of those days? A new-born infant who survives the first massacre of holy innocents and floats in a laughable little ark towards his future mission of liberator of his people; who, from this very moment, is set apart in order to forge a band of slaves and martyrs into a nation, and who will subsequently be introduced to the court (God's stratagems outdo those of the king). In the course of a long training period, such as those who are destined to rule must pass, he was initiated in the mysteries of his time, became a priest and a prince, a strategists and a man of the law. Thus the policy of the kingdom coincided with that of human pride; until the two policies could no longer be reconciled and the entire structure collapsed, following Moses's first encounter with his suffering people and the intervention of the Egyptian taskmaster. The crown prince, who had just divulged his Jewish origin, was henceforth nothing but an outcast. For forty years afterwards he was a ruler of sheep, camels and goats in a desert which he came to know thoroughly with its places of encampment and its rich sources of water. In these forty years the pomp and circumstance of the royal court gave way to a nomadic way of life. Instead of the Book of the Dead he read in the Book of Heaven alone, in an eternal face-to-face encounter with this strange God of his ancestors who, unlike the other gods, cannot be confined in a temple or made visible in an image; this God without priests (as if to demand that all his worshippers be priests), without ritual, without a written law, without sacrifices in any form; this God who is not frightening, this God of the fathers who were interred in a remote country that once was promised to them; this silent God who is nevertheless so near and so powerful.

A God who suddenly revealed Himself in the poverty and fragility of a burning bush; a God whose all-consuming love has for ever been given to the arid soil of the human heart; this God who suddenly speaks, commands and sends away. For the old shepherd and fallen prince with the tender heart did not yet know that he was called to lead an entirely different flock to different meadows. In the hour of his vocation Moses was an old man who had not accomplished anything. He had killed a man, but what is simpler and commoner than this? Now he was called to devote himself with all his might to the service of his people, a mission which he was never able to forget. He who knew to read the silence of the desert, heard the Word of the Lord:

> And the Lord said: I have surely seen the affliction of My people that are in Egypt, and have heard their cry by reason of their taskmasters; for I know their pains; and I am come down to deliver them out of the hands of the Egyptians, and to bring them up out of that land unto a

good land and a large, unto a land flowing with milk and honey; unto the place of the Canaanite, and the Hittite, and the Amorite, and the Perizzite, and the Hivite, and the Jebusite

(Exodus 3:7–8)

When the suffering of Israel became so great that the promise of redemption seemed to be a mockery, the dialogue that had begun with the fathers was resumed:

I am the Lord; I appeared unto Abraham, unto Isaac, and unto Jacob, as God Almighty, but by My name YHVH I made me not known to them. And I have also established my covenant with them, to give them the land of Canaan, the land of their sojournings... And moreover I have heard the groaning of the children of Israel... *and I have remembered my covenant... and I will take you to Me for a people* And I will bring you in unto the land concerning which I lifted up My hand to give it to Abraham, to Isaac and to Jacob and I will give it you for a heritage: I am the Lord

(Exodus 6:3–8)

If God remembered His covenant with the fathers, how could He have forgotten Israel in Egypt? But perhaps He had waited a few hundreds of years for His people to return to the Promised Land *of their own accord*? After all, had not the words of Jacob and Joseph, on the threshhold of death, been marching orders?

God does not forget His covenant with man, but man remembers Him only in his plight. Only then does he cry out to Him, after hundreds of years of forgetfulness.

However this may be, being persecuted is what brings Israel back to God and, likewise, to the Promised Land. Without Ramses II there would have been no Moses. Such are the dialectics of human and Divine policy.

When through a conjunction of circumstances Israel clashes with Caesar and seems to be infernally trapped in an exile which is brutally transformed into a death camp, its yearning for the Promised Land becomes manifest and God intervenes, using for His purpose, if necessary, even a "fuehrer."

Israel's martyrdom thus assumes a redemptive quality. The Jewish people will never say: "If God existed He would not have allowed this," but, to the contrary, cry out: "Why didn't we leave Egypt earlier!"

Did Jacob not come down to Egypt to remind Joseph of another Land that must be conquered and saved from famine, in order to render it into the instrument of another policy and another kingdom? But his people had come to regard this country as "Terra Sancta," where one went to shed a few tears on holy tombs. Other tears had to be shed before Israel learned that this Land must be reclaimed and cultivated in love. Through other tears Israel had to learn that it is its unique historical destiny to chose between a gilded existence in exile and an austere life of independence.

This choice has remained the core of the Zionist epic. It finds its true expression, not in nationalist slogans, but in the cry of the Psalmist:

If I forget thee, O Jerusalem Let my right hand forget her cunning.

Since not Jewish nationalism, but the policy of The Kingdom of which the nations will not hear, is at stake, Israel, like the bush that burnt, but was not consumed, will not perish in its long exiles. If the Zionist epic had, from its beginnings in Canaan and Egypt, merely been one nationalist movement among others, Israel would have ceased to exist thousands of years ago, and we would have had to dig up its relics among the stones of Egypt. All nationalisms have collapsed and only the archaeologists can show us their remaining traces. All imperialist powers were challenged by the historical scandal of which Israel is the exponent, and it is they that have vanished.

This is an additional proof of the extraordinary nature of Jewish history which does not conform to the laws of general history. The Zionist vision of history, first propounded in the days of Moses, is thus elevated to the heights of a theology of history.

The promise to Israel that it would possess Canaan is actually a covert promise to all of mankind. We have seen that the Land was not given to Abraham, the Friend of God, nor to nearly-sacrificed Isaac or to Jacob-Israel. Nor was it given to the people emerging from Egypt or from the concentration camps, or to Moses. For it is not a Land like other countries. As Moses so forcefully proclaimed, it is destined to become the Temple of a new, reconciled mankind. Israel marches in the front ranks of mankind: it shows the way and absorbs the blows. This is the meaning of this first Zionist epic, infinitely deeper than the meaning the nations accord to their own struggle for independence.

Some of the laws that were given on Mount Sinai to guide man's relations with the Land — an entirely new phenomenon in its own time, which has lost nothing of its originality — offer us an additional indication that this people and this land are "set apart" (ontological sanctity).

First of all the following verses:

And the land shall not be sold in perpetuity; for the land is Mine; for ye are strangers and settlers with me

(Leviticus 35:2–3)

Hence the great innovation: the sabbatical year:

When ye come into the land which I give you, then shall the land keep a sabbath unto the Lord. Six years thou shalt sow thy field... But in the seventh year shall be a sabbath of solemn rest for the land... And the sabbath-produce of the land shall be for food for you, for thee, and for thy servant... and for thy hired servant and for the stranger... and for thy cattle, and for the beasts that are in thy land.

(Leviticus 25:2–7)

Jewish tradition has made this sabbatical year into a year in which all of Israel shall study the Scriptures and work for the coming of the Messianic Kingdom on earth. What have the nations accomplished in this respect, after so many centuries of civilization? The most enlightened among them have instituted a few weeks of "payed leave..."

The fastidious minds of Antiquity, and in the first place Tacitus, already derided these Jewish institutions which they regarded, together with the Sabbath, as evidence of Israel's "laziness!"

And which other people has so faithfully observed the following revolutionary commandment of the Jubilee?

> And ye shall hallow the fiftieth year and proclaim liberty throughout the land unto all the inhabitants thereof; it shall be a jubilee unto you; and ye shall return every man unto his possession, and ye shall return every man unto his family.
>
> (Leviticus 25:10)

Unlike other nations, it never occurred to Israel to behave as absolute masters of their land. This piece of land in the Middle East, on the crossroads of the continents, in the very heart of the antique world, is the place the Master of History has chosen to dwell therein among men, and His capital will be this Messianic city where His will is revealed, first to Israel and then, by natural expansion, to all of mankind.

But the people must be worthy of this land and worthy of Him to whom it belongs. That is why Moses, even before the hour of conquest and separation, conveyed to his people these warnings, probably the most terrible to be found in the Bible:

> ...if thou wilt not hearken unto the voice of the Lord thy God... cursed shalt thou be in the city, and cursed shalt thou be in the field... Cursed shall be the fruit of thy body, and the fruit of thy land... and the young of thy flock. Cursed shalt thou be when thou comest in, and cursed shalt thou be when thou goest out... And thou shalt grope at noonday, as the blind gropeth in darkness... Thou shalt betroth a wife and another man shall lie with her; thou shalt build a house, and thou shalt not dwell therein; thou shalt plant a vineyard, and thou shalt not use the fruit thereof... Thy sons and thy daughters shall be given unto another people... And thou shalt become an astonishment, a proverb, and a byword, among all the people whither the Lord shall lead thee away.
>
> (Deuteronomy 28)

Thus, not death, but exile is the supreme penalty. In a mysterious way Israel is no longer God's ideal Israel when it is uprooted from the soil of the fathers. Outside this unique homeland the Jewish people evinces a historical tension which borders on impotence. Exile is lethargy and at times agony. But this has nothing whatsoever to do with some mystical "Blut und Boden" theory, for this dramatic tension is first and foremost expressed in spiritual terms, in the people's estrangement, not only from its biblical origins, but also from the Master of History. Paradoxically, when Israel is "at home" in its own country, the nations seek to turn it into the outlaw of history, while God mysteriously upholds it; but when the nations apparently succeed in their campaign against Israel and lead it into captivity, it is God who places Israel under the ban of His sacred history.

All this is so true that the supreme and most ideal reward Israel has ever been able to think of throughout its history, is the termination of Exile, the Return, as promised in the following verses of Deuteronomy which are the antithesis of those quoted above:

> ...the Lord thy God will turn thy captivity... and will return and gather thee from all the peoples... If any of thine that are dispersed be in the uttermost parts of heaven... from thence will He fetch thee. And the Lord thy God will bring thee into the land which thy fathers possessed...
>
> (Deuteronomy 30:3–5)

It should be evident to every honest historian that no other people could have survived during nineteen centuries of dispersion throughout the world after a national disaster and — what was worse — the destruction of the Sanctuary upon which its entire life depended.

The tensions in Israel's history are never fatal because its vital relationship with the biblical homeland is never irreparably broken. During all these centuries the mystical hope of return and of rebuilding Jerusalem has faithfully been kept alive in the prayers of the synagogue.

The land itself was also in lethargy and agony and its history was similar to that of the people; only the latter's return marked the beginning of its resurrection. Neither its colonization by the Romans, nor its occupation by the Babylonians, the Crusaders or the Turks were able to revive it. Under their rule it remained merely the "Holy Land," that is a land of relics and the cult of the dead.

It became the task of Moses, this spiritual giant and doubtless — though hardly accidentally — the most neglected genius, to develop the dialectical rapport between Exile and Israel, the key to the theology of history which, in fundamental contradiction to all other philosophies of histories, was revealed in the Bible alone.

THE EXODUS FROM EGYPT AND THE STAGE
OF HISTORY

It was not the practice of the Egyptian historians to record the past adversities of their country. There is, consequently, no reason to be surprised about the eloquent silence of the Egyptian sources about the period of Hyksos rule (XIth–XVIIth dynasty), or about the revolt of the Hebrew slaves under the leadership of the fallen prince Moses. The Bible alone, of all the contemporaneous documents, does not shrink back from revealing the defeats and errors of its own people. What should surprise us is that the historians all but ignore this piece of evidence of Hebrew objectivity!

The fact that the first Pharaohs of the XVIth dynasty (1587–1350

B.C.) began to suppress the not so glorious history of the previous centuries should warn us against questioning the historical truth of the Exodus or of any of its details. For we may be certain that Ramses II (if he indeed was the Pharaoh of the Exodus) was just as eager to censor these embarassing events.

Israel has ñever concealed the fact that its ancestors were slaves in Egypt, although historians do not regard this as a provenance to be proud of. What interest could a people possibly have in inventing such a humiliating beginning of its own history if it were not the truth?

The Exodus from Egypt is the first known slave revolt in Antiquity. And it is from this angle, we believe, that the Passover events must be approached. Some Christian theologians go somewhat far when they oppose Passover to the Christian Easter celebration. For in this extraordinary night the Jewish people escaped not only from material slavery, but also from spiritual bondage in an idolatrous world which threatened to wipe out the Hebrew faith once and for all — and thus also the Christian faith, of which it already bore the seeds.

We cannot attach enough importance to this regime of slavery which prevailed in the so-called "civilized world" of Antiquity until the decline of the Roman empire. The pyramid and the other fantastic temples in, among other places, the Valley of the Kings doubtless arouse our admiration. But it is easily forgotten that they were actually built not with mortar, but with the blood and bones of thousands of men, women and children under conditions that came very close to those in the Nazi camps of our time. Herodotus tells us that the Nile–Red Sea canal, built during the reign of Pharaoh Necho II (609–588 B.C.) demanded the death of hundred and twenty thousand slaves. His contemporary, King Jehoiakim of Judah, decided to follow the example of his powerful neighbor and launched sumptuous building projects in Jerusalem. But hear what a certain Jeremiah had to say about this in the name of the Lord of History:

> Woe unto him that buildeth his house by unrighteousness... That uses his neighbor's service without wages, And giveth him not his hire... But thine eyes and thy heart Are not but for thy covetousness and for shedding innocent blood, and for oppression, and for violence, to do it. Therefore thus saith the Lord concerning Jehoiakim, the son of Josiah, King of Judah...: He shall be buried with the burial of an ass, drawn and cast forth beyond the gates of Jerusalem!
>
> (Jeremiah 22:13–19)

His Majesty Necho II, the divine ruler of Egypt, would, no doubt, have been amused if one of his counsellors had dared to entreat him to regard a slave as his neighbor. (This counsellor would soon have found himself in the company of the king's miserable slaves). But the reader of these biblical verses cannot but smile when he thinks of the fastidious spirits of our days who persist to regard the "God of the Jews" — as they express themselves so elegantly — as a wrathful and blood-thirsty God. It is regrettable that even Simone Weil was caught in this web of anti-judaism of the parlor and the academy...

The Exodus from Egypt was also a revolt against idolatry and the cult of the dead in Egypt itself. Was not the Egyptian "bible" called the "Book of the Dead?" One reads in it how the deceased, appearing before the chair of judgement of Osiris, invariably denies that he has committed any of the forty-two cardinal sins in order to escape his torment at the hand of the evil spirits which inhabit the dwellings of the dead. The ideal solution was for a man to become, through sorcery, one of these spirits himself.

Such a spiritual regime, forcefully upheld by a caste of priests whose bread-and-butter it was, could only demoralize the masses. As a matter of fact, the tombs, even the royal tombs, were frequently pillaged.

The silence of the Pentateuch on the subject of death in general should not lead us to false conclusions with regard to the belief and hopes of Israel. It was part of God's (and Moses') pedagogy that the Egyptian customs and practices should not be mentioned. But it is sufficiently clear from the Hebrew writings that the Lord is the God of Life and that death in no way affects his omnipotence. As to the Hereafter, the Hebrew concept had nothing whatsoever in common with the Egyptian netherworld with its population of evil spirits.

In this paedagogic perspective the ten plagues that afflicted Egypt appear as judgments intended to open the eyes of all, not only of Israel. Excepting the last plague, which hit all the country's first-born, they challenged and derided the local deities. The Nile — which was worshipped with no less fervor than the sun-god Ra — the frogs, every animal down to the scarabee (whose image is found everywhere on the stones and in the tombs of Egypt), even the sun itself of which Pharaoh was the incarnation, were put in their proper place. (The orientalist Edward Mahler registered a solar eclipse on 13 March, 1335 B.C., which would fix the date of Passover on Thursday, the 27th of that month...).

It was, once again, Herodotus, who mentioned the solar eclipse of 585 in the heat of the battle between the Lydians and Medians which so much that they hastily asked for a truce! Neither of these peoples worshipped the sun, and if *they* were so frightened, one can imagine the effect of a solar eclipse on the Egyptian contemporaries of Moses. Many of them doubtless abandoned their idols to join the Jewish people, thus provoking a crisis which can only be compared to that caused by the "monotheistic" reforms of Amenhotep IV-Akhenaten, who tried to abolish all cults except that of the Sun. (His son-in-law Tut-en-khamon could be the Pharaoh of the Exodus as this solar eclipse occurred during his reign).

The Exodus from Egypt, sanctified by the institution of Passover, is thus God's intervention in history by means of Israel's revolt against an imperialistic regime of slavery and idolatry.

It was certainly not on tiptoe that Israel appeared on the stage of the antique world, but, rather, tumultuously and, as we have already pointed out, provoking a sociological, political and theological outrage. A sociological outrage because it shook the very foundations of the economic structure of the time; a political outrage because it claimed the right to be independent as well as the possession of a country of paramount strategical importance, and, finally, a theological outrage because in its "mockery" of the Egyptian deities, Israel proclaimed its own unique and sovereign God and Lord.

The gap between Israel and the nations became consequently unbridgeable; a tension was created which would never be alleviated.

Israel, as the first people to have revolted against the injustice of the powers, would therefore throughout history invariably be suspect in the eyes of the established regimes, which realized that a dangerous revolutionary ferment was at work in this people that is so different from other nations.

Because of Israel's passionate fight for its national independence it inevitably clashes with every form of imperialism.

Because Israel raised the victorious banner of monotheism, it will always offend the champions of idolatrous cultures.

However, since Israel always presented its outrageous claims in the name of its Holy Book and in the name of its God, its being outlawed by history makes the "Zionist" tension of its existence all the more manifest.

All things are interrelated: because we despise the Parousia we also despise the Old Testament since it is the Covenant of History. We speak readily of the base and petty nature of the promises of earthly bliss which abound in the Old Testament, and derive from them this little anti-semitic refrain: These Jews, to remain faithful must be promised at least a vineyard and an olive grove, whereas we content ourselves with spiritual goods...

Jean Massin
Le festin chez Levi (p. 96)
Chez Julliard, 1952

NOTES ON THE TORAH AS REVELATION

It would be a serious matter if, while trying to define the historical meaning of the Jewish people's election and having emphasized the revolutionary significance of the Exodus, we would tacitly pass over the upheaval of the legal order on Mount Sinai. For Israel is the nation which, while still in search of a homeland, told the world what justice means.

No other document has wielded such influence on mankind as the few chapters of the Torah (the five books of Moses) that are summarized in the hundred-and-twenty Hebrew words of the Decalogue which embrace not only all aspects of human relationship, but also the secret stirrings of the human heart.

Rabbinical tradition teaches that the two Tables of the Decalogue (the

Ten Commandments) were written at the time of the Creation, even before the appearance of man, and are therefore not dependent on any human culture or thought. The Torah was given to Israel *in the desert,* according to the same tradition, because it does not belong to any specific nation or race but, coming from the desert, all peoples were able to hear it in their own language. The sixth day of Sivan, on which the Decalogue was given, is therefore as important as the first day of Creation.

It is a misconception to say that Moses was inspired by the Code of Hammurabi or even copied it. Hammurabi was a contemporary of Abraham who was himself of Sumerian origin. It is true that the life-story of the Patriarchs often suggests the influence of his Code — which is not surprising. The scholars agree that this royal Code was the most advanced of its time. The Sumerians were the first to build strong cities; they laid the foundations of family life, were the first to have schools, weights and measures and an alphabet; to them we owe the science of irrigation, the division of the circle into three hundred and sixty degrees and of the hour into sixty minutes. It was in Sumer that a notion of justice was conceived, although largely determined by the social hierarchy: the king and the nobles possessed virtually unlimited rights, the people very few and the slaves none. In Israel, on the other hand, a slave was set free for the loss of a tooth inflicted by his master. Moreover, it was forbidden to refuse asylum to an escaped slave or to return him to his master!

The Sumerian code concludes with the case of an escaped slave whose ear is to be cut, and maybe we may read an ironical note in the fact that the Mosaic Law *opens* with the case of the slave whose ear is *pierced* because he wishes to stay for ever with his master!

As to the famous clause "eye for eye, tooth for tooth," scholars agree on this point as well and admit that it seriously curbed the brutal arbitrariness which then prevailed everywhere. The Code of Hammurabi does not contain this law of retaliation about which so much — anti-Jewish — ink has been spilled, but it has its own "a son for a son, a daughter for a daughter" clause, according to which a child must pay with his life for the crime of his father. One notes the progress...

If the Code of Hammurabi was a large step foreward towards genuine justice, the Torah of Israel is entirely inspired by the love of God and the love *of one's neighbor*, even, and in particular if this neighbor is a slave or a stranger, for "ye were a stranger in the land of Egypt."

This Law depends by no means on social distinctions, on the differences between rich and poor, mighty and humble. The king of Israel himself must pay dearly for a fraudulently acquired vineyard, or for a concubine taken by criminal means.

If this were the only accomplishment of the Law of Moses it would suffice to regard it as a revolutionary step forward. Indeed, the mighty of the period understood this all too well, and their blind hostility towards the Jewish people was directed in the first place at this dangerous law of brotherly justice (and consequently at the God of Israel).

God's transcendental intervention in mankind's bloody history was essential to imbue human relations with the sense of egality and fraternity. Israel, as the channel of this intervention for the good of mankind at large, is the people of Revelation, of the renewed dialogue with God, as once in the Garden of Eden. The resumption of the dialogue is a commitment to man's future, a promise and a pledge of unequivocal reconciliation. To be the recipient and trustee of such a redemptive code means to be the vanguard in every battle against the forces of darkness and death and to be exposed to their fiercest blows. The Jewish people has certainly known this.

None of the civilizations that crossed the path of Israel has taken this law that was revealed to Moses seriously. Egypt, Assyria, Edom and the Philistines rejected it by force of arms; Athens and Rome as behooves the strong and mighty, scoffed. And the so-called Christian civilization has betrayed it, in so far it did not underestimate it. Hence the terrifying situation in our twentieth century with its gas chambers and its nuclear arms, which ignores the Word of the Lord Christ that "Torah" does not mean "law" but rather the way to eternal life:

> For verily I say unto you, Till heaven and earth pass, one jot or one title shall is no wise pass from the Torah..."
>
> (Matthew 5:18)

IV

THE DIALECTICS OF EXILE AND RETURN
IN ISRAEL'S PROPHETICAL WRITINGS

If I forget thee, O Jerusalem let my right hand forget her cunning!
If I do not remember thee, let my tongue cleave to the roof of my
mouth!
If I prefer not Jerusalem above my chief joy!

Psalm 137

It was neither chronology nor logic with which the Jewish prophets were concerned in their historical vision of history. These visionaries did not contemplate the ages in their normal successive order, but in the perspective of the two poles of Israel's history: exile and return, thus zooming in on the centuries and the events in a manner which enabled them to experience several exiles and returns simultaneously. On the other hand, there is one, unique element in their vision which cannot be "telescoped" through repetition — namely the culmination of Jewish history (and of History in general) in a perfectly stable human regime and society of genuine justice and peace, on earth as in heaven.

This cycle of exile and return was, as we have seen, first announced to Abraham in the covenant signed with blood and subsequently, in much more explicit words, to Moses. But is was reserved to the prophets to enter the scenario — if we may use this expression — of exile and the vicissitudes of return.

Let us therefore now examine the "Zionist" thought of the prophets and try to understand how this dialectical process was apprehended by each of them.

AMOS

Amos' prophetical ministry took place during the reign of Jeroboam II, King of Israel (784-744 B.C.) and of Uzziah, king of Judah (779-739 B.C.). It was a period of political and economic prosperity: the king of Israel had firmly established his rule over all of Samaria and even been able to conquer several Aramaic cities. In the south the Judean monarch had defeated the Philistines as well as Ammon and Moab. Against this background Amos' prophecies of doom seemed ludicrous, and as such they were indeed received.

If, according to the prophet, this seemingly permanent prosperity was built on sand, this was because injustice and corruption had infiltrated the entire country and in particular the upper class, with the complicity and participation of the clergy. It is with those that Amos clashed when he castigated the High Priest of Bethel, who had ordered him "to eat bread" elsewhere, in such an unusually violent way:

> Thy wife shall be a harlot in the city; And thy sons and thy daughters shall fall by the sword; And thy land shall be divided by line; and thou thyself shalt die in an unclean land; And Israel shall surely be led away captive out of this land.
>
> (7:17)

Not the northern kingdom of Israel alone shall be led into exile, but the House of David as well. And not only to Babylon shall the Jewish people be led into captivity, but to all countries of the world:

> ...I will sift the house of Israel among all the nations, like as corn is sifted in a sieve, yet shall not the least grain fall upon the earth.
>
> (9:9)

But this dispersion will be accompanied by a much worse disaster: the oblivion of the biblical Message and the interruption of the "prophetical succession" among the people of the Bible:

> Behold the days come, saith the Lord God, that I will send a famine in the land. Not a famine of bread, nor a thirst for water, but of hearing the words of the Lord. And they shall wander from sea to sea, and from the north even to the east; They shall run to and fro to seek the word of the Lord, and shall not find it.
>
> (8:12–12)

But since none of the Jewish prophets confined himself to being "a prophet of doom," a message of hope, the hope of Return, is added to this particularly dark picture. The following proclamation, which is of a precision that is not often found in the prophetical literature, concludes the book of Amos:

> In that day will I raise up the tabernacle of David that is fallen, and close up the breaches thereof, and I will raise up his ruins, and I will build it as in the days of old that they may possess the remnant of Edom and all the nations, upon whom My name is called.
>
> (9:11–12)

The expression "in that day" which we encounter here for the first time introduces into the prophetical literature an apocalyptic tonality which links all the nations to the ultimate destiny of the Jewish people; they will either restore Israel's messianic borders of the days of David and Solomon (as in this case) or they will have to pass through an extremely grave crisis bordering on a planetary, not to say cosmic, cataclysm.

And in this context another expression appears: "the Day of the Lord."

This is the day of final judgment for Israel and the nations alike. Thus it may be assumed that the re-establishment of Israel in the Land of the Fathers and the Divine promise will come about against the will of the nations, and in spite of their hostility. That is why the nations are not merely judged by Divine justice which also applies to Israel but by their attitude towards the Jewish people. For by opposing Israel and its Return they in fact oppose God's particular way of guiding history for those upon whom the "name of the Lord is called," even though the nations are not aware of this, or do not want to admit it.

We have said that the message of Return at the end of the book of Amos is distinguished by its rather unusual precision. This is the message:

> And I will turn the captivity of my people Israel, and they shall built the waste cities, and inhabit them. And they shall plant vineyards and drink the wine thereof. They shall also make gardens and eat the fruit of them. And I will plant them upon their land, and they shall no more be plucked up out of their land which I have given them.
>
> (9:14–15)

The last verse casts, to say the least, a confusing light on the fact that after the Babylonian Captivity there was to come the great Exile at the time of the Roman empire. We will come back to this.

HOSEA

A contemporary of Amos, the prophet Hosea performed his ministry in the same historical circumstances. But he opens an entirely new prophetical perspective. To begin with: he is led to identify an intimate conjugal drama with the drama of the relations between YHVH and Israel, thereby giving a pathetic sense to the election of the Jewish people throughout the ages and the millennia.

Every other rejected husband would have left his guilty spouse and his children's degenerate mother to her perverse debaucheries. But at God's command Hosea, more than once repairs to the market place (where the slaves and prostitutes are exhibited) and in front of his scandalized relatives, friends and colleagues he forgives her and leads her back to the bosom of the family. For he understood that the God of the fathers did not demand from him such gestures out of cruelty or sadism, but in order that he, Hosea, would realize how much more profound was the agony of the God of Israel because of the infidelity of his Chosen One in view of the nations who were not scandalized, but to the contrary, rejoiced in holy glee. It is therefore understandable that Hosea understood the intimate aspects of God's love and the unique dialectical process of Exile and Return which casts such a special light on the history of Israel. Like Jeremiah, this other "man of pains," after him, and like Ezekiel he received revelations which only such men as they were could absorb and interpret. The following is one of these revelations without precedent in the biblical writings:

> For the children of Israel shall sit solitary many days without king, and
> without prince, without sacrifice, and without pillar and without ephod
> or teraphim... afterward shall the children of Israel return...
>
> (3:4)

Thus, for a long period, the Jewish people will know neither national independence, nor princes of the House of David (whose genealogical tree will probably be lost) and, even more significant, it will no longer have a national religion with its center in Jerusalem. Amos had already announced that for a long period there would be no prophets in Israel and its faith would consequently wane. Now his colleague Hosea proclaims that the Chosen People will also lose its double ministry of king and priest of the Most High among the nations thereby in fact losing its very *raison d'etre,* its responsibility as a chosen people and a light unto the nations.

But not forever. For "in that day" the Jews of the twelve tribes will return — and where will they return if not to the Promised Land? — and find once again their God and their king David. In other words; they will regain their threefold ministry of King, Prophet and Priest in the midst of the nations.

As Amos had also predicted, the Return and "conversion" will take place in extremely dramatic circumstances:

> The iniquity of Ephraim is bound up; His sin is laid up in store. The
> throes of a travailing woman shall come upon him.
>
> (13:13)

For the first time mention is made here of what was to be called in Rabbinic tradition the "pre-Messianic tribulations." But in this same prophecy Israel's destiny is illuminated and the ultimate purpose of its election revealed. Paradoxically enough, the sufferings Israel must experience to atone for the so frequent betrayals of its election will one day give birth to a new era for the entire world, when the House of David will be reestablished, not by the blissful reign of a worldly prince, but by the coming of the King-Messiah. This is the supreme moment to which the drama of Jewish history, and through it of history in general, aspires. It was to be the role of the prophets to outline this messianic determinism, and of Hosea to lay its cornerstone.

The following revelation announces — again for the first time — the end of the regime of envy and conquest which has ruled in the world since the murder of Abel:

> And in that day... I will break the bow and the sword and the battle out
> of the land.
>
> (2:20)

So long as wars and the satanic arms race which is ravaging our age are not wiped out from the life of the nations and the heart of men, Israel will have no rest, its history will not reach its end. It is evident that this prophecy has never been fulfilled. Neither the return from Babylonian

Captivity, nor Christian society have brought a solution to this fundamental outrage in human relations. This is why the Jewish people, like a woman about to give birth in pain, still bears, in a mysterious way, the advent of the new era in its womb, as it has done throughout history, in spite of the terrible succession of pharaohs, inquisitors and Hitlers. This is why it always returns from every exile whereas its tormentors perish. This is why Israel one day — let us not doubt it for one moment — a day that has been appointed since the Covenant between the Lord of History and Abraham, will return to its promised land, for ever...

JOEL

It is virtually impossible to assign to this prophet a place in history since no king is mentioned by him. The fact that the northern kingdom of Israel is not even once mentioned by him may be an indication that Joel's ministry took place after the fall of this kingdom. But after all, this is of secondary importance for the subject which engages us.

Joel announces the rise of the most formidable nation with which the Jewish people was ever to be confronted on its road through history;

> A great people and a mighty, there has not ever been the like, neither shall be any more after them, even to the years of many generations... The land was as the garden of Eden before them, and after them a desolate wilderness...
>
> (2:2–3)

This obviously refers to the enemy who was to inflict upon the people and its homeland their harshest sufferings and, consequently, their longest exile. To whom else can this prophecy be applied if not to the Roman legions? To what else can it be applied if not to the almost nineteen centuries long exile?

But during this long period God has not abandoned His people, but called them in these words:

> Yet even now, saith the Lord, turn ye unto Me with all your heart, and with fasting, and with lamentation; And rend your heart, and not your garments...
>
> (2:12–13)

With fasting, to be sure, but mainly with tears and lamentation will this Exile end;

> For behold, in those days, and in that time when I shall bring back the captivity of Judah and Jerusalem...
>
> (4:1)

And this promised land, effectively reduced to the state of a "desolate wilderness" by Roman devastations and age-long neglect, will become fertile and joyful again, by the grace of God alone:

And the Lord answered and said unto His people: Behold, I will send you corn, and wine and oil, and ye shall be satisfied therewith... Fear not, O land, be glad and rejoice... For the pastures of the wilderness do spring. For the tree beareth its fruit... For I will give you the rain in just measure in spring and in autumn as of old...

(2:19–23)

And let there be no misunderstanding:

And I will no more make you a reproach among the nations; But I will remove far off you the adversary from the North...

(2:19)

But the threat of the nations will never be entirely removed, for until the very end they will resist the Divine policy and the fulfillment of the Zionist dream of final Return.

Joel makes it clear that the people will be gathered within the borders of a new Israel in a different manner, in accordance with the will of God, in preparation for the great Day of the Lord when ancient accounts will be settled once and for all:

I will gather all nations, and will bring them down into the valley of Jehoshaphat; And I will enter into judgment with them there for My people and for My heritage Israel, whom they have scattered among the nations and for My land which they have divided...

(4:2)

"My people... My heritage... My land..." Let the nations pay heed! For their last attempt to wipe Israel from the map will end in their weapons being broken and cast away like garbage, once and for all.

What a terrible irony — this "encouragement" to take up arms!

Proclaim ye this among the nations: Prepare war, stir up the mighty men! Let all the men of war draw near, let them come up! Beat your plowshares into swords and your pruning-hooks into spears, let the weak say: I am strong! Haste ye and come!

(4:0–10)

But on this terrible "Day of the Lord" mankind will not perish and the world will not come to its end in the way popular tradition and certain apocalyptic sects like to picture it. To the contrary:

And it shall come to pass that whosoever shall call on the name of the Lord shall be delivered. For in mount Zion and in Jerusalem there shall be those that shall be saved...

(2:5)

The long centuries during which Israel will be deprived of its independence and its Temple, as foretold by Amos with such severity, will end when the Word of God has become scarce and the thirst for it great.

It shall come to pass afterward that I will pour out My spirit upon all flesh; And your sons and daughters shall prophesy, your old men shall dream dreams, your young men shall see visions; And also upon the slaves and the handmaids in those days will I pour out My spirit.

(3:1-2)

We see that these few chapters of the book of Joel contain a complete blueprint of Israel's Zionist history, from the great Exile until the coming of the Kingdom of God in the whole world. It is evident that the return from the Babylonian Captivity has not led to the judgment of the nations, nor to the end of mankind's obstinate policy of armament or to Israel's return to its God and its permanent settlement in its land, and certainly not to the absolute reign of the Holy Spirit in the world.

All this places insurmountable obstacles in the path of those Christian exegetes who insist that with Christ's appearance on earth Israel's history has lost its biblical and messianic significance...

ISAIAH

It is not our intention to join those who have performed an "autopsy" on the biblical book which bears the name of this famous prophet and have discovered four different personages, but rather to underline its "Zionist" character by describing its consistent vision of Israel's history.

On the Middle-Eastern scene of the period the new Assyrian power celebrated its triumphs with deportations and massacres. Tiglath-Pileser III, Salmanasser V, Sargon and Sennacherib, who succeeded each other on the throne, led the road roller of their hordes and chariots through the world.

During the reign of the first of these tyrants Pekah, the king of Israel, allied himself with the Syrian king Resin against Jerusalem!

In the face of Assyria's imperialism the children of Jacob engaged in a civil war... This was the atmosphere in which Isaiah grew up.

In 732 Damascus was raised and ten years later it was Samaria's turn, and Israel was deported by Sargon. In 701 Jerusalem miraculously escaped the fate of Samaria. It was in this catastrophic context with the Assyrian armies covering the face of the earth and tiny Judah remaining the only witness of the Lord of History, that Isaiah proclaimed the holiness of Him "whose glory fills the whole earth!"

More than any other prophet Isaiah was politically engaged. There is no doubt that he was the scion of an aristocratic family and that the gates of the royal court were consequently open to him. But he always intervened with the king in his capacity of prophet alone, and as such he became the counselor of king Hezekiah.

As an outspoken opponent of the war faction, the general staff and the false (and salaried!) prophets who propagated an illusionary peace and artificial and incongruous alliances, Isaiah inevitably attracted their attacks during the reign of Manasseh, the cruellest king Jerusalem has ever known.

The lofty flight of his prophecies, the importance of the book which bears his name, and a brief survey of his interpretation of the meaning of Exile allow us to regard his hymns of Return as an expression of the double aspect of physical and spiritual resurrection. According to him, in the course of the Zionist development of history, the Jewish people will "at that time" first of all resettle and revive its land, and only then return to the Lord and the Holy Scriptures. Such a picture was also painted by Ezekiel in his dramatic vision of the dry bones which were revived physically, but not spiritually. Spiritual revival was to come later. In other words: one day in its history Israel will experience a political resurrection in the land of its fathers, and this political revival will later be followed by its re-establishment as a priestly nation among the Gentiles who "will go up to Jerusalem."

At the heart of Isaiah's ministry is the theophany and his answer to God's question: "Whom shall I send, who will go for us?" with the words: "Here am I." Confronted with the harsh message he must convey to the people, a message which recalls the severest warnings of Amos, Isaiah asks: "Lord, how long?"

> Until cities be waste without inhabitant, and houses without man, and the land become utterly waste.
>
> (6:11–12)

The desolation of the land and the exile of the people will last until Israel laments that it has been forgotten by its Creator, that He no longer holds its hands as in the days of yore.

> Zion said: the Lord hath forsaken me... Can a woman forget her suckling child, that she should not have passion on the son of her womb? Yea, these may forget, yet will not I forget thee.
>
> (49:14–15)

Let us begin the series of texts relating to the return to the promised land with the following prophecy, which is unique in prophetical literature, since it refers to two different types of exile:

> And it shall come to pass in that day that the Lord will set His hand the second time to recover the remnant of His people... And he will set up an ensign for the nations... from the four corners of the earth...
>
> (11:11–12)

The Christian exegetes who interpret all the prophecies of return as references to the return from the Babylonian captivity, obviously ignore that after this exile Israel did not return from the four corners of the earth! The just quoted verses solve the problem. And the following text clearly does not refer to the forty-five thousand immigrants who came back from Babylon.

> And it shall come to pass in that day, that the Lord will beat off the fruit... And ye shall be gathered one by one, O ye children of Israel.
>
> (27:12)

51

Then follows the prophecy of an immigration "through the air:

> Who are these that fly as a cloud, And as the doves to their cotes?

> (60:8)

Must we recall here the Jews from Yemen and Iraq who came to Israel by air soon after the rebirth of the Jewish state? Must we recall that these Jews themselves did not doubt for one moment that God, as this hour of ultimate trial, had saved them by carrying them "on the wings of his great eagle?"

Not only the land of Judah, but even the desert of the Negev will revive, and cities will spring up there on their ruins.

> The Negev and the parched land shall be glad, And the desert shall rejoice, and blossom as the rose. It shall blossom abundantly and rejoice even with joy and singing.

> (35:1–2)

> For the Lord hath comforted Zion; He hath comforted all her waste places, And hath made her wilderness like Eden, And her desert like the garden of the Lord.

> (51:3)

> And they shall build the old wastes, They shall raise up the former desolations, And they shall renew the waste cities, The desolations of many generations.

> (61:4)

And must we recall that it was not until this century that the desert began to blossom as a rose and that cities were once again erected on their ruins — cities that certainly had not been archaeological sites in the days of Ezra and Nehemiah...?

Moreover, whenever did Isaiah tell the Jews whom he saw in his vision return from the four corners of the earth, that another exile was awaiting them in the days of the Roman legions? Let us listen to him:

> I will bring thy seed from the east, And gather thee from the west; I will say to the north: Give up, And to the south: Keep not back, Bring My sons from far, And my daughters from the end of the earth.

> (43:5–6)

> In a little wrath I hid My face from thee for a moment; But with everlasting love will I have compassion on thee... I have sworn that I would not be wroth with thee, Nor rebuke thee.

> (54:8–9)

How can these words of God be interpreted as referring to the seventy years of the Babylonian captivity, unless we entirely ignore the nineteen centuries of dispersion "to the four corners of the earth?

For the Lord shall be thine everlasting light... They shall inherit the land for ever.

(60:20)

For when, one day, the children of Israel will be brought back to their biblical homeland, it is not merely in order that the Negev will blossom as a rose:

He that is left in Zion, and he that remaineth in Jerusalem shall be called holy...

(4:3)

But ye shall be named the priests of the Lord, Men shall call you the ministers of our God.

(61:6)

And the nations shall see thy triumph, And all kings thy glory; And thou shalt be called by a new name.

(62:2)

This is the spiritual aspect of the Jewish people's final Return and no one can maintain that this resurrection, this conversion of the Jewish people indeed took place after the return from Babylon.

Isaiah came to tell us that this conversion of all of Israel cannot be separated from the coming of its King-Messiah who will come to judge the nations at the time of the final battle in the Middle East, and perhaps in the entire world. This advent will mark the end of our barbaric pre-history and herald the era of peace and justice to which all peoples more or less consciously aspire and which all mythologies placed in the Golden Age of the past.

And it shall come to pass in that day, That the Lord will punish... the kings of the earth upon the earth. And they shall be gathered together, as prisoners are gathered in the dungeon... For the Lord of hosts will reign in mount Zion and in Jerusalem.

(24:21–23)

Freed of their satanic involvement with bombs and war budgets, the nations will then be able to understand that the Golden Age is still before them, though they had not known it, because they and their leaders and high priests never knew to read the history of Israel or to understand its prophets. When finally the gordian knot of Zionism will be unravelled in the Middle East by the Messiah himself, the nations will acknowledge the Lord:

And it shall come to pass in the end of days, That the mountain of the Lord's house shall be established as the top of the mountains... And all nations shall flow into it. And many peoples shall go and say: Come ye, and let us go up to the house of the Lord... For out of Zion shall go forth the Torah, And the word of the Lord from Jerusalem.

(2:2–32)

At that time, when History will finally have found its fulfilment and Jerusalem will be the capital of a reconciled world, Israel will at last be able to devote itself entirely to its mission which it received from Moses and of which it was reminded by Isaiah;

> It is too light a thing that thou shouldest be My servant, To raise up the tribes of Jacob, and to restore the remnant of Israel; I will also give thee for a light of the nations, that My salvation may be unto the end of the earth.
>
> (49:6)

This has been Israel's mission since the day God called Abraham. It has failed, since the world has not accepted its message. When Israel was crushed under the Roman boot, the Church took over this solemn assignment. But it, too, has failed, and even more seriously, because it has never been able to bring peace and justice to the world.

The last word belongs to a mightier One, who will come to force the nations towards salvation before their folly blows up the entire world.

Finally, to sum up this brief study of Isaiah, we quote one of his most famous prophecies of a world entirely at peace with itself, even in its humblest creatures:

> The wolf shall dwell with the lamb, And the leopard shall lie down with the kid. And the calf and the young lion and the fatling together; And a little child shall lead them.
>
> (11:6)

MICAH

A contemporary of Isaiah, and a member of the class of poor peasants who were groaning under the burden of taxes and exactions, Micah passionately denounced the corruption of the ruling classes, the clergy and the false prophets, who were paid to condone the official policy of the day. Better perhaps than anyone else he exposed "religion" which pretended to be a way towards a successful life.

In the following terrible worlds he announced not only the imminent exile, but even the destruction of the Temple:

> Therefore shall Zion for your sake be plowed as a field, And Jerusalem shall become heaps, And the mountain of the Temple as the high places of a forest.
>
> (3:12)

But not for ever:

> I will surely assemble, O Jacob, all of thee; I will surely gather the remnant of Israel... They will break the gate and go out.
>
> (2:12)

In that day, saith the Lord, will I assemble her that halteth, And all those
that are driven out... And the Lord shall reign over them in mount Zion.

$$(4:6-7)$$

Not a king, reigning in Jerusalem, or even in the entire world, nor a
Jewish nationalist movement will be the triumphant ruler in the Holy Land,
but He who will be born in a humble village, "little among the thousands of
Judah," has been destined since the Beginning by the Lord to reign in the
world in divine majesty:

...He who is to be ruler in Israel, whose origins are from of old, from
ancient days... for he shall be great unto the ends of the earth, and He
shall bring peace.

$$(5:1-4)$$

But before this great turning point in the history of the Jewish people
comes — the goal of Divine policy — the nations will be compelled to
recognize the hand of the Lord of History. They will be judged, but not
destroyed; they too, like Israel, will have to undergo a radical conversion
which will be effected only by the descent of the Holy Spirit (and not by
the endeavors of the "religious").

They will go up to Jerusalem in Israel's footsteps in a spiritual Zionist
pilgrimage, for "out of Zion shall go forth the Torah, and the word of the
Lord from Jerusalem."

Micah faithfully reiterates the great "Zionist" proclamation of his
teacher Isaiah. It is in Zion that the nations will learn not to make war any
more, but to devote all their energy, all their resources to the happiness of
man and his children.

But the prophet, being a man of the land and the fields who has weighed
the cities and found them too light and inhuman, adds the following small
sentence which is the sum and substance of the ideal of genuine
equality:

They will sit every man under his vine and under his fig-tree; and none
shall make them afraid.

$$(4:4)$$

JEREMIAH

Never has there been a man who seemed to be less predestined to play such
important role in the life of his people than Jeremiah of Anatoth, this timid
young man of sad reputation. By obeying the commands he received from
God he soon set the politicians, the military and the clergy as well as
considerably large sections of the population against himself. To be a scion
of a priestly family and at the same time predict the destruction of the
Temple, to preach surrender to the enemy — what a program! But such
was indeed Jeremiah's program.

At the beginning of his ministry Assyria was still all-powerful under the reign of Assurbanipal. Niniveh was destroyed in 612. Judah found itself caught between the two giants Babylon and Egypt. The latter country, under Pharaoh Necho, had again become a power which had to be reckoned with. Twice Jeremiah had to witness the siege of Jerusalem, the second time with the resulting fall of Judah and the Babylonian captivity. But he also witnessed, in 620, the spectacular discovery of the Book of Deuteronomy under the foundations of the Temple and the reform of the good king Josiah, who was unfortunately killed soon afterwards during his helpless campaign against Egypt. He was succeeded by the sombre Jehoiakim who was to reign for many years. Thus evil triumphed and the righteous king with his messianic dreams perished.

The corruption which prevailed everywhere, and in particular in the Temple itself, induced Jeremiah to announce the imminent Exile in terms which Amos could not have improved:

> Behold, I will feed them, even this people, with wormwood, And give them water of gall to drink. I will scatter them among the nations, Whom neither they nor their fathers have known.
>
> (9:15)

> I will cause them to eat the flesh of their sons and the flesh of their daughters... in the siege and in the straitness wherewith their enemies shall straiten them.
>
> (19:9)

But the Exile will not last longer than one generation, for then Israel will repent and return to its God. And if Israel prays for forgiveness they will return not only from Babylon, but also from the countries where Assyria had deported the ten tribes...

> In those days the house of Judah shall walk with the house of Israel... to the land that I have given for an inheritance unto your fathers... Thou shalt call Me my Father and shalt not turn away from Me.
>
> (3:18–19)

> And I will gather the remnant of My flock out of all the countries whither I have driven them, and will bring them back to their folds... And I will set up shepherds over them... And they shall fear no more, nor be dismayed, neither shall any be lacking, saith the Lord.
>
> (23:3–4)

Such a realistic man as Jeremiah was, however, who knew the world of the royal court and the Temple very well, understood that such a change and such a conversion could only be effected by the immediate intervention of God, as at the time of the giving of the Torah on Mount Sinai. Hence his extraordinary prophecy — unprecedented in the Hebrew Bible — of the "New Covenant."

> Behold the days come, saith the Lord that I will make a new covenant with the house of Israel and the house of Judah; not according to the

covenant I made with their fathers... for they broke My covenant...
After those days I will put My Torah in their inward parts and in their
heart will I write it... And they shall all know Me from the least of them
unto the greatest of them.

(30:31–34)

It is certainly not an annulment of the covenant with the fathers, nor of
Deuteronomy, or their replacement by new scriptures, new teachings. In
other words, by no means is it God's intention to found a new religion to
replace biblical Judaism. Such a decision would make the Patriarchs and
the prophets into liars and be the surest way towards the radical
disappearance of Israel as a people, a religion and a nation whose mission
it is to live in the promised land.

The same passage from which we have just have quoted, also contains
the following remarkable verse:

They shall teach no more every man his neighbor, and every man his
brother, saying: Know the Lord! For they shall all know me.

(31:34)

Indeed, one may say that Israel will no longer be merely one religion
among others, but rather that it is predestined to live in perfect harmony
with the Divine will, thereby making its cultural, or rather cultic, way of
life focused on the Temple redundant.

It is to such a mature Jewish way of life that the Great Return must lead,
independent of a doubtful priestly caste and of the life and death of a good-
willing king.

Moreover, this Great Return will herald the advent of the King-Messiah,
a mysterious personage bearing the name of "Lord of our justice" who will
be, in a miraculous way, a descendant of the House of David —
miraculous because at that time the House of David will have ceased to
reign over the Jewish people and have become extinct.

Behold, the days come, saith the Lord, That I will raise unto David a
righteous shoot, And he shall reign as king, and prosper, And shall
execute justice and righteousness in the land. In his days Judah shall be
saved and Israel shall dwell safely... For the Lord hath brought up and
led the seed of the house of Israel out of the north country, and from all
the countries whither I had driven them...

(23:5–8)

It is of minor importance whether Jeremiah, when he proclaimed the
coming of the perfect king, thought of Zedekiah or of somebody else. We
are rather inclined to believe that a man like Jeremiah who knew the nature
of men and of princes so well, had no illusions about the chances of a
wordly sovereign who might one day emerge from the House of David.

The same God who will gather the children of Israel "in that day" will
also reign over them for ever in their recovered land. He alone can guide
history towards the fulfilment of His people's Zionist vocation, in spite of

the obstinacy and hatred of the nations. He alone can engrave in the heart of Israel this new, purifying and redeeming covenant.

Neither humanism, nor "religion" or human politics can bring about both the physical and spiritual resurrection of Israel when it will one day, once and for all, be gathered in its own homeland.

Jeremiah's lamentations will not last for ever and his grief will be alleviated when his children will rebuild Jerusalem in preparation, not only of the rebuilding of the Temple, but of a different advent...

EZEKIEL

Ezekiel is the prophet of exile *par excellence*, since his ministry took place on foreign soil. Like the other prophets he interprets exile as a punishment for his people's shortcoming, but he is even more severe than they, and goes so far as to proclaim:

> I have delivered thee unto the daughters of the Philistines that are ashamed of thy lewd ways... Sodom thy sister hath not done, she nor her daughters, as thou hast done...
>
> (16:27–48)

It is hardly possible to launch harsher and more offensive accusations against the people of Israel and Judah. One wonders how they reacted to the prophet's outrageous insults...

As the prophet of Exile, more than any other prophet, Ezekiel introduces a concept which is entirely new in the prophetical writings, but has nevertheless its origin in the teachings of Moses who was "the greatest of all prophets" according to Deuteronomy. Before Ezekiel the prophets had seen the "Zionist" development of history in accordance with this pattern: sin, punishment, repentance, forgiving and return. But in Ezekiel's message the return is no longer dependent on repentance:

> I do this not for your sake, O house of Israel, but for My holy name, which ye have profaned among the nations... and the nations shall know that I am the Lord when I shall be sanctified in you before their eyes.
>
> (36:22–23)

But, of course, no nation ever repents, Israel no more than any other people. Only a minority of righteous men and martyrs saves the honor of every generation.

Immediately after the episode in the desert with the molten calf, we are told, the Lord wanted to forsake Israel and to make another people emerge from Moses. But like Abraham in the case of Sodom, Moses has recourse to a specific plea which can be summed up in the following words: "You have chosen this people, O Lord, and You, who has created them, know them. You have committed Yourself to them with solemn promises, in front of the nations (that is, of history). What will they say, these nations and their idols, if You renounce Your word?"

This is what Ezekiel in exile also realizes, an exile which is, after all, far from uncomfortable for most of the exiles, whose first contingent consisted of opportunist and realistic members of the bourgeoisie and the aristocracy. Why should these people repent and give up their comfortable lives in the luxury of Babylon in order to rebuild the walls of the desolate and provincial town of Jerusalem?

God therefore compels His people to return, and guides the return with a strong hand, so that the nations, who would do everything to prevent Israel's return, acknowledge that the God of Israel is the true Lord of History, and that this book they hold in contempt, the Bible, is the truth. Thus God "saves His honor" in spite of Israel's lukewarm attitude and in spite of the world's hatred.

The inevitable conclusion must therefore be drawn that the Jewish people returned to Jerusalem by *force majeure* and not because it had been converted to its God — such a conversion is to take place in the future. This is an extremely important aspect without which we cannot understand Jewish history, nor this very special theology of the messianic era as part of the Divine pedagogy.

God does not demand man's conversion as a precondition for his salvation, but salvation will come against his natural inclinations. It is always the Creator who makes the first move towards His creatures — this is what every sound Judeo-Christian theology means by Grace. The Jewish people is indeed the most convincing demonstration of Divine Grace and this fact is the heart of Ezekiel's message.

After its return to the promised land — only after it — Israel will return to its God:

> When I shall bring you into the land of Israel, into the country which I lifted up My hand to give unto your fathers... there shall you remember your ways... and you shall loathe yourselves...
>
> (20:42)

"In that day," after having regained its political independence, Israel will realize that it is still far from safe and that it is not immune to corruption and mediocracy; and, no doubt, the hunger and thirst for the word of God will increase... Zionism, as a political movement alone, cannot satisfy the people of the patriarchs and the prophets, the people that yearn for justice, truth and peace.

Moreover — and this is yet another of Ezekiel's "innovations" — precisely when Israel has regained its independence it will be threatened with total destruction:

> Son of man, set thy face toward Gog, of the land of Magog, the chief prince of Meshech and Tubal and prophesy against him... In the latter years thou shalt come against the land that is brought back from the sword, that is gathered out of many peoples... and thou shall come up against My people Israel as a cloud to cover the land, thou and many peoples with thee...
>
> (38:8–15)

First important disclosure: Israel's final return will take place in extremely dramatic circumstances after a narrow escape from a very real attempt to exterminate them. And the second disclosure: the enemy is not one of Israel's traditional adversaries, for he comes from the north, from the surroundings of the Black Sea and the Caucasus, accompanied (or should we say 'supported'?) by many peoples in a last attempt to suppress once and for all the Jewish people which has just been gathered again in its biblical land. This will be the outcome:

> Thou shall fall upon the mountains of Israel thou and the peoples that are with thee; I will give thee to the ravenous birds... and to the beasts of the field, to be devoured... and the nations shall know that I am the Lord... and they shall bury Gog and all his multitude... seven months this shall last.
>
> (39:4, 7, 12)

The Lord's direct intervention rescues Israel from total destruction, as it did at the time of the Exodus from Egypt. And just as the miraculous Exodus from Egypt was followed by the giving of the Torah on Mount Sinai, the annihilation of Gog and his armies will be followed by a new encounter, by a new covenant between God and His chosen people, sealed by the descent of the Spirit who will engrave the Torah on the tables of their hearts. Moreover, as we shall see later on, one of the prophets who predicted the return from the Babylonian captivity also announced that the Messiah himself, coming upon the clouds, will destroy the forces of Gog and Magog. He, the heavenly liberator, will inaugurate the new Temple and introduce on earth the universal worship of the only Lord and Savior of the nations:

> And the glory of the Lord came into the Temple by the way of the gate whose prospect is toward the east. And the Spirit took me up, and brought me into the inner court. And I heard one speaking unto me. And He said unto me: Son of man, this the place of My throne, and the place of the soles of My feet, where I will dwell in the midst of the children of Israel for ever.
>
> (43:4–7)

One can hardly believe one's ears when one hears Professor Klausner declare with authority that there is no trace of the Messiah in the book of Ezekiel.

But Klausner, of course, like the overwhelming majority of Jewish historians and theologians, regards the Messiah merely as a king who will be more successful than his predecessors and whose role will be essentially political. In their excessive desire to reject every more or less christocentric interpretation these scholars throw out the baby with the bath-water, thereby reducing the hopes of their people to nothing but a nationalist adventure.

But the prophets had no such complexes, and they present us with this messianic hope in all its fulness.

We have reserved for the conclusion of these pages on Ezekiel the text which seems to us the Magna Carta of Zionism and of Jewish history, since it paints with remarkable clarity the phases of the final Return which will be followed by a redeeming upheaval for Israel and the entire world. We refer to the famous vision of the dry bones and the chapter preceding it:

> Because they have made you desolate, and swallowed you up on every side... and thou art the subject of many talks, and of the evil report of the peoples... Behold, I am for you and I will turn unto you... and will do better unto you than at your beginnings... Thou shalt be my inheritance and thou shalt no more be bereaved...
>
> (36:3, 9, 11, 12)

Thus the very Return implies the judgment of the nations and one believes to hear the laughter of the Lord of History at the deliberations and international conspiracies against the Jewish people...

> This land that was desolate is become like the garden of Eden; and the waste and desolate and ruined cities are fortified and inhabited. Then the nations that are left round about you shall know that I the Lord have builded the ruined places, and planted that which was desolate.
>
> (36:35–36)

Without any doubt the neighboring countries of the promised land are reminded here of the wonderful message of Isaiah (in chapter 49) of Israel's reconciliation with its Arab neighbors. For it must never be forgotten that when the Lord leads His people back to its land and revives the desolate desert, He does this also in order to convince its neighbors, the children of Ishmael and Esau, that no league of hatred can prevail against His will, and that the day will come when Jacob and Esau shall find each other, not for a brief reconciliation as in the past, but in repentance and eternal brotherhood.

But let us now turn to what we have called the Magna Carta of Zionism:

> The hand of the Lord was upon me and the Lord carried me out in the Spirit, and set me down in the midst of the valley, and it was full of bones... Son of man, these bones are the whole house of Israel; Behold, they say: we are clean cut off... Behold, I will open your graves, and cause you to come up out of your graves, O My people, And I will bring you into the land of Israel.
>
> (37:1, 11, 12)

It would be foolhardy to pretend that the Babylonian captivity had been a period of concentration camps and genocide for the Jewish people. The bones had not dried out, nor had these few decades killed all hope. On the contrary, it was the Christian era which saw a terrible succession of persecution, culminating in the gas chambers of our own time. Nobody can maintain that it is foolhardy to apply the vision of the dry bones to this seemingly endless exile...

> I prophesied as I was commanded... And lo, there were sinews upon

them, and flesh came up, and skin covered them above; but there was no Spirit in them...

(37:8)

It is not a God-fearing people that returns to its land "in those days." The long centuries of its wanderings from one corner of the western world to the other, as the despised victims of an outspokenly antisemitic society in search of a scapegoat, were time enough for its hope to perish, and for doubt, if not desperation, to take root in its soul. In such a situation the Jews have begun to recover their land — a wilderness. More than just idealism was needed to overcome. That is why in Ezekiel's Magna Carta a Spirit goes out from God after the first phase of "biological" resurrection. Not the Holy Spirit of the return to YHVH, to be sure, but certainly related...

Thus, after having been firmly planted in its recovered soil, after having regained its independence (at a high price!) the second phase begins:

Come from the four winds, O spirit, and breathe upon these slain, that they may live.

(37:9)

For so long as they are a nation like the other nations, they are still dead in the eyes of the Lord of eternal life. They are not the people of witnesses amidst the nations, a task which the Lord has imposed on them since the first days of their history, a history not like that of other nations. But they are afraid to take upon themselves the part of the Chosen people. They no longer understand the meaning of Election. They do not want to be reminded of this redoubtable election, they wish to be "a people like the others." They have wanted this since the days of Samuel when they demanded a king so that they might be like the others, and they forgot that God alone is their King.

But let them nevertheless listen to this promise, which discloses the true meaning of that feared Election:

...I will cleanse them; so shall they be My people, and I will be their God. And my servant David shall be king over them, and they all shall have one shepherd... They shall also walk in Mine ordinance... I will make an everlasting covenant with them... and the nations shall know that I am the Lord, when my sanctuary shall be in the midst of them for ever.

(37:23–28)

THE POST-EXILIC PROPHETS

After we have heard the pre-exilic and exilic prophets announce the Return in exultant words, the time has come to examine under which conditions this Return actually took place, and above all whether this tremendous event in Israel's history was the fulfilment of the prophetical messianic message. In other words: does the return from the Babylonian captivity represent the implementation of all the "zionist" prophecies? If this were the case the Jewish people would have completed its role in history. If, on the other hand, these prophecies were not fulfilled in the time of Ezra and Nehemiah, Zerubbabel the prince and Joshua the high-priest, Israel's election is still valid and will continue to be valid until the Creator estabished His messianic Kingdom on earth as in heaven.

HAGGAI

Haggai began his ministry in the second year of the reign of Darius, in 520, about eight years after the famous Edict of Cyrus which allowed the exiles to return to Judah and to rebuild the sanctuary in Jerusalem. And right away he asks a painful question:

> Is it a time for you yourselves to dwell in your ceiled houses, while this house lieth waste?
>
> (1:4)

More than fifteen years after the return the Temple is still lying in ruins while the aristocrats, the bourgeoisie of the Return, have comfortably installed themselves in their homes! This is all the more disturbing as the imperial Edict had formally affirmed their right to rebuild the unique sanctuary of Judaism and the historical circumstances had been extremely favorable because quiet — though not exactly friendship — prevailed on all frontiers. True, the returning immigrants had found a waste and often entirely desolate land. They had had to start from scratch in a very small territory: the distance from Bethel to Hebron was 66 kilometers, and from Jericho to Lydda 44.

Zerubbabel and Joshua, obviously not leaders of stature, were afraid of their responsibilities and shrank from taking an initiative and in particular from the decision to rebuild the Temple. Indeed, the promises seemed to have been fulfilled to a very limited degree, with only a small number of immigrants (about forty thousand) returning to frontiers that were certainly not those of David and Solomon...

Haggai nevertheless succeeded in arousing these leaders from their torpor and faint-heartedness; and a few weeks after his intervention building activities on Mount Zion already started, but in a mood that was far from messianic.

> But many of the priests and Levites and head of fathers's houses, the old men that had seen the first Temple standing on its foundation, wept with a loud voice, when this house was before their eyes.
>
> (Ezra 3:12)

But Haggai is there to encourage the pioneers. True, the work holds no promise of a magnificent building; gold, silver and precious wood are mainly conspicuous by their absence, but the future has several surprises in store:

> I will shake all nations, and the choicest things of all nations shall come, and I will fill this house with glory... for Mine is the silver, and Mine is the gold... The glory of this latter house shall be greater than that of the former... and in this place will I give peace.

> (2:7–9)

In order to stimulate the imagination and, no doubt, also the ambitions of the timid governor, the prophet recklessly concludes his prophecies with these words:

> I will shake the heavens and the earth and I will overthrow the throne of kingdoms... In that day, Saith the Lord of hosts, will I take thee, O Zerubbabel, son of Shealtiel, and I will make thee as a signet, for I have chosen thee, My servant.

> (1:22–23)

But the least we can say is that prince Zerubbabel never caused any throne to collapse in spite of the prophet's feverish impatience to see the messianic rule established in Judah, when the nations bring their silver and gold for the inauguration of the sanctuary of the Lord, the God of Israel. Surrounded by mediocre men in this tiny country of Judah, Haggai tried in vain to force his people's destiny.

ZECHARIAH

Zechariah relieves Haggai as soon as the reconstruction of the Temple began, in the fourth year of Darius' reign, that is in 518.

A cloud had risen over the horizon of Zion in the person of Tatenai, the satrap of Syria, who apparently suspected the Jews and their leaders of preparing a revolt. (The man must have had a very vivid imagination to take his dreams for reality; he was probably set up against the Jews by Samaritan agents.) In view of this danger it became necessary to encourage the builders with visions of glory. This was the task Zechariah took upon himself:

> Jerusalem shall be inhabited without walls, for the multitude of men and cattle therein, for I, saith the Lord, will be unto her a wall of fire, and I will be the glory in the midst of her.

> (2:4)

Indeed a prophecy in which those who deplored the scarcity of immigrants and the poverty of Jerusalem might find comfort! Next Zechariah turns to those "who have not returned," but prefer the comforts of Babylon to the hard life in Judah:

> Ho, ho, flee then from the land of the north! ...ho, Zion, escape, thou that dwellest with the daughter of Babylon...

> (2:10)

64

Like Haggai Zechariah tries to force the land of fate by evoking the King-Messiah from among his people instead of announcing his advent "in those days." He is even far more audacious than his colleague in as much as he prepares two crowns for Joshua the high-priest, obviously having lost all faith in the weak prince Zerubbabel. This was a gesture of great temerity, for by doing this he actually anointed and consecrated one and the same person both king and priest.

No more than the ousted prince, however, does the high-priest bring about the expected conquests, and no sign from heaven comes to affirm the prophet's daring choice; and once again the people has to pay the price of its illusions...

It is then that Zechariah retires into solitude and silence. Over the years he is to meditate about the total "echelon" of the men he had crowned...

Since only the poorest people have returned from Babylon and are now struggling with the stones and groaning under the many heavy taxes while the aristocrats have installed themselves in Jerusalem to play there their petty ambitious games, it is clear that the time has not yet come and that this return was not the final one:

> ...I will gather them, for I have redeemed them... And I will sow them
> among the peoples, and they shall remember Me in far countries...
>
> (10:9)

The hour of the reconciliation of the tribes, which was announced by the great Ezekiel, has not yet struck; this is why Zechariah, in a symbolic act, breaks the two staves which he calls Grace and Binder, to demonstrate that exile and judgment will continue as long as discord and envy exist.

The exalting messianic program will be realized "at that time... on that day" — the Day of Judgment of the nations. For even Cyrus and his successors, however great their political visions and their undeniable tolerance may be, cannot understand the Lord's plan with His chosen people, nor can they accept that history is made in Jerusalem. The borders of Judah are not wide enough, and how insignificant are these few tens of thousands of immigrants, when the Lord calls all Jacob's children from the four corners of the earth; not only those who were sent in exile, but also those who went to far-away islands of their own free will.

Since even in a time of peace, and in spite of the approval of an enlightened and tolerant king the great Return and national revival proved to be impossible, new sufferings, new destructions must visit this people and this sanctuary. Until the day that Jerusalem becomes an abscess in the body of the nations, an insolvable international problem, and the nations will "go up" to this city for the last time, not to worship the only God, but to destroy it once again, and forever.

> Behold, I will make Jerusalem a cup of staggering unto all the peoples
> round about... a stone of burden for all the peoples, and all that burden
> themselves with it shall be sore wounded, and all the nations of the earth
> shall be gathered together against it. (12:2–3)

So great will be the distress and so formidable the danger that the people will realize the vanity of every political and military alliance:

> ...And they shall look unto me, and they shall mourn for him, as one mourneth for one's only son, him, whom they have thrust through. In that day shall there be a great mourning in Jerusalem.
>
> (12:10-11)

And the Savior of Israel, as so many times in the history of His people, will respond to this distress, this repentance, this mourning:

> Then shall the Lord go forth, and fight against those nations. And His feet shall stand in that day upon the mount of Olives, which is before Jerusalem on the east, and the mount of Olives shall be cleft in the midst thereof...
>
> (14:3-3)

Only then, not by virtue of the wisdom of the council of nations, nor by virtue of Israel's military or pioneering valiancy will the Zionist epic reach its culmination, and the era of the Holy Spirit's omnipotent reign on earth begin.

> And the Lord shall be King over all the earth... And Jerusalem shall be lifted up... and shall dwell safely.
>
> (14:9-11)

To ask the question whether the (very partial) return from the Babylonian captivity has brought about such a succession of apocalyptic events in the history of Israel and the nations, is to answer it. And this answer implies that the theories of the exegetes who believe that Israel's history lost its prophetical meaning with the coming of Christ (incognito and in death), are utterly wrong...

DANIEL

Since the end of Persian rule Judah had gradually begun to prosper, and this more or less happy and "eventless" period continued throughout the reign of Alexander, his immediate successors (333-301 B.C.), and the Ptolemaeans (301-198 B.C.) until the reign of the first Seleucids.

It is therefore not surprising that this "eventless" period has left no trace in the Bible, all the more so since the prophetical canon had been closed and made place for a rich wisdom literature (Psalms, Song of Songs, Ecclesiastes, among many others).

All the prophets had been involved in the political struggles of their days. They had appeared on the scene in times of crisis, not only to interpret these crises, but to shape history. For the subject which occupies us, it is remarkable to observe that almost four centuries separate the Edict of Cyrus from the Maccabees' struggle on life and death for survival and independence against the "nazi" regime of their days. Almost four centuries had passed since the return, centuries during which none of the great prophecies had been fulfilled, excepting the resurrection of a tiny section of the promised land and the return to Zion of an almost negligible number of diaspora Jews. The pessimist tone of Ecclesiastes seemed indeed justified...

It is understandable that the messianic dream and Zionist hope flamed up again in the heart of the people when the threat of extermination loomed with the rise of the satanic regime of Antiochus Epiphanes in Judah. The time for the nations "to up" to Jerusalem had not yet come, but the hour was grave and all things pointed at the imminent rebirth of an independent Jewish state upon which the efforts of the evil powers will be broken.

> The God of Heaven shall set up a kingdom which shall never be destroyed; nor shall the kingdom be left to another people. It shall break and consume all the other kingdoms, but it shall stand for ever.
>
> (2:44)

But Daniel is too realistic to imagine that a new independent Jewish state, even under the most gallant leadership, will be able to break the giants of the time with the tools of this world. Hence the following important proclamation:

> I saw in the night visions, and behold, there came with the clouds of heaven One like unto a son of man... and there was given him dominion, and glory and a kingdom... dominion, which shall not pass away, a kingdom which shall never be destroyed.
>
> (7:13-14)

Thus the "Son of Man," coming on the clouds, whom Christ will later evoke in his own apocalyptic discourses, appears here for the first time in apocalyptic literature. As a matter of fact, Zechariah had already referred to him in his last vision of the cataclysm on the Mount of Olives, and the prophet Ezekiel had also predicted that he would come when the messianic Temple would be inaugurated, after the defeat of the armies of Gog and Magog.

We see it: under the pressure of the events and the long wait for messianic salvation the apotheosis of the Zionist epic is now conceived, not as the result of "natural" means, but as part of a cosmic drama, as a transcendent intervention in the course of history, a real invasion of our little planet by "the other world."

The only remaining question is: how long will the period of exile and oppression last? There is no doubt that the book of Daniel has given rise to many speculations and calculations with regard to the time of the Messiah. We shall not indulge in such speculations about the last, mysterious verses of this book written by Daniel. We prefer to quote the following, more important text, which cast a clear light on the biblical, "Zionist" vision of history:

But thou, O Daniel, shut up the words, and seal the book, even to the time of the End.

(12:4)

Apparently it is not the period of the Maccabees that offers the key to this history, and the author of the book has no desire to lure his contemporaries into the snare of false hope. The Maccabean revolt, even if it came up to the most optimistic expectations and indeed re-established genuine Jewish independence, was not the End of Days and could not claim to be the manifestation of the Kingdom that will put an end to all the kingdoms of this world.

Moreover, even if we would indulge in such speculations, and start calculating from the time of Antiochus Epiphanes, or more precisely from 25th of Kislev in 168 B.C. when his lieutenant Apollonius ordered the sacrifice of a swine in the sanctuary of YHVH, it would lead us nowhere and certainly not to the Kindom of justice and eternal peace on earth as in heaven.

Indeed, this book must remain "sealed" as long as possible and certainly until the moment in history when true Jewish independence will be installed not only in the province of Judah, but in the entire promised land, and the children of Jacob will return from the four corners of the earth after long centuries of exile and suffering.

V

GENERAL CONCLUSIONS

After having analyzed the specific prophetical vision which we have defined as the dialectical process of Exile and Return, let us now try to summarize. Let us try to define what may be called the biblical, Zionist scenario which began with the alliance of the Creator and Lord of History with a man named Abraham, whom so many believers call "the Father of the Faithful," and which will reach its culmination at the Omega of our history (which we have characterized as "prehistory") with the advent of "him who comes on the clouds" on the Mount of Olives.

Amos affirms that the Great Return will bring about the permanent settlement of the children of Israel in the holy land. He concludes his book on an almost proverbially severe note with a message of forgiveness and messianic bliss.

Hosea reveals that the Jewish people will pass through a very long period of cruel exile, during which the royal dynasty will be extinct and the Temple lie in ruins. Indeed, until the beginning of the Christian era Judaism preserved the genealogy of the House of David and of the tribes.

Joel emphasizes the judgment of the nations and the consequent end of the policy of war and of the arms race.

Isaiah (and his disciple *Micah*) reaches the sublime height of a vision of universal redemption. All the nations will share the Zionist epic and come to worship the Creator on Mount Zion in Jerusalem which will be the re-established spiritual center of a new world. The entire creation, down to its humblest creatures, will be reconciled and live in peace, free from violence and bloodshed. It was Isaiah's destiny to reveal the mysterious essence of this Zionist vision of history: the servant of the Lord who gives his life to atone for the sins of all of mankind, thus personifying Israel as Moses had described it in Deuteronomy.

Jeremiah, in his agony and martyrdom, sang of the new covenant.

Ezekiel, the great bard of the Babylonian captivity, was granted the privilege to draw up the Magna Carta of Zionism, the national revival of Israel, in two clearly distinct successive stages: a physical, biological revival of flesh and bones — the political and economic aspect of Zionism — followed by a spiritual resurrection, the final return culminating in Israel's conversion to its God. It was also Ezekiel who announced the last hostile act of the nations, represented by Gog and Magog, whose armies will be crushed at the gates of Jerusalem.

Zechariah, disillusioned by the small number of pioneers and the mediocracy of their leaders, predicted the Great Exile and painted in vivid colors the last battle for Jerusalem and the messianic coming on the Mount of Olives in an atmosphere of repentance and national mourning.

Daniel announced the coming on the clouds of the Son of Man, and exhorted his readers not to scrutinize his book too closely until the "last days" when the Great Exile comes to an end and the Jewish people recovers its land and its independence.

All the prophets regarded the Zionist epic as a process which develops along the lines of a divine plan and pattern: sin, punishment, repentance, return and the coming of the Kingdom.

In other words: since the people of God has forgotten and betrayed its Master, it was dispersed among the nations and had to pass through terrible ordeals. But nevertheless it continues, in a mysterious way, to be the witness of the God of love and of the faith of the fathers. Then, either because it repents and yearns for the promised land, or because God Himself decides to save His honor in face of the nations (we have seen that this is Ezekiel's view), Israel will recover and revive its desolate land, within the borders of David and Solomon's kingdom, with the help of the Holy Spirit. But revival does not stop here: the people must return to their God and thereby bring about the conversion of all the nations who will come to worship the Creator of heaven and earth in Jerusalem, the center of a new, reconciled world.

But Israel's revival at the end of days, in two phases (material and spiritual) will not occur by itself, not in peace and quiet with the consent of the nations. Once again the latter will violently resist the Jews' attempt to recover Jerusalem and to render it into their capital city. And ultimately a number of nations will form an alliance to destroy the city and wipe the Jewish people once and for all from the face of the earth.

But this will provoke the personal intervention of the Creator — for this is the only way towards the salvation of both Israel and the world — and the Parousia of the King-Messiah, whose origin must be traced back to the very act of creation, to God's most intimate thoughts when He created man and did not want his downfall.

This Parousia is a cosmic event and will cleanse the hearts of men and of all creatures. All arms will be destroyed, forever, and the politicians of this world will be judged and found wanting.

Thus our prehistory draws to an end, marking the beginning of a new era which indeed deserves the beautiful name of human history, because it brings happiness to all.

We hope that at this point of our study one aspect of the "zionist problem" has been clarified: the return from the Babylonian captivity has not brought the fulfilment of the prophetical promises. It is true that the Temple was rebuilt, but Rome would destroy it again, together with Jerusalem. It is true that for a brief period a certain degree of Jewish independence was maintained, but this independence, too, would be crushed.

Israel was not gathered from the four corners of the earth. Those who returned from Babylon, in response to the call of Zechariah and others, were but a small minority, and certainly did not return from the four corners of the earth. They recovered the province of Judah alone, not the whole promised land.

The King-Messiah has not established his Kingdom of peace and justice in Jerusalem. The nations have not laid down their arms and not gone up to Jerusalem in love and repentance. It is not of this world, not yet of this world, the Kingdom of universal brotherhood, radiating its light from a new Jerusalem.

They are wrong, the theologians and exegetes who maintain that the return from Babylon was the fulfilment of the prophetical promises. They must have read the text of these prophecies very superficially, they must have taken great liberties with it, if they can say exactly the opposite of what these texts proclaim...

But it is true that these theologians have a strong argument when they deny the messianic role of the Jewish people in the modern world by asserting that in Jesus Christ all the prophecies, including that of the Return, were fulfilled.

In the second part of this book we intend to examine the value of this argument.

PART TWO
FROM JESUS TO HERZL

Jesus then gave his disciples strict orders not to tell anyone that he was the Messiah.

Matthew 16:20

I

THE ZIONIST CLIMATE AT THE
TIME OF JESUS

It would be a mistake not to linger somewhat over the period between the last prophet of the Hebrew canon and the birth of Jesus and, subsequently, of the Christian church. In spite of the silence of the Bible, an amazing spiritual revolution had taken place in the Jewish soul under the influence of the political upheavals in Palestine.

These few centuries, in which Jerusalem was confronted with Athens, were the first period in history — with the possible exception of the time of the Exodus from Egypt — in which antisemitism was an openly declared policy aiming at the annihilation of the Jewish religion and not just the Jewish nation, as had been the case under Ramses II.

Moreover, the very important Jewish diaspora in the then known world (the entire mediterranean basin) constituted a serious problem for the rabbis and would drastically change Israel's *Weltanschauung* with regard to the gentile world. And finally, the concurrence of all these new different factors at this time of Jewish history contributed to the birth of a very vivid messianic hope. In this time of feverish expectations a Jewish child was born who was to be known in history as Jesus of Nazareth, and who was to give to history, and consequently also to the Zionist expectations, a new meaning.

THE POLITICAL SITUATION IN PALESTINE

It was not Palestine that was revived by the pioneers who had returned from Babylon, but Judah alone. It was not political independence that was granted them, but merely religious autonomy. These two facts led to the failure of the great hope aroused by the message of the prophets of exile, and projected into the future the fulfillment of the Divine promises of salvation of Israel and the nations.

The province of Judah was of very secondary importance in the vast satrapy of Trans-Euphrates of which it was a part, even to such an extent that the great historians of the time and first among them Herodotus never mentioned it. For almost four centuries the "Jewish world" was entirely unknown and remained unnoticed on the political chess-board of the time. During these four centuries Israel passively waited and hoped for the return of its (mostly voluntary) exiles on the one hand, and on the other for national independence which would lead to a reign of peace and justice in the whole world of which Jerusalem was to be the center, if the prophets had been right and YHVH would fulfil His promises.

The megalomania and mad antisemitism of a Seleucid king, Antiochus Epiphanes, was needed to bring Judah forcefully back to the scene of history and to revive the hope of Israel and the ancient Zionist dream with unprecedented intensity. Towards the end of December of the year 168 B.C. the "abomination of desolation" predicted by Daniel was installed in the heart of Jerusalem: a swine was sacrificed in the Temple for the glory of Zeus the Olympian of whom the Gauleiter of the time was believed to be the incarnation. (This was certainly not the final abomination of desolation spoken of by Jesus in the Olivet discourse, Matthew 24:15-22, as we shall note in greater detail later in this book.) The practice of circumcision, the observance of the Sabbath and the Jewish religious holidays and even the simple possession of biblical scrolls was punished with death. The cult of Zeus became compulsory throughout the Jewish land.

The priest Mattathias of Modi'in raised the banner of revolt, together with his five sons. In the wake of victory after victory Jerusalem and the Temple were cleansed, exactly three years after the sacrilegious act of Antiochus IV. He died a few months later and his death was greeted by liberated Judah as a token of God's judgement. In May 142 Simon Maccabaeus captured the Syro-Greek fortress which dominated Jerusalem, thereby restoring his people's political independence. This independence would last until 63 B.C. with the arrival of Pompey.

The new Jewish dynasty set itself the task of conquering the entire territory of messianic Palestine as it had been during the reign of Solomon. This feat had practically been accomplished at the time of the death of Alexander Jannaeus in 76 B.C.

Thus the circumstances seemed to be opportune for the fulfilment of the Divine promises and in particular for the return of all the children of Israel to their recovered land...

But these calculations and hopes did not reckon with a calamity that had more than once befallen the Jewish people: civil war; in this case the open hostility of the two "ruling brothers" of that time: Aristobulos and Hyracanus, who even went so far as to plead their cause before the Roman general Pompey. This was the lion's mouth: in 61 Aristobulus was forced to walk in the triumphal procession of the Roman general together with a mass of Jewish slaves who were to "enrich" the Jewish diaspora...

This was the hour of Herod. What a downfall for a nation so proud of its dynasty, to be ruled with an iron rod by an Edomite slave, and to be forced to accept his poisonous present of a reconstructed Temple of the Lord!

The fact that there was still a Hasmonaean pretender to the throne became the hope of all the rebels, in particular in Galilee. Never would the tyrant be able to wipe out entirely the blood of the Maccabees in spite of his brutal measures.

In the year 40 Herod was greeted by the Roman Senate as "king" of

Judah. It took him almost three years to establish himself in Jerusalem, and in 30 B.C. Octavian, the future Augustus, reaffirmed his title.

During almost thirty years this "King of the Jews", under the pretext of a messianic dream, made constant efforts to firmly establish the universal rule of his master the Emperor for the greater glory of Graeco-Roman culture, until his death in Jericho in the year 4.

His son went to Rome to obtain Augustus' consent for the succession. This was all that was needed to provoke a revolt in Galilee and Jerusalem against the Roman garrison, a revolt that was to end in the execution and enslavement of tens of thousands of Jews.

It was in these circumstances, in this atmosphere of bloody revolt that Jesus was born in the vicinity of Jerusalem.

THE JEWISH DIASPORA

It was the sad privilege of the Assyrian empire to introduce into history the policy of "displaced populations." The Jewish people have known it from its own bitter experience.

But since the dawn of Greek rule in the Middle East many children of Israel had gone into exile of their own free will, following the example of the Phoenicians and of the Greeks themselves, either for adventurous reasons or because of economic interests. At the time of Caesar there were, consequently, approximately one million Jews in Mesopotamia, a comparable number in Egypt and Europe, and more than a million and a half in Asia Minor alone. Against the hardly three million Jews in Palestine, the Diaspora Jews formed a considerable majority. Against every Jew in the Holy Land, there were two "in Exile."

This was a double problem for rabbinical theology in Palestine. How could this state of affairs be reconciled with the Divine command of Return, and how should Israel in Exile relate to the pagan world in which it lived?

The first aspect of the problem was thornier than the second one. Had not God commanded Israel to be a light unto the nations? Did this not imply that Israel had to go out to the nations, in order to bring them the good tidings?

On the other hand, how could this "missionary" vocation be reconciled with the messianic command of Return?

This missionary vocation was often referred to in the religious literature of the intermediate period between Malachi and Jesus, especially in the pseudo-epigraphic books, such as Tobias, The Testaments of the Twelve Patriarchs, Henoch and the Sibylline Oracles. Moreover, had not Malachi himself concluded the Hebrew canon with this message:

> For from the rising of the sun even unto its going down My name is great among the nations? (1:11)

In this context we should mention an event which had far-reaching consequences for the Jewish and, subsequently, the Christian missionary vocation, namely the completion of the Greek Bible translation, the

Septuagint, in Alexandria. Through this contribution to the religious literature of the time Israel provoked a chain reaction of revolutions in the mentality of the world of antiquity. Through this translation the name of the God of the Jewish Patriarchs was indeed "made great from the rise of the sun even unto its going down."

It must be added that the moment was highly opportune for the expansion of the Jewish religion. If I may use this expression, the gods of the Olympus had for some time been in disgrace. Every philosopher who respected himself could only indulgently, and often ironically, smile about the lives of the gods as related by the ancient myths. Pessimism and cynicism had become the fashion in Athens, and Rome, with its own men of letters proved to be a worthy successor.

The biblical message had a striking success in the entire empire, in particular among the lower classes of the population and the women of the bourgeoisie and even of the aristocracy.

At the same time, it goes without saying, antisemitism grew among the higher classes, strongly encouraged by the "refined spirits" of the time who discovered a disquieting revolutionary ferment in the Jewish scriptures which called for justice and brotherly love. Let us not forget that the entire civilization of the time, with its commerce and its laws, was based on the exploitation of a multitude of slaves.

The first large-scale pogrom (and the first ghettoes) were organized in Egypt. This is the price Israel must pay when it assumes its "missionary" vocation. This is also the price so many of the early Christians had to pay, because for more than two centuries they were simply regarded as Jews by the Roman authorities.

That Caesar, and Augustus after him, were so tolerant towards the Jewish diaspora in the Empire, only encouraged the emigration from the Jewish country, thereby weakening Palestinian Jewry. It is true that the majority of the "exiled" Jews maintained more or less sentimental ties with Jerusalem and made their yearly pilgrimage. Many even went up to the Holy City more than once every year.

Thus, paradoxically, Ceasar's good-will towards the Jews was instrumental in the weakening of their messianic hope. and whenever the nations are openly hostile to Jerusalem, as was the case in the time of Antiochus Epiphanes, the source of this hope is in danger of running dry, and the policy in favor of life in exile gains! For how could those millions of Jews be persuaded to return to their promised land, when it was threatened by extermination, or when it groaned under the oppressive rule of the Gentiles? This had been the case since the death of Herod the Great. The dilemma was not simple, and it is difficult to see how under such circumstances all the children of Jacob could be gathered and thus herald the coming of the Messianic Era in Jerusalem and in the entire world.

The last word remained therefore with the "terrorists" in Galilee and Judah. their only hope was a policy of violence, a policy which would provoke the occupier to take extreme measures, which in turn, would force God to intervene.

In their view the Messianic coming would be followed by the return of the exiles, and not the other way round.

To sum up: two political conceptions can exist simultaneously. The one leads to the promised land, for better for worse, while the other leads to the Diaspora under the slogan of Judaism's "missionary" vocation. It is therefore not surprising that we find in the Talmud this maxim of Rabbi Elazar: "God has dispersed the Jews in order to enable them to make proselytes." (Pesahim 78b)

But it is no less surprising that the Talmud also contains this rabbinical saying, which breathes a spirit of Greek pessimism:

> The schools of Hillel and Shammai discussed for two and a half years in order to decide whether it would have been preferable if man were not created. Finally they agreed that it would indeed have been better if man were not created. But since he does exist...
>
> (Eruv 13b)

This leads us to the third subject of this chapter: the nature and quality of the Jewish expectations in Palestine itself.

AN ANALYSIS OF MESSIANIC HOPE IN PALESTINE

The short-lived triumph of the Maccabean dynasty on the one hand and the catastrophical Roman occupation on the other, aroused unbridled hope in Palestine, which was shared by the overwhelming majority of the people, with the exception of the leading class of the Sadducees. Since the latter could maintain their position of power only by the grace of the Romans, they had no desire whatsoever that the regime be forcefully changed, since they would be the first victims of such a change. Their theology was opposed to that of the Pharisees since it rejected every mystical and apocalyptic trend, and even the entire prophetical literature which at one time had been regarded by them as the smallest danger to their privileged position. The Sadducees were the established caste of priests who kept the Temple accounts, and they believed that this pious bank brought them nearer to God!

A Messiah, whoever he would be, could only be a serious threat to this bank, and this was sufficient reason for them not to do anything which hasten his coming and to do everything to prevent it.

With the exception of this privileged class and of the wealthy, with the exception of these "collaborators," the people as a whole had joined the ranks of the Pharisees and the Essenes, wishing for the forceful overthrow of the regime.

The common people, who were generally called *am ha'aretz*, in particular in Galilee, were groaning under the heavy taxes and duties which were levied by the priests and the Romans alike. They had everything to gain and nothing to lose but life in the great messianic upheaval. This had become their attitude, and over the years the Roman crosses had become a common sight along the roads of Palestine. What they were waiting for, after the long series of successive gang leaders, was a "successful" Messiah who would be no less God-fearing than they and who would be well-versed in the prophets.

The Pharisees tried to canalize this revolutionary movement and to limit its damaging effects, because they were convinced that the Lord had His own plan which He would carry out at His own time for the good of all. but all of them were good patriots who deeply detested the Roman, pagan occupiers.

As to the Essenes, they too prepared themselves, and day and night they searched heaven and earth for the sign that would augur liberation and the final war between the sons of light and the forces of darkness.

Let us have a closer look at the situation and open the New Testament at the first pages of the Gospel according to St. Luke:

> Praise to the God of Israel! For He has turned His people, saved them and set them free, and has raised up a deliverer of victorious power from the house of His servant David. So he promised by the lips of His holy prophets that He would deliver us from our enemies, out of the hands of all who hate us...
>
> (1:68-71)

In other words, the Romans had better watch their steps, for the hour of revenge will certainly come; the times are ripe and the Messiah is at the gates.

In these words the priest Zechariah expressed his faith after the birth of his son John the Baptist, convinced that he had reiterated the message of the last chapter of Malachi concerning the coming of Eliah.

But this is not all. An even more revolutionary hymn awaits us, and not from the lips of a priest...:

> ...wonderfully has He dealt with me, the Lord, the Mighty One... The arrogant of mind and heart He puts to rout, He brings down monarchs from their thrones but the humble are lifted high. The hungry He satisfies with good things the rich he sends empty away. He has helped His servant Israel, His servant firm in His promise to our forefathers, He has not forgotten to show mercy to Abraham and his children's children, for ever!
>
> (Luke 1:49-55)

What a program from the lips of a young girl from Galilee! But we know already that Galilee was the cradle of revolutionaries of every type, and this passage from the New Testament discloses that the young girls of the time were also among their ranks. For these were the words of Mary, the mother of Jesus, a few months before the birth of her child. Fortunately for her, there was no spy of Herod lurking in the quiet garden in Nazareth, for this patriotic young woman would have paid with her life if the agents of Herod or of the Romans had heard her hymn.

These were the sentiments that were aroused in both a priest and a young woman of Galilee by two children whose birth marked the beginning of Christianity among the oppressed Jewish people in the Holy Land.

The future mother does not doubt for one moment that her child will bring about the realization of the messianic program for which the overwhelming majority of the Jewish people had been yearning so ardently: Herod and the Roman procurator thrown from their thrones, the priestly caste of the Sadducees deprived of their employment; those hitherto held in contempt (one is inclined to say "the cursed of the earth") uplifted to the place of honor by the Lord Himself, and Israel for ever enjoying peace and justice.

Such expectations were not merely the product of the exalted spirit of an old retired priest or of a young woman who might have been seduced by some gang leader. No, they were based on God's promises to the Fathers, and in particular on His promises to Abraham.

We have read these promises, we have analysed them, and we know that all of them are linked, in one way or another, to the presence of the Jewish people in its land that was promised to them for ever. We have called them Zionist promises, because they are deeply rooted in the soil of Mount Zion, under the foundations of the Temple.

And here is a third Zionist and messianic proclamation:

> This day, Lord, thou givest Thy servant his discharge in peace. For I have seen with my own eyes the deliverance which thou hast made ready in full view of all the nations: a light that will be a revelation to the nations and glory to Thy people Israel.
>
> (Luke 2:29-32)

These words were spoken by the old priest Simeon who was serving in the Temple when Jesus' parents came to present their infant to his Creator. We are told that the Holy Spirit had disclosed to Simeon, who waited every day for the "Comforter of Israel" that he would not die before he had seen him.

Simeon's words are in harmony with the prophetical doctrine of the nations. As a matter of fact, the King-Messiah is not only he who comes to crown and deliver Israel, he is also and equally the one who brings the light to the Gentiles who are erring in the darkness of idoltary and cynicism, thereby fulfilling the missionary command which Israel had received from its Creator. Here we have the messianic hope in its purest and loftiest form, because the salvation and peace of the nations are considered equally important as those of Israel. Mary the mother, being a girl from Galilee without much culture, hoped above all for a just settling of accounts. Simeon, being a priest in Jerusalem, linked the salvation of his people to that of the world, even though the Gentiles were occupying and mal-treating the promised land and the chosen people.

These three hymns of liberation from Jewish lips herald the coming of Him whom the nations will call the Christ, in recognition of the fact that it is this light which must lighten them, and in fulfillment of part of the biblical promises.

But it remains nevertheless true that the unique adventure of Jesus of Nazareth on earth has not brought the reign of peace and justice to the world. Rome emerged as the victor from the unequal battle; Palestine ran towards its fall and the Temple towards its destruction. Hundreds of thousands of slaves were to join the ranks of the Jewish exiles.

Once again the failure seemed absolute, and the promises withdrew to the remote future. The hour of the Great Exile had struck, and the land that was promised to the children of Abraham, Isaac and Jacob was for many centuries to be covered with sand and pestilent swamps.

Why then do the Christians call this Jesus the Messiah? During His life in the Jewish land He fulfilled not even one of the Zionist promises and soon after His death the agony of exile reached its nadir. Why?

Isn't Christian theology right when it claims that all the Zionist promises were fulfilled "spiritually" by Jesus' resurrection and ascension, and that the Jewish Zionist hopes and messianic pretensions were reduced to naught, leaving the Jewish people with the only alternative of conversion, of entry into the Church?

JESUS AND THE MESSIANIC MYSTERY

We know which hopes Jesus' mother and some of his relatives had placed in him. We also know that the time came when the family united in an effort to put an end to this misleading ministry which seemed to consist entirely of opposition to, and clashes with the rabbis and scribes. This blatant change of heart of Jesus' family in the key to the messianic mystery of him who appeared to seek an open conflict with the Temple authorities, a conflict that was bound to result in His being sentenced to death. Instead of leading the struggle against Herod and the Roman occupying forces, Jesus turned against traditional doctrines using a formula which none of the prophets before him had dared to use, and which could not but put the spark to the tinder: "It was said by them of old time, but I say unto you..."

It is evident that a dramatic misunderstanding existed between Jesus and His relatives, because of the discrepancy between the way he performed His ministry and the hopes that were placed in Him, even before He was born. How could this systematic opposition to the doctors of the law lead to the fulfillment of the Zionist promises, to the Return for Exile, to the expulsion of the Roman legions? The dilemma was never better formulated than by John the Baptist who, from Herod's dungeon on the shore of the Dead Sea, asked his cousin:

Are you the one who is the come, or are we to expect some other?

(Luke 7:19)

Jesus' ministry began, as it should, in accordance with the prophetical tradition, with a retreat to the desert. This retreat sets us on the right track.

THE TEMPTATION IN THE DESERT

Everybody knows that Satan is an experienced theologian, well-versed in the Scriptures. Jesus discovered this during the forty days of solitude, prayer and fasting. Satan opened his attack with a temptation that was very down-to-earth under the circumstances: food. To change those stones into manna of the wilderness — is that a big thing for you if you are the King-Messiah, the Incarnation whose origin is in the act of creation? A false approach. For Jesus was a man of a different stamp, and the long years in Nazareth of which we know nothing, but which—we may assume — had been years of extreme austerity, had undoubtedly hardened him so that it was not difficult for him to resist this rather rude attempt to make him break his fast. The Devil therefore changed his tactics, and passed on to a higher level, beginning with a quotation from the Scriptures after having taken place on the highest pinnacle of the Temple overlooking the valley of Jehosaphat:

> No disaster shall befall you... For He has charged His angels to guard you wherever you go, to lift you on their hands, for fear you should strike your foot against a stone...
>
> (Psalms 91:11)

If you are the Son of God... If you are the son of David... For maybe you are not? They have put ideas in your head with their old-women's tales. After all, how can you know for sure, if you don't prove it yourself? Or perhaps you are the one? In that case you must not lose time, but impress the masses with your almightiness and your deeds.

But such a spectacular conjuring trick obviously does not tempt the Man of Nazareth. The Devil therefore brings his heaviest artillery into action, appealing to Jesus' heart, to his loftiest messianic ambitions:

> Once again, the devil took him to a very high mountain, and showed him all the kingdoms of the world in their glory. 'All these,' he said, 'I will give you, if you will only fall down and do me homage.'
>
> (Matthew 4:8–9)

The text of Luke is even more revealing:

> All this dominion will I give to you... for it has been put in my hands and I can give it to anyone I choose...
>
> (Luke 4:6)

He, whom the Bible calls "the Prince of this world," does not bluff, and Jesus knows it. The devil offered Him an extraordinary short-cut toward the fulfillment of some of the Jewish messianic hopes and the quick solution of the Roman-Herodian problem." Why should He not accept it and later extricate Himself and deceive the devil with his own game as in certain popular legends...

But Jesus answers:

> You shall do homage to the Lord your God and worship Him alone.
>
> (Matthew 4:10)

What no gang leader, no pseudo-Messiah had done, Jesus accomplished in Galilee for the poor and miserable of His people: not only did He heal their illness, He also gave them to eat, free and abundantly. And the people exclaim: "Surely this must be the prophet that was to come into the world" (John 14:6). Who they are referring to is the prophet announced by Moses himself:

> I will raise up for them a prophet like you, one of their own race, and I will put My words into his mouth, and he shall convey all My commands to them.
>
> (Deuteronomy 14:18)

Thus the people of Israel, and in particular the humble and oppressed, had thirsted for the messianic liberation, had waited for this second liberator. In Jesus' days they expected that the Messiah would liberate them from the Roman yoke with signs as great as those that had heralded the liberation from Egypt.

This man Jesus, like Moses in the desert, distributes manna, but his manna is even better than that of Moses for it is accompanied by fish and by marvellous sermons. No doubt, he must be the one...

This is the reason why, according to John 6:15, after the multiplication of bread and fish "Jesus, aware that they meant to come and seize him to proclaim him king, withdrew again to the hills by himself."

One can imagine that it was an even greater temptation for the pious Jew Jesus to accept power from the hands of his own people, if only over Galilee, than to accept Caesar's crown from the hands of "the Prince of this world" and to rule the Empire. It would be more in agreement with the biblical message and with God's will as revealed in the history of the Jewish people. It was therefore a much greater temptation for the man of Nazareth. At this very moment he could have been well on the way towards the implementation of the entire messianic program and the fulfilment of all the hopes placed in him.

Any other revolutionary gang leader—of which there were more than a few at that time — would have accepted. Jesus, however, refuses and withdraws by Himself.

And His numerous followers ask themselves, as John the Baptist had asked in Herod's dungeon: "Is He really the one that has been announced, or should we offer power and arms to someone else?"

After having rejected supreme power over the entire Empire in the wilderness of Judah, Jesus now rejects the powers offered to Him by His own people.

After having rejected the crown in Galilee, all that remains is for Him to reject the crown in Jerusalem itself. This is what He is going to do in circumstances and in an messianic atmosphere which undoubtedly were more tempting than anything else in His short life on earth.

THE GREAT TEMPTATION IN JERUSALEM

Riding an ass, in accordance with the prophecy of Zechariah, Jesus entered the capital which was preparing itself for Passover, together with the stream of pilgrims from all over the Empire. The multitude of His followers is not slow in understanding this messianic gesture, all the more since they have just witnessed the resurrection of Lazarus in Bethany. The fact that there were Zealots, Sicarians and other enthusiastic patriots, most of them Galileans, among the multitude increases the tense atmosphere.

As they approach the famous fortress Antonia where the Roman garrison is stationed, nobody doubts that the prophet will now definitely settle His accounts with the hated Temple authorities, the "collaborators" and certain doctors of the law.

The people rejoiced when they saw how the "pious" traders were cast out, and the "pious" bank was overthrown, for they regarded the pieces of gold and silver that were thrown into the alleys as symbols of their coming freedom from taxes and duties, and they thoroughly enjoyed the trick played on the Sadducees whom they detested even more than they did the Romans. Moreover, this brave and angry act of Jesus' encouraged the most violent and rowdy elements among His followers. The Romans had better watch their steps, for their turn would surely come at the height of the Passover celebrations...

One can understand that the Sadducees and leaders of the Jewish people cunningly seized Jesus during the night when the people were asleep. One can also understand that they held a mock trial which violated the Torah in more than one respect, and even went so far as to execute a man during the festival. One understands all this, as one understands the grief of the people who realized the next morning that once again one of their prophets had been murdered.

But how can one understand Jesus who let such an opportunity, such a fortunate concurrence of circumstances pass?

THE MESSIANIC MISUNDERSTANDING

More than once (Matthew 16:20; Mark 8:20; Luke 9:21) Jesus forbade his disciples to disclose that he was the Messiah, though at the same time admitting that He indeed was:

"And you," he asked, "who do you say I am?" Simon Peter answered: "You are the Messiah, the Son of the living God." Then Jesus said: "Simon son of Barjona, you are favored indeed! You did not learn that from mortal man; it was revealed to you by my heavenly Father..."
He then gave his disciples strict orders not to tell anyone that he was the Messiah.

(Matthew 16:15–20)

How to explain this mystery? The best explanation is given in the same chapter of the Gospel according to Matthew:

> From that time Jesus began to make it clear to his disciples that he had to go to Jerusalem and there to suffer much... to be put to death and to be raised again on the third day. At this Peter took him by the arm and began to rebuke him: "Heaven forbid" he said. "No Lord, this shall never happen to you." Then Jesus turned and said to Peter: "Away with you, Satan. You are a stumbling-block to me. You think as men think, not as God thinks."
>
> (16:22–23)

Jesus did not come to the world in that night in Bethlehem in order to expel Herod and the Romans. He did not come to bring Jewish political independence within the borders of the Davidian kingdom. He did not come to convert the nations by force to the ritual of the Temple and the Synagogue.

But he came to suffer and to die, to bridge once and for all, in the name of God and in the place of God, the vast gap which had separated man and his Creator since the Fall in the Garden of Eden. He came to restore the dialogue between the entire creation and the Creator and not only that between YHVH and Israel. He came to bring light and salvation to all men through His death as the fulfillment of the Day of Atonement.

What God had not accepted from Abraham, the sacrifice of his only son Isaac the trustee of all the promises, He accepts from him who preceded creation. This is the meaning of "the new Passover" and of the new "liberation from the bondage of sin."

One understands that the people, and more than anyone else Jesus' own disciples, were not greatly inclined to welcome the coming of a Messiah who must suffer and will be put to a shameful death on a Roman cross! For they were suffering under the Roman boot and had just experienced the crushing in blood of the Maccabean dynasty.

In thirty years of silence, work, prayer, retreat and intensive study of the Scriptures the Man of Nazareth had had sufficient time to understand perfectly well the messianic plan and mystery and the seeming contradictions in the Scriptures themselves. He had understood that since the days of Moses no call for repentance had rendered Israel into the people of priests in the midst of the nations (not to mention that it had never put an end to the latent hostility of the nations...). He had understood, like Isaiah, that Messiah must give his life to atone for the sin of all men:

> ...yet on himself he bore our sufferings, our torments he endured, while we counted him smitten by God, struck down by disease and misery; but he was pierced for our transgressions, tortured for our iniquities; the chastiment he bore is health for us and by his scourging we are healed... The Lord laid upon him the guilt of us all...
>
> (Isaiah 53:46)

They are mistaken, those rabbis who assert that this hymn of suffering refers to the Jewish people as a whole paying for the sins of the nations. For nowhere in the Bible, nowhere in the words of Moses do we find a trace of a vicarious ministry of the Jewish people or of its atoning mission. To the contrary, the Bible and the words of Moses affirm that Israel will return to its God through trial and suffering and repentance.

On the other hand, the prophetical writings portray the Redeemer as a victorious personage who comes to impose His reign on earth, to judge the nations and save the Jewish people in extremis from total annihilation in its recovered promised land. Daniel, describing the advent of the one he calls "the Son of Man coming on the clouds" and Zechariah, placing this event on the Mount of Olives at the moment that Jerusalem is on the verge of utter destruction, brought the discussion in the Hebrew Bible of the nature of the Messiah to its final point.

There is apparently a formal contradiction between the Messiah who dies for the sins of all and the Messiah who comes in all His might in a cosmic upheaval. He who enters Jerusalem on an ass, in humility, cannot be the one who comes "on the clouds", from another world. The rabbis of the talmudic period were aware of this contradiction and worked out a theory of two Messiahs: the Messiah, the son of Joseph, to be delivered to death, and the Messiah, the son of David who will be the triumphant and glorious liberator of Jerusalem and Israel and the judge of the nations (Succoth 52a). They based this concept of the Messiah ben Joseph on Zechariah 12:10: "They shall look on him whom they have pierced."

If Jesus forbade His disciples in particular to disclose that He was the Messiah, it was because the people expected at that time the coming of the Messiah ben David, who would expel the Romans. He did not want to mislead his followers and his people, surrounded as he was by Zealots and "terrorists" who demanded an armed revolt. Is was therefore playing with fire on His part when He threw the traders from the Temple court, for this was a revolutionary gesture which no prophet before Him had dared to risk and which could easily be interpreted by the Galileans as the sign for the final revolt.

Jesus is deeply aware of His mission: to carry out the first phase of the messianic program of redemption; to launch the great movement of "evangelization" of the gentile masses and to bring them the light of the Holy Scriptures and faith in Him who is the Lord of life and death; to open for all of mankind a direct road to God, and not only for the children of Israel, by breaking down what every Gentile regarded as national barriers; the practice of circumcision and the loyalty to the Temple and the policy of Jerusalem. And, if it is possible *to reform the Synagogue* by imposing on it its prophetical responsibility towards the pagan world. All this in order to pave the road towards the second phase of the messianic program: the parousia of "the Son of Man."

For Jesus did not believe that there are two Messiahs, but rather that the mission of redemption belonged to one Person. After the suffering Messiah has voluntary given His life, and has prevailed over death through His resurrection from the dead at the "new Passover," He will be ready for the parousia in the history of men and in particular in the history of Israel, as had been foretold by the prophets.

Jesus offers the key to the mystery of messianic hope and the solution to its apparent contradiction.

Let us now listen to the answer Jesus of Nazareth, who is regarded by so many Gentiles as their Savior, gives to the theologians of the Church and the rabbis of Israel. We shall soon discover that this answer is in full agreement with the great Zionist vision and perspective that are developed in the Hebrew Bible, from Abraham to Malachi.

THE ZIONIST VISION OF JESUS

The Gospels show, on several occasions, that Jesus developed a vision of history which the theologians, rather thoughtless, use to call "apocalyptic," a convenient term because it implies that this vision is esoteric, fantastic and consequently rejectable. However, Jesus' vision is clear enough.

Now that we have analysed Jesus' words about the beginning of that period of history we use to denote as "christian," we can proceed to the next phase: a long period of evangelization of the world (we shall see that Jesus has a different word for this period); the era of the "pre-messianic tribulations," and, finally, the parousia and the judgment of the nations.

Let us see what Jesus Himself says about these three moments of history.

THE EVANGELIZATION OF THE WORLD

Jesus' principal preoccupation in his so-called apocalyptic sermons is with the salvation of the Gentiles. He takes the great announcements of the universalist prophets such as Isaiah and Jeremiah very seriously. We have already seen that there were very active Jewish communities everywhere in the Roman Empire, and that their synagogues were centers of attraction for the gentile proselytes, whether they had or had not accepted circumcision. According to the Acts of the Apostles Paul systematically used the local synagogues as his points of departure for his work of evangelization among the Gentiles, convinced as he was that a minority of born Jews would accept the message of good tidings and that a fair number of actual or potential proselytes would become disciples of the Messiah of death and resurrection. In using this approach Paul obeyed Jesus' official command:

> And this gospel of the Kingdom will be proclaimed throughout the earth
> as a testimony to all nations; and then the end will come.
>
> (Matthew 24:14)

Note that Jesus does not speak of the "conversion" of the nations but of a testimony, which simply means preaching. He has no illusions about the heart of man and his inclination to repent. Had He not said:

> When the Son of Man comes shall he find faith on earth?

Forceful conversion of the Gentiles, after the example of some of the Maccabean princes, is altogether out of the question. It is simply a matter of charging them with their biblical responsibilities, to the extent that the peoples have learned what they are and that their leaders claim to be Christians. By these criteria will they be judged.

But soon after Jesus' appearance on earth a terrible disaster will befall Jerusalem and the promised land marking the beginning of a long period of Exile for the children of Israel:

> ...they will be carried captive into all countries, and Jerusalem will be trampled down by foreigners until the time of the nations has come to its end.
>
> (Luke 21:24)

It is evident from this text that so long as the biblical and Christian message is being preached to the Gentiles, the Jewish people will remain in exile among the nations, and Jerusalem will continue to be occupied by foreigners. In other words: during the entire era of evangelization of the world Israel will deprived of its national independence and its biblical capital.

And for the first (and only) time Jesus uses here the curious expression *the times of the nations.* (Gentiles) This is the time when the nations will be called to repent and to convert, while they are still occupying the land of Israel and Jerusalem, until the crucial moment when their domination over Jerusalem comes to an end and the children of Israel return from their world-wide exile.

When will that be?

Before Jesus' ascension, the disciples gathered around Him and asked Him this same question, which had been burning in their hearts and which we must call the Zionist question:

> Lord, is this the time when you are to establish once again the sovereignty of Israel?
>
> (Acts 1:6)

We see the apostles, as true Galileans, still hoped to see in their lifetime the downfall of the Herodian dynasty and the Roman legions and their replacement by the rule of the Son of David and his disciples... Let us not laugh, as certain Christian exegetes do, about what they call the "worldly hopes" of the Jewish people. These hopes are not despisable, for we have seen that they have lived in Jewish hearts since the first promises to Abraham, and that they were affirmed by the prophets, from Amos to Malachi.

Moreover, Jesus himself also took them seriously, as is witnessed by His entirely satisfactory answer:

It is not for you to know about dates or times, which the Father has set within His own control.

(Acts 1:7)

Is it not clear that this answer means that the Father has appointed the precise moment for the reestablishment of Israel's independence? How can one read into this text an entirely reversed meaning, or argue about the obscure meaning of the Greek words of this response? This is a petty game to which we will have no recourse for the simple reason that Jesus did not answer his disciples in Greek.

Moreover, if we relate this answer to the text we quoted earlier and which announces the end of Jewish captivity and exile how can we still doubt Jesus' Zionist views?

Let us return to the first point. Israel must go into exile a second time, and for a much longer period. Jerusalem and the Temple will be destroyed and this catastrophe is the beginning of a period in which Israel will remain "without kings and priests" as was prophesied by Hosea. Throughout this period the gentiles will rule Palestine and Jerusalem, while at the same time being placed before the crucial choice: to accept or to reject the message of Jesus.

The "time of the Nations" might as well be called the time of Mission. But it is also the time of the great dispersion of the Jewish people and of their hardest sufferings. What then must happen for the Time of the Nations to be fulfilled and for the Jewish people to be gathered in their land in order to devote themselves to rebuilding Jerusalem and reclaiming the desert? In this respect too, Jesus has no illusions.

THE MESSIANIC BIRTH-PANGS

In accordance with the teachings of the prophets, Jesus foresees that the final return will take place in an extremely dramatical historic context:

When you see the abomination of desolation, of which the prophet Daniel spoke, standing in the holy place, then it will be a time of great distress; there has never been such a time from the beginning of the world until now, and will never be again. If that time of troubles were not cut short, no living thing could survive...

(Matthew 24:15–22)

Let us note first of all that Jesus gives new significance to the book of Daniel respecting, however, the seal with which this book is sealed until Israel's Messiah comes. Jesus certainly did not regard the sacrilege committed by Antiochus Epiphanes in the Temple as an event to which the prophets had alluded. He saw the fulfilment of the prophecies as a mysterious state of affairs in the future when the children of Israel will return from their last and long Exile. That certain theologians of the Church continue to regard the prophetical writings as a dead, ossified letter merely relating to the ancient history of the Jewish people, is their problem, but let it be clear that Jesus rejects their theories, and attributes a biblical and prophetical significance to Israel's future history.

Jesus implies that the substitution of independent Israeli rule of Jerusalem for gentile domination will occur when the political situation in the world has reached the point of worst degeneration. The world would then probably be faced with total destruction, "if that time were not cut short."

What may be the meaning of this "abomination of desolation standing in the holy place?" One thing is obvious: the text refers, and can only refer, to biblical Jerusalem, and more precisely, to the Temple place. There will reign in those days an "anti-messianic" and, consequently, anti-Jewish and anti-Zionist power, endangering the people of Israel's life as in the days of Antiochus Epiphanes.

But not Israel alone will bring forth in agony the glorious parousia of the Messiah — the Gentiles, too, will suffer birth-pangs. Jerusalem will be threatened by a League under the aegis of Gog and Magog and the situation will become so desperate that God Himself must intervene to save Jerusalem, Israel and the world from total destruction, "cutting short" this really apocalyptic time.

THE PAROUSIA OF THE SON ON MAN

Once again Jesus, in his apocalyptic teachings, is entirely in agreement with the prophets, and in particular with Zechariah and Daniel:

> Then will appear in heaven the sign that heralds the Son of Man. All the peoples of the world will make lamentation and they will see the Son of Man coming on the clouds of heaven with great power and glory.
>
> (Matthew 24 : 30)

We have seen that the rabbis of the talmudic period had worked out the doctrine of the two Messiahs as, on the one hand, a reaction to the prophecy of Isaiah, in chapter 53, and, on the other, as an attempt to justify the unfortunate predictions of the most famous rabbi of the last Jewish revolt, Rabbi Akiva, who had greeted the leader of the revolt, Bar-Kochva, as the expected Messiah. But Bar-Kochva fell in 136, in his last battle against the legions of Hadrian. For obvious reasons Jesus could not share such views. More often than was usual in his days, Jesus referred during His brief ministry on earth to Himself as the Son of Man, not in the general sense of the term as Ezekiel, among others, had used it, but in the very specific meaning it had in the apocalyptic literature of the time. Jesus knew that He was the one who will one day come in glory after having voluntarily given His life to atone for the sins of all men. It is a fact that neither His disciples, not His relatives understood this. But it became an accepted reality to them after the resurrection, and especially after the ascension, as we learn from the following passage from the Acts of the Apostles:

> This Jesus, who has been taken away from you up to heaven, will come
> in the same way as you have seen him go.
>
> (Acts 1:11)

The next verse of the same chapter discloses that the ascension took place on the Mount of Olives, overlooking Jerusalem and the pinnacles of the Temple. We may therefore assume that the disciples had been waiting on this mountain for the return of their risen Messiah after they had heard the extraordinary tiding from two men in shining garments. Let us once again stress the admirable harmony of these pages of the New Testament with the hebrew text of the prophets. For this is what Zechariah had announced:

> The Lord will come out and fight against those peoples... On that day
> His feet will stand on the Mount of Olives which is opposite Jerusalem
> to the east.
>
> (14:4)

We know, that day will mark neither the triumph of the Church, nor that of the Synagogue. The Jewish people will not enter that era through the gates of one or another Church, for the Christian world will also be judged and be found wanting.

The Synagogue, as was also foretold by Zechariah, will recognize in tears this Messiah and Redeemer in His glory, but with pierced feet and hands. For this is the Synagogue's destiny: to prostrate in repentance before her King who once was nailed to a Roman cross out of love for her and for all Israel.

In spite of some of the Talmudic rabbis the Synagogue will recognize that the Gentiles are also worthy of redemption, that their salvation is also part of the Creator's plan of justice and love. She will recognize her own shortcomings and supineness.

And she will find at her side the Church, also on her knees, also in tears. It will be the hour of the great pardon for the Church, who throughout her long history has been so ungrateful, so haughty and, alas, often so cruel toward her Jewish sister; who, for such a long time, has remained indifferent to the final Return to the promised land, so dangerously silent in the face of the permanent threats to revived Jewish Jerusalem.

THE APOSTLE PAUL'S ZIONISM

This chapter would not be complete if we did not reserve a place for the Zionist sentiments of the man who without any doubt is the great unknown of the Synagogue. It has become the fashion among Jewish theologians and historians, and Jewish intellectuals in general, to regard the rabbi of Tarsus as the traitor *par excellence*. This is certainly more understandable if we remember that it was Phariseism that has become the dominant trend in the Synagogue and in Jewish religious life. This trend would not easily forgive one from among its own ranks for having broken away so openly, and with such great success. This is why Paul for centuries has been accused by his former colleagues of having violated the Torah even though he never rejected the Torah itself, but only the rigid system that had been developed on the basis of the Torah. On the other hand, the Synagogue has never been willing to recognize that Paul regarded circumcision and the other precepts of the Torah as irrelevant only for the Gentiles. He himself remained an observant Jew until his last day.

In his famous Epistle to the Romans, which is the backbone of every sound Christian theology, he devotes three whole chapters to what he calls the "mystery of Israel." We will see that in these chapters definitely Zionist concepts are developed in full agreement with the concepts of Jesus himself. In order to lay a firm foundation for his arguments in favor of his people, he starts with the following introductory remarks:

> They are Israelites: they were made God's sons; theirs is the splendor of the divine presence; theirs the covenants, the Torah, the Temple worship; The promises, the patriarchs...
>
> (9:4)

Obviously having a premonition of future developments, the author of the Epistle to the Romans right away applies himself to forestalling the fathers of the Church and the Christian theologians who, throughout the centuries, were to argue that God had rejected His people and that the latter merely continues to exist as witnesses of God's punishment and will eventually seek refuge under the wings of the Church.

After the resurrection, in the early days of the missionary Church, Paul declared that the divine promises remained in the first place the prerogative of the Jewish people, and most of all the promise to the Patriarchs that they will possess the Holy Land for ever.

In other words, throughout Christian history God has reserved Palestine and Jerusalem for Israel in the Diaspora, for this promise was given to Abraham, Isaac, Jacob, Moses and the Prophets.

It is also simply a fact that being adopted by God, together with other privileges, likewise remains in the first place the prerogative of Israel. The same is true of the Torah and the covenant, and this implies that the Synagogue will continue to exist until the Messianic time which the House of David will be re-established.

In the 11th chapter of his Epistle the apostle implicitly acknowledges that henceforth the history of redemption will be divided into two periods: the first under the sign of the nations hearing the good tidings, and the second under the sign of Israel being reintegrated in its own land. Indeed, how else can one interpret these words of Paul:

> I now ask, did their failure mean complete downfall? Far from it! Because they offended, salvation has come to the Gentiles... But if their offense means the enrichment of the world and their falling-off the enrichment of the Gentiles, how much more their coming to full strength!
>
> (11:11–12)

The blindness of the Jewish leaders for the teachings and the person of Jesus has, in a way, projected the biblical message into the gentile world: the first missionaries took the torch of Hebrew proselyting from the hands of the Synagogue. Let us assume for a moment that the Sanhedrin had accepted Jesus and that his message had received the imprimatur of the synagogue and the Temple.

The Gospel would then have been "nationalized" if we may use this expression, and the Gentiles would have been deterred from joining the ranks of the Jewish people because of such obstacles as circumcision. For the Pharisees would never have accepted the compromise in favor of the Gentiles for which Paul fought all his life. The message of the Gospel would certainly not have penetrated the contemporary world. It is precisely because the Sanhedrin and the Temple authorities hardened their hearts that all the superfluous obstacles on the gentiles' path toward the only God the Bible were removed.

Consequently, Paul continues, if this blindness has brought redemption to the gentile world, how much more will the future messianic maturity of the Jewish people contribute to the unprecedented spiritual enrichment of the entire world...

> For if their rejection has meant the reconciliation of the world, what will their acceptance mean?
>
> (11:15)

At this point of his exposition the Apostle obviously had in mind Ezekiel's vision of the dry bones which we have called the Magna Carta of Zionism.

But let us go on to the Apostle's most original concept which is akin to Jesus' own view of the historical situation in the days of the End.

For there is a deep truth here, my brothers of which I want you to take account, so that you may not be complacent about your own discernment: this blindness has come upon part of Israel only until the fullness of the time of the Nations has come.

(11:25)

It is regrettable that almost all Bible translations, including the beautiful Jerusalem Bible, render this verse in a way which falsifies the entire concept of Christian history and, consequently, obscures the destiny of Israel. They translate Romans 11:25 as if it says: *"until the Gentiles have been admitted in full strength,"* thereby revealing the "wishful thinking" of the Church, but certainly not conforming to the text and the Apostle's intentions. For this translation actually says: until the Church has converted the entire world to its doctrine. This hope is understandable, but neither Jesus' allusions to the days of the End, nor the present state of the world allow us to be so optimistic — that is the least one can say in this time of nuclear arms, a time in which the Afro-Asiatic world is, more or less openly, in revolt against the so-called Christian world.

But let us return to the text. One must take certain liberties with the text to translate the Greek words *pleroma ton ethnon eiselte* in this way. This literal meaning is: the fullness of the nations has come.

However, all this becomes clear and evident if we call to mind that the Apostle not only thinks in Hebrew terms, but also expresses himself in purely Hebrew notions which are far from every Greek philosophical thought. Jesus himself, we have heard, mentioned this mysterious "time of the Nations" which will end when the Jewish people recovers both its independence and its biblical capital. What else does the expression *pleroma ton ethnon* in Paul's epistle mean if not the equivalent of "the end of time of the nations?" Why should the Apostle evoke, on the one hand, the Return of Israel, and on the other its spiritual integration in a world which is not related to the biblical and Zionist vision of history, a vision held by Jesus of Nazareth and the Prophets who preceded him alike?

To avoid all misunderstandings the Apostle of the Gentiles, after having mentioned the end of the time of the Nations, immediately recalls the redemption of all of Israel by quoting these words of Isaiah:

...the whole of Israel will be saved in agreement with the text of Scripture: From Zion shall come the Deliverer; he shall remove wickedness from Jacob...

(11:26)

We find here again the classic pattern of the biblical, Zionist vision of history: Exile, Return, Redemption, which may also be summed up as follows: fullness of the time of the Nations, political anti-Zionism of the nations, Parousia and Judgment of the nations.

"What will their acceptance mean? Nothing less than life from the dead!" When we think of what the centuries of exile among the nations have done to the Jewish people, we see with our mind's eye a vast valley of dry bones lighted up by the flames of the Inquisition, by the burnt-down ghettoes and — only yesterday! the frightful glare of the crematoria. That Israel has survived this perpetual, satanic conspiracy of the nations and has recently recovered its land and made Jerusalem once again its capital — what is this, if not life from the dead?

Since in biblical perspective the final Return must bring in its wake the Parousia of the Deliverer placing his feet in Zion and putting an end to our blood-stained history and our deadly arms-races, yes, what does Israel's reintegration mean for *the world* if not life from the dead?

> *The Christians place themselves between the Messiah and the Jews hiding to them the true face of the Redeemer...*
>
> Nicolas Berdiaev

III

THE CHURCH AND ISRAEL

But while he was still a long way off his father saw his and his heart went out to him. He ran to meet him, flung his arms round him... Now the elder son was out on the farm... He called one of the servants and asked what it meant. The servant told him: "Your brother has come home, and your father has killed the fatted calf because he has him back safe and sound." But he was angry and refused to go in.

The Parable of the Lost Son
Luke 15

First of all a preliminary remark: during the first forty years of its existence the community of disciples of Christ was not a "church" as opposed to the Synagogue, but rather a *Jewish sect* within a Synagogue, deeply attached to the prayers and worship in the Temple in Jeruslem.

We cannot say it often enough that the first conflicts, the first dramatic events — starting with the complot of some of the Temple chiefs and Synagogue elders and ending with the stoning of Stephen and the arrest of Paul in the heart of the Holy City — were expressions of an inter-Jewish crisis and certainly not of a policy of contempt for and persecution of the "Christian Church." By saying this we do not diminish the terrible responsibility of the Sadducees and the Pharisees, but merely emphasize that these were no question of violent opposition of the Jews against the Christians, as if the latter were non-Jews. Without losing our sense of proportion we may say that the crisis was very similar — to use only one example from Jewish history — to that in which Amos confronted the priestly clan of his days. Not only physically, but also *theologically*, this conflict at the dawn of the Christian era placed Jews against Jews, and in particular the people of Galilee against the intellectuals of Judah.

In the early days in Jerusalem not the Jews as such opposed the Christians, but it was the Temple authorities who entered into a, sometimes bloody, conflict with a religious *Jewish* minority whose members went up to the Temple three times a day.

It was not until the revolt against Rome and the destruction of the Temple in the year 70 A.D. that the relations deteriorated, not in the first place because of a violent aggravation of the theological dispute, but rather

96

because of the disappearance of the Temple as a place of common worship. This dramatic event drove the young community of Christ towards the pagan world with greater force than previously.

The break became almost absolute with the revolt of Bar-Kochva, hundred years after Jesus' appearance, because this brave resistance fighter proclaimed himself the "Messiah", a title which the disciples of Christ for obvious reasons had to reject. By doing so they placed themselves in the camp of the non-belligerent and were therefore an easy target for those who accused them of treason (just as Jeremiah had been accused of treason in different circumstances).

Nevertheless, until the radical change brought about by Constantine's "conversion" to Christianity in 312, Jews and Christians were often united by the contempt and persecutions of the Romans. Until that fateful date the majority of the Romans regarded.every Christian as a Jew.

It was the rise to power of this "converted" emperor that inaugurated the anti-Jewish "Christian" regime which was so rightly (alas!) described by Jules Isaac as a school for contempt.

Thus, as the terrible legacy of pagan anti-semitism, a new, "Christian" form of anti-semitism entered the lists against the Jewish people, an anti-semitism which, in the words of Marcel Simon in his main work "Verus Israel" was "official, systematic and consistent... the handmaid of theology and nourished by it... with one clear purpose: to render the Jews into a hateful nation."

A legacy, we said.

Indeed, it was not so much their bad exegesis which made them develop this specific form of anti-semitism, but rather their own pagan, anti-semitic past which led to their bad exegesis. In other words, a more or less subconscious primitive pagan mentality, seeking justification in certain passages of the Gospels and words of Christ, explains — but does not excuse — the anti-Jewish inclinations of the first great Christian theologians. Inclinations that were, of course, foreign to the Apostles, because they themselves were Jews and shared with their Master the feelings of profound love for their people and their oppressed nation.

Christians from among the Gentiles could only free themselves of such inclinations through the Grace of God. St. Paul was so deeply aware of this that he included three whole chapters on this subject in his most important Epistle (addressed to the Church of Rome...) in order to forestall this secular anti-Jewish movement which was so dangerous for the faithful in the Empire, and in particular in its capital.

To make us realize the scope of this tragic development and the universality of this misunderstanding and to expose the severity of this wrong exegesis of the Church fathers, a few quotations will suffice. They certainly suffice to make us understand why for so many centuries the theologians and exegetes of the Church neither understood, nor accepted — in spite of the teachings of the prophets, of Christ Himself and of the greatest theologian of all times, St. Paul — the fact that Israel was elected for ever. They also suffice to make us realize why the overwhelming majority of the Christians, represented by the same theologians and exegetes, has remained silent in the face of the Zionist epic and the unique and formidable adventure of the State of Israel...

Justin Martyr regarded circumcision as "an infamous mark imposed by the divine foreknowledge on the murderers of Christ and the Prophets..." (Dialogue, 16). "You have exceeded your own perversity by your hate for the Righteous One whom you have killed."

We note that from the 2nd century onwards there was a growing tendency among the fathers to draw inspiration from certain apocryphical writings, such as the Gospel of St. Peter and the Acts of Pilate. And from this same time onwards we can also observe that the infamous and stupid accusation of deicide is launched against *all* Jews. After Justin, all the Church fathers were to take up his accusation which became the backbone of every manifestation of "Christian" anti-semitism.

The following is the image of the Jews drawn by *Gregory of Nyssa* in his sermons:

> Murderers of the Lord and the Prophets, enemies of God and the laws, enemies of Grace and of the faith of their fathers, advocates of the devil, a race of vipers, slanderers, scoffers, people whose spirit errs in darkness, the leaven of the Pharisees, a congregation of demons, sinners, stoners, malicious beings who hate justice...
>
> (Oratio in Christi resurrectionem, p. 685)

His style is not different from that of the man whom tradition has given the name of "the goldenmouthed" — *St. John Chrysostom*:

> Since the deicide the Jews have been delivered into the hands of the demons... they are only fit to be butchered... their behavior is not better than that of swine and oxen in their gross lewdness... The synagogue is a brothel, a cave of brigands, a den of ferocious animals...

The Nazis would not be ashamed of the terminology of these "Six homilies against the Jews"... One can easily imagine the effect of such vulgar and rude utterances on a population which was only superficially christian and ready for every form of violence. Indeed, Chrysostom, whether it was his intention or not, was not of the most fervent advocates of pogroms and massacres. But there was somebody even worse than he, who did not content himself with encouraging pogroms, but actually organized them. We are referring to *St. Ambrose*, and in particular to the following fragment from a letter to Emperor Theodosius in answer to the latter's demand to open an inquiry into the riots that had occurred in Ambrose's diocese:

> I declare that I have set fire to the synagogue, or at least that those who did it acted under my orders, so that there would be no place where Christ is rejected... Moreover, the synagogue was in fact destroyed by the judgement of God...
>
> (Eleventh letter to Theodosius)

Let us also note in passing that it was the bishop of Alexandria, *Cyril*, who expelled the Jews from this city which had been the home of the most important Jewish community in the Mediterranean basin for such a long time.

Even men of the stature of Tertullian, Origen and Irenaeus, though refraining from crude language and open attacks, "stayed in line" with the policy of accusing the Jews of deicide. The same is true of Jerome.

It would be a grave mistake if we did not linger on the teachings of St. Augustine, since his influence on Christian tradition has been only second to that of Paul. Hear what he has to say:

> ...greedy, rude people, incessantly preoccupied with material pleasures...
> a worldy people.

Here we have the great accusation which was to be taken up by a choir of theologians after Augustine: Israel understands its own Scriptures only in a "worldy" manner. If they dream of liberation, expect a glorious Messiah and wish to recover and revive their land, well, let us try to excuse their deplorable worldy inclinations! For, of course, neither the Christian nations, nor the papacy can be accused of such aspirations...

> Of all nations the Jews were dispersed as witnessed of their own iniquity
> and of our fruit... thus our enemies serve us to disconcert other enemies.
>
> (Commentary on Psalm 18, par. 22)

Why then was Israel, somehow, preserved? Because the Creator has promised them a happier destiny?

> They who trampled Jesus under foot were doomed by God to disgrace...
> they merely exist to carry our books for their own confusion... they
> have become our book carriers in the manner of the slaves who walk
> behind their masters...
>
> (Commentary on Psalm 56, par. 9)

St. Augustine offers several examples of false exegesis with the evident intention of accusing the Jews. Thus he, who ranks among the most prestigious theologians, does not hesitate to falsify the text in order to add his stone to the anti-Jewish structure. The following is the most pernicious example, taken from his "Sermons for catechumens":

> The end of the Lord has come. They hold him, the Jews, they insult him,
> they bind him, the Jews, they crown him with thorns, they taint him with
> their spittle, the Jews, they crush him outrageously, they hang him on
> the cross, they pierce his flesh with their spears...

Thus Augustine, with all the weight of his undisputed authority, substitutes the Jews, and why not, *all the Jews*, for the cruel Roman soldiers, in front of his catechumens who had just emerged from a pagan world which was anti-semitic by nature! Nobody will ever be able to evaluate the effect of such a catechesis on the minds of dozens of

generations who were exposed to these doctrines of the bishop of Hippo...
But there is no doubt that he prepared the ground for future pogroms...

After the pogroms have thus been evoked, we advance through the centuries and reach the period of the Crusades which, as we know, were preceded by massacres of Jews throughout Europe. Thus, for example, expressed himself the most famous preacher of the time, *Bernard of Clervaux.*

> O rude intelligence, like unto that of the oxen, which does not recognize God, not even in His own work. And if the Jews complain that I insult them... let them read what their own prophet Isaiah said about them... You will see, you Jews, that I am less harsh than your own prophet (Isaiah 1:3) for I have merely compared you to a dumb animal...
>
> ...To say the truth, what is there in this Jewish people that is not crude and vile, if we consider their occupations, their inclinations, their understanding and even their way of worshipping God. For war is their occupation, wealth their only desire, the letter of the Law the only food of their foolish spirit, and the slaughtering of vast herds their way of worship...
>
> (Ep. 149 — De incredulitate judaeorum)

There was certainly no better way to prepare the massacres of the Crusades than by preaching that the Jews had nothing human, and it is not incidental that a monk of Clervaux, Rodolph, organized in 1146 the pogroms in Cologne and the Rhineland...

Over and over again in his sermons (saint) Bernard identified the Jews with the children of Satan, thereby reiterating the exegesis which had been the official one since the time of the Church fathers, and according to which the few sworn enemies of Christ must be placed in the same basket with all Jews of all times (a doctrine that was denounced by Christ himself). The venerable Peter of Cluny even went so far as to distinguish various degrees of horror:

> I do not demand that these doomed creatures be put to death... God does not want to destroy them... But they must be subjected to terrible anguish and be preserved for an even greater ignominy, for an existence more bitter than death.
>
> (Tractatus adversus judeaorum inveteratum duritiem)

We see it: the crude diatribes of Chrysostom and others had borne fruit. Henceforth every tyrant who wishes to persecute Israel can have recourse to the teachings of the doctors of... the Church. (I had almost written: the doctors of the Law...).

Leaving the great theologians of the Christian tradition, we will now discuss another slogan which, together with that of deicide, has caused so much anguish to the Jewish people during its long martyrdom in Europe: the slogan which says: "his blood will be on us and on our children." Let us quote St. Thomas:

Until our days this curse continues to rest on the Jews and they cannot cleanse themselves in the blood of the Lord.

(Commentary to St. Matthew 27:25)

It is a shocking fact that none of the great theologians of the Christian tradition has ever been willing to grasp the implications of this curse, even though they all had developed, after the example of St. Paul, a theology of the *redeeming blood*. But what they meant, of course, was: redeeming for the non-Jews and condemning for Israel. It must be put on record that the theologians, since they have occupied themselves with the destiny of Israel, have been the victims of the spiritual blindness which they prefer to attribute to the Synagogue (see for example the famous statue on the cathedral of Strasbourg).

The persistent virus of anti-semitism which was born in Egypt in Moses' days, spares no-one. Without any doubt it is the most subtle and effective weapon of Satan in his fight for the corruption of the Church from within (seeing that a massacre of martyrs only strengthened and glorified the Church).

After this brief survey of the doctrine and tradition of the Church we will now proceed to an examination of the anti-Jewish measures it has taken over the centuries.

In 315 the first anti-Jewish law was promulgated, under which every convert to Judaism was punished. Then, in 339 the same law was applied to every Jew marrying a Christian.

Such measures — of which we do not known to which extent they were indeed implemented — are proof that Judaism was expanding among the pagan masses, and without any doubt also among the members of the Church... The Church, brought to power by a cunning and far-seeing emperor, soon realized that the Synagogue from whom it had emerged in the days of the apostles, was to a growing degree becoming its rival and that it was therefore essential to "absorb" her by all possible means.

In 397 the right of asylum in the churches was denied to the Jews; certainly a telling measure.

The Council of Nicaea, the exact date of which is difficult to determine, but which was certainly held during the reign of Constantine, applied itself to cutting all the ties which somehow still linked the Church to the Synagogue. The Council decided, for example, that the religious festivals would henceforth be celebrated according to a new calendar. It also ordered all the faithful never to attend the "Jewish sacrileges." We have come a far way from the days of Paul who always held his sermons in the synagogues. The Church would like to forget that the Mediterranean region had witnessed its birth from the womb of the Synagogue. This is one of the manifestations of the sin of which the Church of Ephesus is accused in the first pages of the Revelation of St. John: "you have forgotten your early love...".

A decree of 409 put every form of Jewish propaganda on a par with lese-majesty, which makes us suspect that the Jewish religion still held great power of attraction for the masses in the Christian empire.

There were many manifestations of Christian life in this period of expansion that were not particularly appealing to the Synagogue. The numerous theological conflicts, of which the Aranian controversy was the most outstanding; a certain degree of "paganization" of the ritual, especially with regard to baptism and eucharist; and finally, the struggles for influence and power among the bishops — all these made the Synagogue rather thoughtful...

Towards the end of the 3rd century, for example, Stephen, the bishop of Rome, who opposed Cyprian, the bishop of Carthage, and most of the Asian bishops, excommunicated them. The latter reacted with the statement that the bishop of Rome himself was "the real schismatic who, by excommunicating the others, had placed himself outside the community of the Church." The luxury and pomp of the religious services rapidly spread throughout the Church, at the personal instigation of Constantine and his mother who wanted the Church to compete successfully with the splendor of the pagan temples. One can imagine the effect of these developments on the faithful of the Synagogue.

This process of paganization also became apparent in the prayers for the dead, in the belief in a "purgatory", and the worship of saints and relics. In the last mentioned matter, for example, Cyril of Jerusalem (approximately 350) related that the wood of the genuine cross had been distributed throughout the entire world...

In 438 the Code of Theodosius was promulgated which subsequently served as a model in several kingdoms of the West. Among the articles applying to the Jews were: the death penalty for converts to Judaism, even in the case of a slave who was converted by his Jewish master; exclusion from all official and administrative functions and from the army ranks.

The quote again Jules Isaac:

> In the course of one century, and for many centuries to come, the Jew had become, through the will of the Church, a debased, if not to say a hunted man.

Thus, in the first half of the 5th century the Byzantine Church set a mechanism into motion in whose wheels the Jews would be caught in every "Christian" country where they were allowed to settle. This mechanism of contempt and oppression inevitably led to its logical consequence: Auschwitz.

Baptism was another point. From 634 Heraclius had enforced baptism notwithstanding the restrictive measures of one of the rare enlightened popes: Gregory the Great (590–604). Indeed, forced baptism was to remain a dark chapter in the history of the Church, regardless of the occasional opposition of a bishop or pope, for what was at stake was the salvation of the most precious and challenging soul — that of the Jew.

Over the centuries the Synagogue was often confronted with this tragic alternative: baptism or death; and sometimes, baptism or expulsion. Pope Leo VI (936–939), for example, in a letter to Frederic, the archbishop of Mainz, who had asked for guidelines for the policy towards the Jews, recommended firm evangelization, and in case of failure, expulsion.

From time to time a "pagan" or merely "enlightened" prince would try to slightly alleviate the fate of Israel, but invariably the Church would intervene and call him to order or anathematize him.

It is a sad fact: precisely under the rule of the "barbaric" Goths and Visigoths the Jewish population was given some respite. It is therefore not surprising that in various parts of the two rival empires the Jews supported the "barbaric" rebels.

In Spain discriminating measures against the Jews were taken after the conversion of king Recared by Leandre, the bishop of Sevilla and a relative of Gregory the Great. In a letter of 599 the pope congratulated the king for having put the *perfidia Judaeorum* in its proper place.

And in Carolingian, Gaul Louis, the son of Charlemagne, who tried to ease the lot of the Synagogue, immediately encountered the hostility of Agobard, the bishop of Lyon in two letters to the Emperor Agobard justified with theological arguments the oppressive measures against the Synagogue. The following are extracts from these missives:

> They boast that they are dear to you for the sake of the Patriarchs... When we forbid Christians to drink Jewish wine they assure us that your counsellors have bought wine from them for considerable sums of money... They flaunt the glory of their ancestors; they boast that they were granted by you — in contravention of the law — the right to build new synagogues...
> ...Antichrists, sons of the devil, these impious Jews, the enemies of the Son of God, hold themselves aloof from the true House of David, which is the Church... all the threats and curses regarding the Synagogue of Satan have been confirmed...

Let us also mention in this context that whenever the Church called a prince to order it was usually to demand that he curb the prosperity of the Jewish community. Pope Gregory VI (Hildebrand), for example, wrote in 1081 to King Alphonse VI of Castile:

> Allowing Jews to be the superiors of Christians and to have authority over them means to oppress the Church of God and to exalt the Synagogue of Satan. Trying to please the enemies of Christ is to scoff at Christ himself.

> (Regesta XI:2)

At the height of the drama of the crusades when all voices preached in unison the massacre of the Infidels, one isolated voice was raised in defense of the persecuted Synagogue, even going so far as to declare that "the Jews are not responsible for the death of Christ," thereby inviting the ire of the monks of Clairvaux and Cluny and eventually the condemnation of Rome.

Let us pay tribute to this man who saved the honor of Christ before humiliated Israel: Pierre Abelard.

The time has come to turn to one of the most fateful dates in the history of the Synagogue. The year 1215 witnessed the meeting of the Council of Lateran, presided over by Pope Innocent III. Four of its sessions were devoted to Judaism. In addition to such oppressive measures as the prohibition to stroll outside one's house on Christian holidays, and to wear festive garments on Sundays, the Council issued a law which ordered the Jews to refund (to Christians) the money they had gained in public functions...

But above all, it took a measure that is wrongly believed to have been an innovation of Hitler: the obligation to wear the yellow badge. Thus, for centuries to come the fate of Israel as an outcast of the human race and of Christian society, was sealed. We have already arrived half-way to Auschwitz...

We said that anti-semitism is a satanic virus from which one can escape only through the Grace of God. As proof of the persistence of this virus we relate that the good and saintly King Louis himself was the first to order the strict implementation of the decisions of the Lateran Council (no doubt at the instigation of his detestable mother...)

Halfway to Auschwitz... In fact, we are already at the gates of Auschwitz: in 1278 pope Nicolas III ordered that every baptized Jew who relapsed into his "Jewish blindness" was to be delivered to the secular arm. In other words: to the stake. Ten years later pope Nicolas IV amended the decree in such a way that it also applied to Jews who had relapsed after having been baptized by coercion.

It was pope Paul IV who, in 1555, radically isolated the Synagogue in its ghetto through a bull worthy in its style and intentions of the basest decrees of the Nazis, the bull *Cum nimis absurdum*, which revived a favorite thesis of Chrysostom by rendering the Jewish people into a nation "for ever condemned by God to slavery." An expression which was to be repeated by many popes until the end of the 18th century.

The inane accusation of ritual murder, which was perhaps first propagated by the Orthodox Church, was repeated in 1754 by pope Benedict XIV. Few accusations have done so much harm to the Jewish people as this one, and we even encounter in in the 20th century... especially in Austria.

The Reformation did not bring respite to the Synagogue. Chrysostom found in Martin Luther a disciple who surpassed him in ferocity and vulgarity...

It is of little importance that these horrors are found in his "table speeches" and not in his theological discourses, for these speeches were much more popular among the German masses, and with reason. Nobody can estimate to which degree Luther influenced the German, popular subconscious and thus contributed to the rise to power of the Nazis on the one hand and, on the other, to the acceptance of more or less violent steps against the Jews by the overwhelming majority of the German people. This is a tragedy which the Lutheran world thus far has not acknowledged and one day it will have to confess and repent. But it is not enough to condemn anti-semitism. We must call a spade a spade and not be afraid to pull up the evil from its deepest, oldest, most unbending and — alas! — often its most "respectable" roots...

We have come to our own century, which will always remain for Israel the century in which Auschwitz was possible. We do not intend to elaborate on the responsibility of the Christians of this century. Suffice it to say that if Adolf Hitler had been denounced for having written *Mein Kampf* (and did this book not deserve a denunciation?) and if he had been excommunicated after the promulgation of the terrible Nuremberg laws, it would have been much more difficult for him to seize power and even more difficult to stay in power. But how could an ecclesiastic regime which itself was the heir of a tradition that had issued the outrageous decrees of the fourth Lateran Council denounce him?

Let nobody say: "Other times, other days," let nobody take recourse to the pretext of the "dark middle ages." These are false consideration, for the Gospels and Paul's Epistles are much older than that! Nothing should prevail over the brotherly love which the Jew Jesus commanded his Church, not even in barbaric and superstitious times such as the Middle Ages or our own cruel century.

The Church must ask for forgiveness, not so much for the yellow badge of 1215, not so much for the ghettoes it has invented, but for the fact that it has tolerated Hitler and sometimes even encouraged him. For the written evidence is there and there is no need to elaborate on the horrible ambiguity of the pontificate of Pius XII...

To sum up; not only has the Christian world in its overwhelming majority never understood the unique destiny of the people of Israel, not only has it condemned this people to being the outcast of history, it has left it with only one solution, only one way of escape: conversion, entry into the Church. And when the people of Israel presented to the world a different solution, called Zionism, the Church in general, and the Church of Rome in particular, grumbled.

Vis-à-vis Israel in exile, the great Exile that lasted from the days of Titus until the famous Balfour Declaration, the Christian world and its official representatives did everything they could to make this exile even more bitter.

And faced with Israel's return to its promised land, the Christian world and its official representatives have persisted in their silence, in so far they did not openly express their scepticism, not to say their hostility. A few examples will prove this.

First the most striking and "official" example:

Not long before his death the great visionary Theodore Herzl was received in audience at the Vatican by the Secretary of State and by the Pope himself.

It is 22 January 1904. Herzl is introduced to Cardinal Merry del Val who plunges straight into the heart of the matter:

> I don't see how we can take an initiative (in favor of the Zionist Movement). So long as the Jews reject the divinity of Christ we cannot support them. Not that we don't wish them well. On the contrary, the Church has always protected them. To us they are the necessary witnesses of the past when God walked on earth. But they reject the divinity of Christ. How then can we, without denying our highest principles, declare ourselves in favor of the seizure of the Holy Land by the Jews?

Let us in passing express our admiration for the Cardinal's extraordinary view of Judaeo-Christian relations and the aplomb with which he declares that "the Church has always protected them..." Let us also admire the truly baffling logic of his argumentation and his apprehension that the Holy Land and the "holy' places be controlled by the Jews!

Herzl then declares that the holy places will be internationalized... and perhaps the Holy See, if it cannot declare itself in favor of Zionism, could be indulgent enough not to declare itself against it... But the Cardinal adheres to his fixed idea and evades the real issue:

> A Jew who recognizes the divinity of Christ — but that is St. Peter, that is St. Paul. The history of Israel is our history, our very foundation. But for us, to declare ourselves in favor of the Jewish people the way you ask for — let it first convert.

Finally, on the 25th of January, Herzl meets with Pope Pius X who also makes it very clear where he stands:

> We cannot support your movement. We cannot allow the Jews to recover Jerusalem, but neither can we prevent it. The soil of Jerusalem was sanctified by the life of Jesus Christ. This is all I can say in my capacity of Head of the Church. The Jews do not recognize our Lord, we cannot recognize the Jews... I know, it is not a pleasant idea that the Turks are holding our holy places, we have to admit it. But to install there the Jews, no, we cannot do that.

Herzl then recalls the pogroms and their horrors and the need of the Jewish people to find a country of their own. "But why Jerusalem?" the Pope asks surprised and adds:

> If one day you will come to Palestine and settle it with your people, we shall have there enough churches and priests to baptize you all!

Let us ignore the insolence of this kind of language and grant the Pope the right to express himself in this manner. But isn't it as if we were dreaming? Notwithstanding the biblical prophecies, notwithstanding the fact that St. Paul has declared that "the promised are theirs" (including the promise of the holy land), the Head of the Church of Rome makes such a statement! What a tragic and symbolic event, this dialogue of the deaf between the uncrowned prince of Israel en route for Jerusalem and him who pretends to be the vicar of Jesus of Nazareth on earth!

Over the centuries the Church has held the Jews in contempt and persecuted them. It does not admit it, but reminds them of their protection by the Church. Even though they are the victims of the pogroms, it is better that the Turks control the holy places than that the "unconverted" Jews return there. Could there be something more absurd than this?

It is therefore not surprising that in June 1921 Pope Benedict XV, on the basis of false information supplied by the observers he had sent to Palestine, sounds the alarm about "the condition of the Christians in the Holy Land, which is worse than in the time of the Turks," and appeals to the governments of the Christian nations, even to those of non-Catholic countries, "to submit a joint protest to the League of Nations." Again: isn't if as if we were dreaming?

But perhaps we'll understand this better when we read what Monseigneur Baudrillart wrote in his *Lettres d'un pelerin francais* which were published in 1924:

> At this moment there exists a two-fold danger in Palestine: a Protestant danger and, consequently and almost inevitably, the danger of English influence; and a Jewish danger as the result of the Zionist aspirations. The joint efforts of all Catholics is needed to withstand this two-fold threat.

The least one can say is that these two "threats" were certainly not in concert. To the objective student of the history of the British Mandate it is clear that the mandatory authorities were eager to smother the Zionist venture in Palestine. From the day of the publication of the Balfour Declaration the British military and the majority of the civil administration had resolved to sink the Zionist ship. The White Paper of 1939 which closed the gates of Palestine before the millions of Jews who were caught in the snare of the Nazis remains one of the most vicious documents of international politics. And the "sudden discovery" of the crematoria in the concentration camps did not lead to a change of the British policy, but rather, the contrary.

One example of a theological nature; when the last international Commission of Inquiry convened in Jerusalem in the summer of 1947, it heard the evidence of the Anglican bishop of the capital. The bishop calmly declared that in his opinion the Jews had *no right whatsoever* to Palestine, since all the promises of the Old Testament were *revoked* by the New Testament. Once again, it is as if we were dreaming, but this really happened. And we cannot but smile when we contemplate the statue on the cathedral of Strasbourg, which is an exponent of the theological school of thought that insists that the Synagogue was condemned to eternal blindness. For another moment should be erected in the heart of Jerusalem to commemorate the spiritual blindness of the Christian theologians... for "they have eyes and see not" the extraordinary return of the children of Israel from the four corners of the earth, nor the revival of this holy land that was abandoned by the nations (but not by God) to the desert, to pestiferous swamps and to death.

Let us conclude with a truism. Whether the theologians of the Church see it as the Hand of God or not, it is a fact that the State of Israel exists. It is a fact that within a few decades the desert has been conquered to a degree that is nothing but a miracle. It is a fact that in spite of the hostility and indifference of the world the survivors of the Nazi death camps have recovered their country. And it is no less a fact that an objective study of the relations between the Church and the Synagogue cannot but fill the heart of every honest Christian with shame if not with horror.

The Christian world rightly regards the promised land as just as holy and precious as the Jews do. But it has done *virtually nothing* to reclaim it. It has left this task to the Zionist pioneers. This task and this sorrow.

Is that just? Is that biblical? Is that evangelical?

Until this day the Vatican has not recognized the State of Israel, and the World Council of Churches remains prudently reserved in spite of the brave work of some of its leaders, such as the Reverend Charles Westphal.

And nevertheless — if there is one nation which the Christian world should have saluted with emotion, with affection (and in repentance) it is this nation that bears the name of Israel, whose people was so cruelly maltreated throughout the centuries, and of whom only a few have escaped the "tombs" into which the countries of Europe had turned and of which the prophet Ezekiel spoke...

IV

ZIONISM BEFORE THEODOR HERZL

It should be kept in mind that the Exile did not begin in the year 70 with the fall of the Temple. In the course of this study we have already discussed the problem and the reality of the Jewish diaspora in the then known world before the appearance of Jesus and thus before the national disaster brought upon Israel by the legions of Titus.

But from this fateful year the Jewish people, two thirds of whom already lived in a more or less voluntary exile, entered a new era with the loss of the Temple, an era that has lasted until our days and in which the Talmud took the place of the Temple.

It was only in 1948 that the world witnessed the restoration of national Jewish independence which had ceased to exist in the days of Pompey. National independence is one of the preconditions for Messianic liberation and the aim and foundation of every Zionist aspiration; the almost twenty centuries of exile were therefore a period of grim hope and often of desperation.

The overwhelming majority of the fathers of the Church, from Tertullian to Augustine, interpreted this Exile as a sign of Divine punishment for the Jews' rejection of Christ. They developed a logic corollary: the Jewish people has no longer a history of its own and has no other hope than conversion and entry into the triumphant Church... This curious vision of history, this astonishing disregard of the biblical promises to Israel, and in particular of the promise of the holy land, was to become a characteristic feature of Christian thought and theology for almost nineteen centuries, without any consideration for *Jewish thought and theology*.

What the thinkers and theologians of the Synagogue said and wrote about the final Return during these long centuries was regarded by the doctors of the Church as a mere fairy-tale! Israel, like the blindfolded woman on the cathedral of Strasbourg, is no longer able to understand its own future nor to interpret its present. Israel is blind.

But, as we shall see, the hope of Return never died in the Synagogue, not even in the heart of those of her children who had abandoned her. It is without any doubt this phenomenon, unique in the history of the nations, that has preserved the community of Israel up to the days in which kibbutzim were founded and the Negev began to blossom.

The time has come for the Christian world to break with its tradition of spiritual pride and to listen, through the centuries of persecution, to the moving voice of the Synagogue and her children who entreated God and fate to return Jerusalem and the Temple to the people of Abraham, David and the Prophets.

ZIONISM IN THE TALMUD

Like the Synagogue, the Talmud is a product of the Diaspora. Since the relatively short period of exile in Babylon (which also came in the wake of the destruction of the Temple) the sages and doctors of Israel have realized that the Jewish people will not vanish if the Temple is replaced by a "spiritual" sanctuary, by a rigid and comprehensive system which will prevent the people from being assimilated — that is, lost — in the pagan masses.

That is why Ezra is regarded by the Synagogue as a second Moses. As the man who may be considered the instigator of the vast edifice of the Talmud, this great scribe saved the dispersed Jewish people from "servitude to the nations."

As the product of Exile, the Talmud — in agreement with the teachings of the prophets — regards the end of the diaspora as a miracle no less great than the Exodus from Egypt.

What will bring about the Return?

On the basis of Isaiah 30:15: "In repentance and peace shall ye be saved" Eliezer Ben Hyrcanus makes the end of Exile contingent on the repentance of all of Israel. And against the scepticism of Joshua Ben Hananiah, who doubts that Israel will ever repent, Eliezer believes that God will call forth in the future a tyrant no less cruel than Haman who will cause the Jewish people to repent and to return to their God. Joshua Ben Hananiah quotes Isaiah 52:3: "Ye were sold for naught, and ye shall be redeemed without money," and concludes from this text that the redemption of Israel will come in God's time with or without Israel's conversion. He concurs with Joshua Ben Levi who believed that although the conversion of Israel will hasten its redemption, it will come in any case at a time known by God alone, regardless of the spiritual state of the Jewish people. This view is in line with the promised made to the prophet Habakuk:

> For the vision is yet for the appointed time, and it declareth of the end, and doth not lie; Though it tarry, wait for it, because it will surely come, it will not delay.
>
> (1:3)

One thing is certain: the Return will be the work of God, whose Holy Presence (the Shekhina) will accompany the miracle of Return even from the furthest reaches of the Diaspora.

Since the promise does not lie and God Himself will direct the Return it is futile and even dangerous to calculate the time of Redemption, and Samuel Bar Nachman goes so far as to curse those who engage in speculations on "the time and the hour." And it is just as futile and dangerous to try to force the Hand of the Lord by taking up arms, for example.

Let us not forget that one of the most famous rabbis, Rabbi Akiva, had paid with his life for the illusions he had cherished with regard to his messianic candidate Bar-Kochva, who fell in battle in 135 after three brief years of national resurrection. This catastrophe was to leave a perhaps even deeper mark on the rabbis who succeeded Akiva than the disaster of 70 had left on the rabbis of that time.

So long as Rome rules the world it is out of the question for the sages of Israel to encourage the advocates of revolt. History must run its course and everything must be done to consolidate and strengthen the faith of Israel and to prevent its spiritual disintegration and deadly assimilation.

Great hopes were placed in the Parths whom Rome never was able to crush. And we are not surprised to see that in the 4th, 6th and 7th centuries the Jews of Palestine allied themselves with, successively, the Parths, the Samaritans and the Persians against the emperors Constance and Justinian and against Byzantium. But never again did a second Akiva arise among the rabbis of Israel to anoint another patriot as the Messiah.

As the centuries of captivity rolled on and the promised land passed from the hands of one "pagan" occupier to those of another, the belief of the rabbis was strengthened that God alone, in miraculous ways and without Israel's active cooperation, could end the long exile and gather the children of Jacob in Zion.

ZIONISM IN THE PRAYER BOOK OF THE SYNAGOGUE

In his famous Epistle to the Christians of Rome the apostle Paul lists among the prerogatives of the Jewish people which are still theirs even *after* the coming of the New Covenant, the Election, the promises, the patriarchs, the covenants and the Messiah, but in the first place *worship and the Torah*.

The Temple, which was still standing in his days, would be destroyed, but the Torah, we know it, is eternal because it is the Word of God. The apostle does not see any reason why this prerogative of being the "guardian" of the Word of God should be taken away from the people that had been its trustee since the encounter on Mount Sinai.

The reading of the Torah in the synagogues and Israel's prayers have not lost their value in the eyes of the Lord after the appearance of the Church in the world.

Moreover, it is well known which great importance was attached to the Hebrew Bible in the time of the Renaissance and the Reformation by the Reformers themselves who had rediscovered it. Incessantly the Jewish people has read and studied the Torah and the Prophets even in the worst of times; they recited them even in the gas chambers...

It is a moving experience to follow, through the prayer book of the Synagogue, Israel's yearning for Jeruslem and Zion.

Ten times, in the morning prayers alone, the pious Jew implores the Lord for the return to Zion, the rebuilding of the Temple and the promised land, and for final Redemption:

> O cause us to return in peace from the four corners of the earth unto our own land, for the God that worketh salvation art Thou... Rock of Israel, rise to the help of Israel and free, according to Thy promise, Judah and Israel!... Cause the great trumpet to resound for our liberation, and the banner to be reared for the gathering of our exiles, and do Thou bring us together from the four corners of the globe. Blessed art Thou, O Lord, who gatherest and deliverest the scattered of Thy people Israel... Blessed art Thou, O Lord who comfortest Zion and rebuildest Jerusalem... Let the scion of David, Thy servant, flourish speedily and enhance his power with Thy salvation... Restore the service to the sanctuary of Thy House...

And the following is one of the central "Zionist" motifs in every service in the synagogue:

> May our eyes behold Thy return to Zion in compassion...

Thus the Zionism of the Synagogue is not merely a form of nationalism with the blessing of the priests, but rather a call for the beneficial Parousia in Jerusalem and in the world at large. It is not enough for the Synagogue in exile that the Negev be revived, that the Temple be rebuilt, but all this must be blessed, cleansed and consecrated by the presence and reign of the mysterious Messiah.

> Incline, O God, Thine ear, and harken; open Thine eyes and look upon our desolate places, and upon the city that was called by Thy Name. For it is not because of our righteous deeds that we bring our supplications before Thee... Our Father, Father of compassion, gather together our dispersed from the four corners of the earth, in order that all nations may recognize and acknowledge that Thou art the Lord our God... O our brethren of the House of Israel who are in captivity and suffer on sea or on earth, may the Eternal have pity on you, deliver you from oppression, free you from servitude and render your darkness into a great light, Amen!

And in his evening prayers the pious Jew adds:

> God of compassion, return to Thy city, to Jerusalem as Thou hast promised. Rebuild her in our days and make her into Thy abode, that she may be an eternal memorial and let the throne of David be established in her speedily. Blessed art Thou, O Lord, who rebuildest Jerusalem.

It is clear that Zionism is conceived as a way, a pilgrimage towards the reign of God in Jerusalem and in the whole world. Return to the promised land and prosperity are not enough.

Let us now listen to some of the prayers of the Sabbath service:

> For in Thy Holy Name, great and sublime, do we confide; we rejoice in Thy salvation. Cause us to return in peace from the four corners of the earth unto our own land, for the God that worketh salvation art Thou... In Thy inexhaustable benevolence, sustain us and gather our dispersed in Thy holy place, that they may observe Thy commands and serve Thee with a pure heart... O Lord, our God and God of our fathers, may it be Thy will to rebuild the Temple speedily in our days, that we may serve Thee in accordance with Thy will...
>
> Cause us to rejoice, Lord our God, by the coming of Thy prophet Eliah and by the restoration of the kingdom of David, Thy Chosen one. May his kingdom speedily restore the joy in our hearts, and let no stranger sit on the throne of David and no longer tarnish his glory...

The Synagogue experiences it as a miracle, that moment in history when the dispersed of Israel will be gathered in the promised land and rally around the Temple and the throne of David, and not under the banner of some form of nationalism or of a political regime. The presence of the Messiah alone is the guarantee of biblical Zionism.

In the service at the beginning of a new month, the Synagogue prays as follows:

> May the Lord who worked miracles for our fathers and delivered them from their bondage in Egypt, deliver us speedily. May He gather together all our brethren in Israel who are dispersed throughout the earth, Amen! Lead us back to the city of Zion with songs of joy, to Jerusalem with everlasting joy...

And here are a few extracts from the special prayers of the three great festivals whose celebration is commanded by the Torah: Passover, Pentecost, and the Feast of Tabernacles:

> By reason of our sins we have been exiled from our land and removed far from our native soil, so that we are no longer able to go up and appear and prostrate ourselves before Thee... because of the violent hand that has been laid upon Thy sanctuary... Reveal the splendor of Thy majesty and reign over us in the sight of all living. Approximate our scattered ones from amongst the nations, and assemble our dispersed ones from the extremities of the earth. Bring us unto Zion, Thy city, in jubilation, and unto Jerusalem, the place of Thy House in everlasting joy...

"In everlasting joy...". We dare hardly hope that the nations will rejoice at the sight of Israel returning to its land after so many centuries of suffering. We can only hope that they will be able to participate in the rejoicing of the new and reconciled world...

And finally two fragments from the prayers of the New Year service:

> O Lord, reveal the honor of Thy people and the glory of those that worship Thee. Sustain the hope of those that seek Thee and strengthen those that confide in Thee. Cause Thy land to rejoice and Thy city to

jubilate. Reveal the glory of David Thy servant and cause the torch of Jesse, Thy Messiah, to burn, speedily, in our days...

O Lord our God, cause the great trumpet to resound, and the banner of freedom to be reared. Gather us that are scattered amongst the nations from the extremities of the earth. Gather us and bring us in triumph to Zion, Thy beloved city and to Jerusalem Thy holy above...

ZIONISM IN THE PSALMS OF ASCENT

The prayers of the Day of Atonement repeat some of the prayers already quoted in this chapter, namely those that speak of the sins and transgressions of the people and the need for repentance and return to God.

It would be a pity to take leave of the prayer book of the Synagogue without mentioning the biblical writings that we have thus far not quoted, but that make up such an important part of the Jewish liturgy: the Psalms, and in particular the so-called Psalms of Ascent, which are Zionist hymns *par excellence* since they sing not only of the pilgrimage to Jerusalem, but also of the final "going up" in the time of the Messiah.

Of these fifteen Psalms, 120 to 135, we will quote the most suggestive fragments which place the final return of the Jewish people to the holy land and to their God, in a clear biblical perspective.

These Psalms of Ascent, of Zionist pilgrimage, immediately immerse us in the atmosphere of exile:

> Deal kindly with us, O Lord, deal kindly with us for we have suffered insult enough... (123:3)

> Often since I was young have men oppressed me, let Israel now say...
> (129:1)

> Out of the depths I call to Thee, O Lord... (130:1)

> My soul waits for the Lord more eagerly than watchmen for the morning... (130:6)

The years and the centuries wear on in the ambiance of contempt and persecution, but the faithful know that God has not renounced His promises:

> The guardian of Israel never slumbers, never sleeps... (121:4)

> If the Lord has not been on our side when they assailed us, they would have swallowed us alive... (124:2)

> He alone will set Israel free from all their sins... (130:8)

> O Israel, look for the Lord now and evermore! (131:3)

The hour of liberation, when it comes, will be even more miraculous than the Exodus from Egypt, for the Jewish people will be "in extremis" at the time of this final Redemption:

> We have escaped like a bird from the fowler's trap. The trap broke, and so we escaped... (124:7)

When the Lord returned the prisoners of Zion, we were like dreamers...
The word went around among the nations: The Lord has done great
things for them... Return once again our prisoners as streams return in
the Negev!

(126:1, 2, 4)

However, it is not sufficient to revive the Negev or to rebuild the Holy
City — we have stressed this crucial point already more than once.

Unless the Lord builds the house its builders will have toiled in vain.
Unless the Lord keeps watch over the City in vain the watchman stands
on guard...

(127:1)

Another advent, another Return must come to put the crown on the
work, to sanctify and purify it:

Arise, O Lord, and come to thy resting-place, Thou and the ark of thy
power...

(132:8)

For the Lord has chosen Zion and desired it for its home...

(132:13)

The most Zionist cry of the entire Hebrew Bible, the cry we have
reserved for the end of this chapter, is this extraordinary fragment from
Psalm 137:

If I forget you, O Jerusalem, let my right hand wither away; let my
tongue cling to the roof of my mouth if I do not remember you, if I do
not set Jerusalem above my highest joy...

(137:5, 6)

Large sections of the Synagogue, large sections of the Jewish people feel
very comfortable in Exile and have forgotten Jerusalem and erased from
their hearts all memory of, all yearning for the final Zionist pilgrimage,
even to the extent — as we will see — that they not only oppose, but even
denounce the partisans of Return. How many of these anti-Zionists were
caught in the deadly trap of the Nazis in Europe? How many of them, in
the comfortable lands and cities of their exile, have broken their last weak
links with their people and their biblical homeland? As ossified religion,
entirely oriented on the past, fanatically attached to life in an absurd
spiritual ghetto; or simply an accommodating religion reduced to some
form of social conformism — isn't this the picture of large sections of the
Synagogue in the world, and paradoxically enough, even in the State of
Israel?

It is not enough to live in the promised land in order not to "forget"
Jerusalem.

But we know that this terrible biblical warning is also aimed at the
Church, for wasn't she, too, born in Jerusalem? We are among those who
believe that the critical state of the contemporary Christian world can only
be explained by the fact that it has lost the Messianic and biblical hope

which, according to these Psalms and to the whole Bible, has once and for all been linked to Jerusalem of the Prophets and the Messiah.

ZIONISM IN THE PASSOVER HAGGADAH

This popular book, which has such a central place in the Passover ritual, is the most pregnant exponent of Israel's hopes and expectations.

For it is not in the first place the liberation of their ancestors from Egypt which the Jews throughout the world commemorate, but their own hope of liberation from Exile, and their even deeper yearning for spiritual freedom and oneness in God. This is the haggadah's first reference to Zion;

> Be merciful, O God, to thy people Israel, to thy city Jerusalem, to Zion, the seat of thy glory, to the kingdom of the House of David, thy anointed, and to the great and holy Temple which is called by thy Name...
>
> May the thoughts and memories of this day ascend and reach Thee: the memory of our fathers, the memory of the Messiah, son of David thy servant, the memory of Jerusalem thy holy city, the memory of thy people, the house of Israel. May it all be remembered for life and peace. Our eyes are turned to Thee, for Thou art a God of grace and compassion...
>
> O merciful God, break the yoke from our neck and lead us upright to our Land!

When the Passover ritual reaches its most moving moment, with the last blessing over the wine, the solemn vow with which the Synagogue and the Jewish people have entreated God even in their hardest trials, is heard once again:

> *Next year in Jerusalem!*

This is almost immediately followed by a litany of Return in which ten times, and with great insistence, this prayer is recited:

> Speedily, speedily, in our days and soon again. Pray, God, build! Pray, God, build! Build Thy House up soon again!

But it is preceded by a messianic prayer which is particularly moving for the Churches of the Reformation who in their liturgy of the Last Supper entreat God that all His children may one day be gathered in the Kingdom of God, "as grapes that were scattered in the vineyard." With that prayer we conclude this chapter:

> Lord, lead us, the offshoots of the vine Thou hast planted, home to Zion in song, redeemed!

> *Many will come claiming my name and saying: "I am the Messiah!" and many will be misled by them... This gospel of the*

Kingdom will be proclaimed throughout the earth as a testimony to all nations. And then the end will come...

(The Gospel according to Matthew,
Chapter 24:4 and 14)

THE FALSE HOPES

Within one generation, between 70 and 135 AD, the Jewish nation had experienced two such shocking catastrophes that for more than eighteen centuries the Synagogue was haunted by the fear of new armed revolts, even to such a degree that she excommunicated everyone who called for the recapture of the promised land.

With the closure of the Talmudic canon the messianic issue had been settled: God alone, through wonders worthy of, and even superior to those that attended the Exodus from Egypt, will lead His people to the land of Israel. Every form of active intervention on the political level aiming at the recovery of the biblical homeland and at "hastening" the days of the Messiah are from the outset doomed to a sanguine failure, of which the Jewish people will never be able to recover.

Especially the revolt of Bar-Kochva had given the Synagogue a traumatic shock from which it was to suffer for a very long time, all the more so since the most celebrated rabbi of the period, together with his disciples, had committed himself completely to this "Son of the Star" and even implicitly greeted him as the Messiah and Redeemer.

In 135 the legions of Hadrian massacred approximately half a million Jews and led as many into slavery. The historian Dio Cassius relates that all of Judah had become a desert. Ten of the rabbis who had sided with Bar-Kochva, paragons of the Synagogue, died as martyrs. Hanina Ben Teradion was burnt alive, wrapped in Torah scrolls... Rabbi Akiva himself died under cruel torture in Caesarea with the words: "I was granted the privilege to praise God in a sublime way, and to fullfil the commandment: 'Thou shalt love the Lord thy God with all thy might...'.".

Almost a thousand settlements burnt down, fifty fortresses razed to the ground, Jerusalem ploughed and rebuilt as Aelia Capitolina, the Temple compound devoted to Bacchus, Venus and Jupiter Capitolinus, and the entire Jewish population banished from the City this was the balance of the "messianic" revolt that had been supported by celebrated rabbis.

But in the midst of Israel, which throughout the centuries never ceased to recite the wonderful psalms and Zionist litanies which we have just read, men were to arise who, without taking up arms, proclaimed themselves the Messiah and called the people to return to Zion. And in order to gain the support of the spiritual leaders, they forestalled their opposition by insisting that Redemption would come from God alone in a miraculous way and that they were merely the instruments who knew how to decipher the hour and the exact time.

The Jewish doctrine known as Cabalah was probably born during the first exile under the influence of Babylonian occultism, Zoroastrian teachings, Pythagorean numerology and neoplatonic mysticism. Its roots reach without any doubt even farther back, to the occult science of Moses' Egypt and Abraham's Mesopotamia. The practice of attributing numerical value to the Hebrew text must probably be traced back to the same remote past.

By juggling with the numerical value of the characters of the Hebrew text the Cabalists of the Great Exile believed to be able to discover the hidden meaning of that text, to reveal the most secret plans of God Himself, and thus to calculate the hour of the Messiah and to evoke his advent by magical means. It was in times of desperation that the cabalistic movements flourished, for they were the last trenches of hope.

We have chosen four examples of such "false messiahs," all of them products of particularly turbulent times, all of them influenced by cabalistic doctrines, and all of them impatient to open the gates of the promised land to their people by various means. The failure of all of them will perhaps tell us why the time was not ripe, and why, much later, at the turn of our century, the time was ripe for the success of the Zionist idea.

In the 13th century Abraham Aboulafia proclaimed himself the Messiah and announced his intention to appeal to Pope Nicholas II and to convert him to Judaism with scientific arguments! But immediately upon his arrival in Rome Aboulafia was thrown into jail. That was the end of this adventure, especially since at that very moment the Pope died under mysterious circumstances... A pope converted to the religion of the Synagogue that seemed a fairly certain manner of bringing Israel home without hindrance, certainly if we remember that Palestine was at the time under the reign of the Crusaders! But it was nonetheless an attempt that was never to be tried again...

Towards the turn of the 15th century a certain Asher Lammlein proclaimed himself, not the Messiah, but more modestly, the reincarnation of the prophet Elijah. He had calculated that the Messiah would come in 1502, and called for a whole year of repentance which was indeed scrupulously observed by hundreds of thousands of his followers. One can image their mood on the 1st of January 1503...

This call for repentance was in accordance with the Talmudic dictum that the Messiah will not tarry if all of Israel faithfully observe one single Sabbath.

In 1527 Rome was sacked. Wasn't this an event which heralded the final judgment of the nations and, consequently, the return of the Jewish people to the Holy Land? At that time Prince David Reubeni appeared at the European royal courts, claiming that he was the ambassador of his brother Joseph, king of Khaibar. he proposed to king John of Portugal, the Pope and Charles V to form an alliance against the Turks. This extraordinary phenomenon of a Jewish prince something which the Jews were not particularly used to see attracted thousands of messianic enthusiasts who joined the ranks of the "army" of this Prince David. He himself, however, denied that he was the awaited Messiah, probably for tactical reasons, and no doubt on the advice of his second in command, the marrano Cabalist Solomon Molko. But the situation rapidly deteriorated and the two illustrious leaders fell victim to the Inquisition...

And once again, in 1648, towards the end of the Thirty years war (which had been particularly cruel for the Jews), and at the height of the organized massacres by the Cossacks of Chmielnicki, the masters of the Cabalah announced that the year 1648 would see the coming of the Messiah.

They did not have to wait long, for in the same year a young Cabalist in Smyrna, Sabbatai Zevi, proclaimed himself the expected Redeemer. His immediate excommunication by the rabbis of Smyrna had no effect whatsoever. For in all the countries of the Diaspora the Jews were greatly agitated by the news, mainly through the influence of another cabbalist celebrity, Nathan of Gaza, who declared that he was Elijah. In missives to all Jewish communities he ordered a period of repentance and fasting in preparation for God's judgement of the nations and for the call to return to the land of Israel in jubilation. The enthusiasm which seized the communities of Europe and Asia Minor is almost beyond description. A Christian eyewitness from the Ukraine related: "Many abandoned their homes and possessions and stopped working, saying that the messiah was about to come to carry them upon the clouds to Zion. Others were fasting, refused to feed their children, and, in this terrible winter, immersed themselves in the frozen rivers while they recited special prayers..."

Sabbatai Zevi announced that in 1666 he would go to the Sultan, the ruler of the promised land, and lead Israel personally to Jerusalem once the Sultan had been "converted."

Without much ado the Sultan had the pseudo-messiah arrested and put in chains in a fortress on the Dardanelles. But his hundreds of thousands of followers immediately acclaimed him the suffering Messiah and their enthusiasm knew no bounds.

And then suddenly the dramatic turn of events: placed before the choice, conversion to Islam or decapitation, Sabbatai Zevi decided to save his skin and to convert. Many of his adherents followed his example, in the belief that their master's conversion was merely another device in his struggle for Israel's liberation from the shame of Exile.

As one can easily imagine, the Synagogue, never entirely recovered from the national disaster of the Bar Kochva revolt, drew her conclusions from the fact that all these non-violent "messiahs" had failed as well. More than ever she was convinced that God cannot be forced and that only a manifest wonder can bring about the gathering of the exiles in Jerusalem and the coming of the Messiah and Redeemer.

The Synagogue became more rigid and withdrew even more into the closed world of the Talmud and the Shulhan Arukh, from which nothing would ever make her budge again, not even the astonishing developments in Palestine since World War I.

Which lesson should one derive from this series of failures, from the Roman period until the end of the 17th century? And especially: which lesson should the serious student of the biblical texts and the Cabalah derive from them?

This much had become evident: pseudo-diplomatic intervention with Popes, kings and with the ruler of the promised land, the Sultan, should henceforth be as much avoided as armed revolts.

Only the revolutionary developments in the Middle East and Palestine, which led to the collapse of the power of the Sublime Porte, could give a new lease of life to the Zionist aspirations, in particular as a new power came to the fore which was favorably inclined towards these aspirations (although these inclinations appeared to be rather ambiguous...). It is true that during the whole period of its martyrdom Israel could never forget Jerusalem. However, when liberal regimes began to arise in all the western countries, the Jewish people inevitably could not resist the temptations of a comfortable exile. Another serious subject for cabalistic speculation!

The believing Christian, whose faith commands him to share the Zionist hope of Israel, may not forget that Jesus himself *mentioned two sure portents of the messianic era*, namely the conclusion of the period of evangelization of the world (not of its conversion!) and the removal of the pagan yoke from the neck of occupied Jerusalem.

No Zionist venture will prevail if it contradicts either of these conditions that were laid down by him whom the Church hails as the Savior and Messiah who will come in glory...

FORGOTTEN JERUSALEM

During fifteen centuries the Jewish religion and unity were, paradoxically enough, safeguarded by the consistent hostility and discriminatory measures of the surrounding world, and by life in the ghettoes. Only conversion could open the gates to a normal life. This state of affairs sustained the Zionist hope among the rank and file of the Jewish people, and induced it, as we just have seen, to cherish the most fantastic illusions of liberation as we have just seen.

In the wake of the French Revolution, which was rapidly "exported", first by the armies of the Republic, then by Bonaparte's troops, the walls and heavy gates of the ghettoes were torn down, and the Jewish population was invited to taste the flavor of liberty, equality and fraternity, often in an atmosphere of extreme exultation. It is not exaggerated to say that since the fatal year 70 there has been no date of greater significance in Jewish history than the 28th of December 1791, when the National Assembly approved the decree which granted the Jews civic rights.

When Israel ceases to weep by the rivers of Babylon it tends to install itself comfortably in Babylon itself and to forget the return to Jerusalem.

On the other hand, however, whereas Zionist hopes may be entertained with fervor in times of oppression, they can be dangerous in a time of emancipation. A benevolent and liberal monarch does not like it when some of his subjects — who have just been emancipated — cast glances at another homeland, instead of showing signs of gratitude...

Thus, soon after the promulgation of the emancipation decree by the National Assembly, Clermont-Tonnerre declared: "All rights for the Jews as human beings — yes! But as a nation — none whatsoever!

A declaration which was to be reiterated by Napoleon at the session of the Grand Sanhedrin in February 1807, just as earlier, on 12 July 1806, the Imperial Commissioner Mole had asked in a meeting of the Council of Notables the insolent question: "Do the French Jews cherish feelings of loyalty towards France?"

Soon prayers for the Emperor were substituted for the prayer for return to Jerusalem...

Thus, as the European Jews became more and more involved in the tempting world of industry, culture and politics (even reaching the British House of Lords), their links with the ancient, desolate capital in the hills of Judah became increasingly weaker, and the passionate call of the prophets increasingly muffled and choked.

Parallel to this development, "conversion" to Christianity assumed tremendous dimensions. Our use of quotation marks is deliberate, for only rarely was such a conversion ("the ticket of admission to Society," as Heine called it) the result of personal religious experience.

The Synagogue, with her orthodox forms and ritual — not to mention the talmudic casuistry and the way of life of the ghetto — was a seemingly unsurmountable obstacle on the road towards the so deeply desired admission to society. But it was this same Synagogue who preserved the Zionist yearnings, notwithstanding the failure of the successive pseudo-messiahs.

It is natural that an attempt to reform the Synagogue should be made but this reform was very different from the protestant Reformation. Whereas the Reformation constituted an irresistable return to the biblical sources, the Jewish Reform of the 19th century was a movement of considerable estrangement from these same sources.

The first seeds of reform had already been sown at the session of the Grand Sanhedrin where the rabbis were compelled to accept the validity of civil marriage. The break was manifest. In 1856 the synod of French rabbis recommended a number of moderate reforms in — rather late — imitation of some of their German colleagues. Indeed, since the late 18th century Reform congregations had already been founded in Seesen, Hamburg and Berlin at the prompting of Moses Mendelssohn. In 1840 Rabbi Abraham Geiger of Breslau introduced the first changes in the prayers referring to the Messiah. Three years later, in Frankfurt, the Reform Union denied the authority of the Talmud in matters of custom, declared that the Jewish religion was evolutionary, abolished the prayers relating to the Return to the promised land, and replaced the messianic hopes of the prophets in the coming of a Redeemer with the belief in the social and moral evolution of man.

The movement spread, with greater success and in a much more radical form, to the United States and from there it passed on to Paris in 1906.

In Eastern Europe, however, the Jews continued to be oppressed. In Rumania they were regarded and treated as "vagabonds." In Bulgaria the inane accusation of ritual murder was launched regularly. In Greece the Jews were the scape-goats of fanatic nationalism. In Poland general Chlopichi told the Jews who had expressed their wish to support his movement: "Jewish blood must not be mixed with noble Polish blood!" And in Russia the few reforms that had been introduced in favor of the Jews were abolished, and at the consistent incitement of the Holy Synod of the Orthodox Church, the discriminatory measures, the expulsions in the middle of the winter, and the pogroms were regular and recurrent events. It was among these persecuted Jews that the flame of Zionist hope continued to burn, and it was from among their ranks, as we shall see, that the great exodus to Palestine was set in motion. Awakened by the martyrdom of their eastern brethren some of the assimilated Jews in liberal Europe would understand their collective responsibility and embark on the march towards Zion.

THE ZIONIST RABBIS

This may seem a strange expression, for, since Zionism is deeply rooted in the Bible alone, every self-respecting rabbi should share the Zionist expectations.

But, as we have seen, following the terrible deceptions and religious crises provoked by pseudo-messianic movements, the doctors of the Synagogue had assumed a more passive Zionist stance, leaving the initiative of Redemption to God alone and refusing to support any movement of Return of a political nature. Only the Messiah himself, coming upon the clouds accompanied by his heavenly hosts could, through his miraculous intervention, bring about the return to Zion and bring it to its happy ending.

In the fact of this united orthodox front a number of rabbis rose up and tried to develop what must be called a Zionist theology, proceeding, not from the contemporaneous state of emergency — the sufferings of the Jews — but from God's own plan for the redemption of his chosen people and of the desolate country on the bords of the Jordan.

No! these rabbis said. God does not demand from us a passive faith. On the contrary, He demands that we participate in the final work of national and spiritual liberation. He is not afraid of man's collaboration with Him. He knows that man is not a saint and that mistakes, failures and even treason are inevitable. But what is at stake is this land, unique among all lands, this City, the heart of the Divine policy, the axis of redemptive history; what is at stake is our people which, as in the days of Moses, must fight to secure and to guard the land that was promised to the fathers and to the prophets. God will purify our imperfect work, He will put the final touches to it, but we must start it, as the soldiers of Joshua, as the exiles in Babylon, as the sons of the Maccabees.

We shall review the writings of some of the rabbis of the great Exile: Ibn-al Dabi (14th century), Zvi Kalisher (1795–1874), Yehuda Alkalai (1798–1878), Samuel Mohilever (1824–1898) and Isaac Kook (1865–1935).

In 1360 the Spanish rabbi *Meir Ibn al-Dabi* published a devotional Hebrew book, *Shvile Emunah* (The Paths of Faith), in which he discussed theological and philosophical, as well as scientific questions, and of which the following is a brief extract:

> When many Jews, pious and wise, knowing the Torah, voluntarily go up to Israel and to Jerusalem, driven by the desire to serve, by the purity of their souls and their love of holiness; when they come there, one by one and two by two, from the four corners of the earth; when many settle there and even more say their prayers on the holy hill of Jerusalem — then the Creator will hasten the Day of Redemption.

We see that according to this rabbi neither fasting nor mortification in exile can hasten the coming of the day of salvation, but the presence of pious Jews in the promised land, coming from all the countries of their dispersion. The ties that once united the chosen people with the chosen land must be restored, that is the precondition for the descent of the Holy Spirit.

Rabbi Kalisher was a party in the first controversies in his native Poland with the advocates of a reform of the Synagogue. he defended the cause of the Messiah and the duty to return to Zion in the last of days. In 1836 he wrote to the head of the Berlin branch of the Rothschild family that "Redemption begins with natural human efforts and the willingness of certain governments to gather the scattered Jews in Israel." In 1860 he participated in the founding meeting, in Frankfurt an der Oder, of a society that aimed at the Jewish colonization of the Holy Land and which, for that matter, would come to nothing, but was for him the occasion to write his Zionist work *Drishat Zion* (In Search for Zion).

In his many travels through Europe and his meetings he succeeded in laying the first foundations for Jewish colonies in the vicinity of Jaffa, and later he was among the founding fathers of the first agricultural school, Mikveh Israel, of which the Alliance Israelite was the patron (1870). Here are a few fragments from his Zionist treatise:

> "The Redemption of Israel" which we await will not come through a sudden miracle. The Almighty, blessed be His name, will not descend from His heaven to order the departure of His people. He will not send His Messiah from heaven on a cloud and with resounding trumpets, to assemble Israel in Jerusalem. He will not surround the holy city with a wall of flames, He will not make the holy Temple descend from heaven.

The miracles announced by His servants the prophets will certainly occur — everything will be fulfilled — but we shall not have to flee in panic, for the Redemption of Israel will be a long process and the light of salvation will appear gradually...

Israel will not return from Exile all at once but they will be gathered slowly, as the grains of corn are gathered after the corn is threshed.

So much for the rigid orthodoxy which expects that the Return will be effected by the lightning wonder of the messianic coming alone! Being a good rabbi, Kalisher strengthens his thesis with a quote from Isaiah (27:6):

The meaning of "in time to come Jacob's offspring shall take root" is that the Lord will render those who come first in the time of Redemption, into the corn that is planted in the earth and gives abundantly fruit... This same concept of Redemption is also implicit in Isaiah 11:11: "And it shall come to pass in that day, that the Lord will set His hand again the second time to recover the remnant of His people..." Evidently two ingatherings are foreseen, the first in order to revive the land, and then Israel shall flourish in an unprecedented manner...

Fearing that this exegesis of the Isaiah text will not convince his opponents, rabbi Kalisher supports his theory with theological arguments:

Can we offer a logical explanation for the fact that the Redemption will begin in a natural way and that the Lord, in His love for His people, will not send His Messiah right away as a sufficient sign? Yes, we can. We know that our worship of God is performed under the sign of the trial with which He puts us to the test. When God created man and placed him in the Garden of Eden, He also created the tree of Knowledge and ordered him not to eat thereof... Why did He allow the serpent to penetrate the Garden if not to test the faithfulness of man? When Israel left Egypt, once again God tested man's faith with hunger and thirst in the desert. The commandment of the Torah not to eat of unclean animals are also continuous tests, for if that were not the case why has the Creator made them so palatable? And all along our dispersion we have suffered martyrdom for His name, we were chased from country to country... out of love for His holy Torah and as a constant test...

If the Lord were to appear suddenly one day, with manifest miracles, it would not be a trial. What kind of test would it be for our faith... if a heavenly command were to send us to the Land to taste its delicious fruit? In such circumstances, who would be foolish enough not to go, not for the love of God, but for selfish reasons?

Only a natural beginning of Redemption constitutes a real test for those who will participate in it. To devote all one's energy to this holy work, to abandon one's hearth and comfort for the sake of Zion even before "the voice of joy" is heard — there is no greater merit, no greater test than this.

Let us note the amazing expression he uses with regard to the work of the pioneers in Palestine: "holy work." Kalisher is here in concert with some of the talmudic sages who regard life in the promised land as one of the most sacred commandments. Not only study and prayer, but manual work as well is an act of sanctification.

Kalisher was attacked in a pamphlet from Jerusalem and charged with encouraging the immigration of pioneers, which would jeopardize the study of the Torah and the Talmud. In fact, the pious Jews in Jerusalem 'lived entirely from the charity of the Jews in the world, and feared the "competition" of the pioneers who applied themselves to the hard work of reclaiming the land. But Kalisher reacted charitably to these attacks:

> ...the Jewish colonization will hasten the messianic Redemption. By bringing to the Land a natural, wordly redemption, we shall evoke the dawn of heavenly salvation.
> And let no one among the opponents of these views claim that those who work day and night are prevented from studying Torah... On the contrary, our plan honors the Torah even more: "If there is no flour, there is no Torah!" If grain grows in the Land, man can study in tranquility. On the other hand, we know that there are many in the Land who are not students of the Torah and are looking for work. They will support the sages who are unfit for manual labor and to whom nobody will say: "Go toil the land!"
> Such activity will raise our dignity in the eyes of the nations who will then say that the children of Israel, too, have the courage to build their ancestral land which now is desolate and abandoned...
> All nations have struggled for their national honor. How much more should we follow their example, for our duty is not merely to work for the honor of our Fathers, but for the glory of God who has chosen Zion!

This is indeed a real crusade, a peaceful crusade of rather unusual farmers. God wills it! For God wants that man holds Him to His Word, that His promises to the fathers, which nobody can abrogate, be taken seriously. There is a mysterious bond which links the Creator to the land of Israel, a bond which even Israel cannot reduce to mere nationalism: the prophets came to keep watch over it. This land is partly the Holy Land. How can God not secretly rejoice when He sees that it is being revived by Jewish hands? In an adventure in which arms do not have the last word, in which the soldiers do not lead the way, an adventure which was intended to be the prelude to the era of peace and justice for the entire world. An adventure under the protection of the Holy Spirit.

YEHUDA ALKALAI was born in Sarajevo, the son of a rabbi, but he spent his youth in Jerusalem where he was influenced by cabalistic teachings. His years in the Balkan, at the height of the revolt against the Turkish yoke, had rendered him as a matter of course into a theoretician of national independence. In 1834 he wrote a study under the title *Shema Israel* (Hear O Israel), in which he pleaded for the establishment of Jewish colonies in the holy land as the first phase toward messianic Redemption.

Unlike his colleague Kalisher, and under the influence of the Cabalah, he believed that the land will eventually have to be conquered in a war against the hordes of Gog and Magog, which will be led by the first Messiah, the

Messiah Ben Joseph who is predestined to die. In 1840 Alkalai was provoked by the events in Damascus, where the infamous blood libel was once again used as pretext for a massacre of the Jews, to sound the alarm and to declare that the Return was the only solution to Israel's suffering in all the countries of its despersion. He sent letters to Jewish bankers and politicians in the Western World, such as Moses Montefiore and Cremieux, proposing to wrest the promised land away from the Sultan, to convoke a "Great Assembly," to establish a national fund for the purchase of land and to issue a loan among the Jewish people.

We note that the rabbi with his cabalistic leanings stood with both his feet on the ground. In the course of his many travels he founded small "Zionist" committees. Among the people he converted to his cause was a certain Simon Herzl, the grandfather of Theodor Herzl...

Let us listen to rabbi Alkalai's Zionist sermons:

> It is written in the Bible (Numbers 10:36): "Return, O Lord, unto the ten thousands of Israel!" On this verse our sages of the Talmud comment that the holy Presence can only become manifest in Israel when tens of thousands of the faithful are assembled...
>
> On what does this Presence rest? On sticks and stones?...
>
> At the time of the first conquest under Joshua the Almighty led the children of Israel to a land that expected them: the granaries were full, the wells filled and its vines and olive trees heavy with fruit.
>
> The new Redemption will, alas! be different because of our sins: our land is a desert and we shall have to build our dwellings, to dig our wells and to plant our vines and olive trees. That is why we have been ordered not to go up in our multitudes to the holy Land, but that at first many must remain for a while in the countries of the Dispersion in order that they may come to the help of the first Palestinian pioneers, who will certainly be the poorest of the people...

We detect the Cabalist behind the exegete, and we note it even more when he plays with the meaning of the Hebrew term which means both "return" and "conversion":

> There are two categories of return: individual and collective return. Collective return means that all Israel must come back to the land of their fathers in order to hear the will of God and to accept the yoke of heaven. This return was announced by our prophets in spite of our unworthiness. Heaven will help us for the sake of our Fathers.
>
> Individual return implies that every person can turn his back on his evil inclinations and convert.

Here, without any doubt, he touches the heart and basis of every Zionist theology. *It is in the first place to bring His people back to Him that God will one day lead them back to the land that was promised to them for ever.* The reviving desert is actually the image of the Jewish heart regenerated in the New Covenant that was announced by Jeremiah in the middle of another exile. The Zionism of the blossoming rose in the desert and the Zionism of the Jew who encounters his God are one and the same reality, the two phases of the same resurrection: the resurrection of flesh and bones through the heroic work of the pioneer emerging from the valley of death, and the resurrection of the spirit that was foreseen in the great vision of another prophet of Exile, the prophet Ezekiel.

After having shown what will be necessary for the accomplishment of the resurrection of the Land, Alkalai turns to the aspect of spiritual resurrection propounding a daring and — it must be admitted — even prophetical solution.

> I must confess that I am pained by the mistake of the previous generations who have allowed our language to perish. That is why our people has been divided into seventy different nations and our language replaced by the seventy languages of Exile.
>
> If the Lord shows us His grace by gathering us together, how can it be that we do not understand each other, how can such a divided nation survive?
>
> Let nobody try to "solve" this problem by saying that at the time of Redemption the Lord will send us an angel to teach as the seventy languages of the nations, for that is a false concept. Such things do not occur in a miraculous way, even though it is almost impossible to imagine that our Hebrew language will be revived by natural means. We must nevertheless have faith in that this is what will happen, in with the prophecy of Joel: "I shall pour out My spirit on all mankind, and your sons and daughters shall prophesy..."

If we remember that even Herzl believed that it was impossible to revive the Hebrew language, we are filled with respect for this rabbi of Sarajevo and his vision, and admit that the enlightenment of the Holy Spirit is not the exclusive prerogative of the doctors of the Church and certainly not in questions pertaining to the resurrection of Israel...

Rabbi MOHILEVER was born in a Lithuanian hamlet near Vilna and lived long enough to witness the glorious hour of the dawn of Israel's Redemption after its long Exile. Extremely gifted, he was ordained rabbi at the age of 18. He was thrown into the arms of Zionism by the bloody pogroms of 1881 which led to the flight of tens of thousands of Russian refugees. Mohilever immediately suggested that this stream of refugees be directed towards Palestine, but his suggestion was not accepted. In Warsaw he was given the opportunity to establish the first cell of intellectual pioneers who were to call themselves "Hovevei Zion" (Friends of Zion) and among whom he was virtually the only theologian. These pioneers were agnostics who were mystically attracted by the Land of Israel which they regarded as the only refuge from the hatred of the nations. Thus Samuel Mohilever had to fight a lonely battle on two fronts.

On the one hand he had to react to the constant attacks of the orthodox non-Zionists who were shocked by his support for such a movement, while on the other he had to defend the rightful place of religious thought in this essentially secular community.

In 1882 rabbi Mohilever won in Paris a "convert" whose future involvement in Palestinian affairs was to be of vital importance: Baron Edmond de Rothschild. Until his death in 1934 Baron de Rothschild would remain the most generous maecenas of the Palestinian pioneers.

The following are extracts from Mohilever's address which was read by his grandson Joseph before the First Zionist Congress in Basel, in August 1897:

> Let all the "sons of Zion" believe with perfect faith that the resurrection of our Land through the purchase of land, the building of houses, the planting of orchards and vineyards and the cultivation of the land is one of the most fundamental commandments of our Torah. Some of our sages of old even went so far as to assert that it *is* the Torah, since this task constitutes the basis of our people's existence. True Zionist is he who believes this with all his heart and all his might.
>
> The foundation of Zionism in all its manifestations is the Torah... it is the source of our life and it must be the basis of the regeneration of the land of our Fathers...

In this most solemn of hours when the delegates of the Jews of the world united to call upon the children of Israel to embark on the road of final Return, the voice of this visionary rabbi reminded them that God is the Lord of History, the Lord of the Holy Land and that the Zionist building cannot be erected on merely nationalist foundations.

In this hour he sent a message to all the children of Israel who had lost the messianic and Zionist faith, to all those who had decided to resist this Jewish Renaissance:

> For two thousand years we have waited for our Messiah to extricate us from our bitter exile and to gather our dispersed from the four corners of the earth in our land where everyone will live in peace under his vine and his fig tree. This faith, firmly established in our hearts, was our only consolation in the days of infinite misery and degradation.
>
> Some have arisen among us in this century, who reject this faith, tear it from their hearts and even go so far as to erase it from their prayers — but the masses of our people have remained faithful to this hope for the fulfillment of which they pray morning, afternoon and evening. Recently some rabbis in western Europe have stood up, and one of them declared that the promises of consolation of our Prophets are nothing but parables and symbols. The coming of the Messiah, they say, does not signify the ingathering of Israel in its Land, but the establishment of a heavenly kingdom on earth with Israel remaining in the midst of the nations as a light unto the nations. Others assert that our Zionism contradicts the messianic faith. I beg to say that all this is false...
>
> We do not ignore the well-being of mankind, we believe, no less than others, in the universal promises that were given us through our prophets...
>
> May He whose name be praised and exalted for ever, the Guardian and Savior of Israel, fulfill the prophecy of Zechariah: "Thus sayth the Lord: See, I will rescue my people from the countries of the east and the west, and bring them back to live in Jerusalem. They shall be My people, and I will be their God, in truth and justice."

There were not many rabbis and theologians at this prophetical congress
...at was called by Herzl, the uncrowned prince of the time of Return, but
the voice of the prophets was heard and God was praised and thanked. Not
through the mouth of some chaplain who was merely doing his duty, nor
with a brief ritual prayer. All these representatives of Jewish martyrdom
from Russia, Poland and Rumania were of one heart and of one mind and
their very sufferings had brought forth this wonder.

Samuel Mohilever, who spoke in defiance of the majority of his
colleagues, was in good company, the company of all the servants of God
who arose and cried out against the guardians of cold dogmatics, the
established doctors and priests without vision.

He who was to become the first Chief Rabbi of Palestine, was in the first
place a man of prayer, a friend of God, a visionary to whom it was given to
interpret the signs of his time.

ISAAC KOOK was born in Lithuania in 1865. In his early years he
showed a marked preference for Hebrew as a spoken language, to the
horror of the sages of the Talmud schools of his days. In his first Zionist
writings he already pictured the movement of Return, even in its most
secular aspects, as the natural road towards the messianic era. Although he
was offered several very honorable posts in his native country, in 1894 he
preferred to become the chief rabbi of Jaffa, thereby setting an example of
settlement in, and of "going up" to the holy land. His unusually liberal
views and his defense of the non-observant pioneers soon brought him into
conflict with orthodox Judaism both in Palestine and the diaspora. The
work of the pioneer is hard and one should not demand of him to be
ritually clean. For the Zionist pioneers are in fact laying the foundations of
a new community which is called to become messianic and holy; it is
normal that these "tools" are somewhat crude — and stand firm in every
test — but, in the words of Kook himself, they will one day "become the
receptacles of the highest and most intense illuminations." To the question
of the orthodox fanatics in Jerusalem: "Why don't you separate between
holy and profane?" (meaning: between us, the pure ones, and this bunch of
impious and indecent pioneers) he answers with a parable:

> Only one man might enter the Holy of Holiest in the Temple, and only
> once a year: the High Priest on the Day of Atonement. But what was
> the situation when the Temple was being built? Was it built by the High
> Priest, or even by the priests? The simple carpenters and stone-cutters
> moved freely on the site and rendered their work into a offering to God.
> The same is true of the work of our days: we are building and are far
> from having reached the Holy of Holiest...

Indeed, a great parable which casts a clear light on the mystery of the
Zionist work in the Holy Land. This is truly the mystical aspect of sound
Zionist theology. Only if we can distinguish the eschatological future of
Israel, gathered again in its ancient biblical land, only then is the work of
rebuilding, which is inevitably profane, inevitably part of a political context,
biblically justified.

One can understand the consternation of the orthodox fanatics when they heard this parable, which reminds us of those of the Gospels. For didn't Rabbi Kook present them with this outrageous thesis: in the eyes of God, who in a mysterious way guides what is happening here in the Land of Israel, the humble pioneer fighting malaria in the Jordan valley, and the young "indecent" girl cleaning the table in her kibbutz are just as precious as the High Priest of old. And, what is more, more precious than those men of the dead letter and the easy condemnation who oppose the building of the Temple of the future!

For this Land was called to become the Temple of all mankind in the messianic era:

> The Land of Israel cannot be separated from the soul of the Jewish people... it is the heart and essence of our nation, organically linked to its intimate life... To regard the Land of Israel as the instrument with which to establish our national unity, or even to sustain our spiritual life in exile is a sterile notion... The hope of return to the promised land is the source of Jewish uniqueness...
>
> The divine revelations, whatever their degree, are purer in the Land of Israel... The spirit of man is here more lucid, purer... Here his spirit is willing to receive the light of the prophetical word, the enlightenment of the Holy Spirit...

Incomprehensible and ridiculous words for those who have no faith. Monstrous nationalistic words which deify the land in a manner recalling ancient and modern manifestations of paganism... But for the children of Abraham, whoever they are, an evident and constant reality. Rabbi Kook compares Israel to the Nations:

> All peoples, we know it, are influenced by their respective civilizations. We know their values exactly, we are able to measure their degree of light and darkness... In the course of History we have overcome the most cruel and sinister manifestations of paganism... the darkness from which stems the inaptitude of the non-Hebrew mind to grasp the full significance of the divine order which unites heavens with the earth, the body with the spirit, faith with action, this world with the world to come, the beginning of Creation with its end...

The Chosen Land and the chosen people must find one another again, some day, not in order to rejoice in their own happiness, but to set in motion the process of messianic liberation. That is why, in spite of all appearances, there is no break between promise and exile, no contradiction between the ways in which the Return is taking place and the announced Redemption. The history of Israel is a continuum, through exiles and catastrophes, because in the last instance it is the history of the Redemption of the world:

> The liberation from Egyptian bondage and the final Redemption are both parts of the same process... Moses and Elijah appear in the same role of Redeemer... and the spirit of Israel is in accord with the

messianic melody, with the sound waves of the birth pangs of the Messiah.

Outside its rediscovered land Israel has no substance, since an extraordinary destiny awaits it only there. When the Land is rediscovered, the Diaspora is no longer an alternative:

> ...Judaism in exile has no other foundations, but lives only by the grace of a mighty vision and the remembrance of our glory, by the grace of the past and the future. But there is a limit to the powers of this vision to carry the burden of life and to give a meaning to the destiny of a people; this limit appears to have been reached. The Jewish diaspora is disintegrating at an alarming pace, and there is no other hope for it than the Land of Israel...

Isaac Kook was well aware that his people had not yet been redeemed and that the unique and formidable experiment in the desolate country of Palestine must pass through the flames of Sinai and through trials before the measure of its destiny is full:

> There exists an eternal Covenant which ensures that the Jewish people will escape total corruption... it can never entirely break its bonds with divine life. Many adherents of the current national resurrection pretend to be secularized people. If a secular Jewish nationalism could be imagined, we would indeed be in danger of such a deep fall that redemption would be impossible... The spirit of Israel is so closely linked to the Spirit of God, that a nationalist Jew, even if he insists that he is a secular Jew, cannot but be a witness of God...
>
> An individual can cut off his ties with eternal life, but not the House of Israel, for its most precious national assets: its land, its language, its history and its tradition are the assets of the Spirit of the Lord...

Finally, Chief Rabbi Kook introduces us to the heart of his own Zionist theology when he justifies his nonconformist vision of the work that is being accomplished in Palestine with the thesis that we are living in the time of the pre-messianic tribulations, which is a time of revolutionary upheaval of the highest degree, a time in which even rabbinical thought and tradition are shaken:

> Notwithstanding the grave mistakes of which we are aware in our life in general and in Israel in particular, we cannot but feel that we are going through a second birth, that we are being created for a new life at the beginning of time. *We must believe that we are in the first stage of final Redemption.*
>
> This deep faith is the secret of our people's existence and the divine mystery implicit in its current historical experience.

Let us sum up his deep thought which is so faithful to the way of thinking of the prophets. The messianic time of Israel opens with the Return to the Holy Land; the entire task of rebuilding is placed under Divine blessing. It is the sacred duty of every Jew to carry his stone, and, possibly, to give his life. It is always the same history which is moulded on the potter's wheel of God's policy and which will lead the world towards salvation. The Land of Israel is the laboratory where the elements of a new life are compounded and the mystic bonds between heaven and earth, in stead of being broken, are strengthened so that the Messiah of salvation can make his appearance in the bloodstained history of man. How could this accumulation of coincidences be the result of some law of nature? At the moment that the Zionist pioneers are engaged in their heroic struggle against malaria, the desert and the lack of comprehension on the part of the orthodox Synagogue, a Chief Rabbi is given to them to take their defense. A supreme theologian who is also a visionary, and whose untimely death in 1935 could not obliterate from the heart of the new Israel his call for purity and justice, for the consecration of a State to the service of God alone.

When we read the pages of his work how can we doubt that God still speaks through the mouth of one of the sages of the Synagogue? How can we doubt the truth of his testimony or the authenticity of his inspiration?

And if one is a Christian theologian, how can one not accept with joy and in humility this theological lesson which reminds the Church of what it had forgotten in its long history of relations with pagan wisdom and of power, in which it lost its own Zionist hopes?

V

THE ZIONIST SIGNIFICANCE OF
ISRAEL'S MARTYRDOM

*The Shekhina was, in a manner of speaking, the reflex of Divinity
and although it had no detached existence it could reveal itself to
man independent of Divinity; just as man can see and receive
only the rays of the sun. Thus, whereas Divinity cannot come near
man, the Shekhina hovers over him and enfolds, somehow, the
Temple... The Shekhina follows the people into exile... The
Shekhina is the first hypostasis of Divinity. It is not conceived as
an emanation of Divinity but as Divinity itself, revealing itself in
the form it chooses to be visible to the human eye...*

Joseph Klausner, *Jesus of Nazareth*

Without the persecution in Egypt following the expulsion of the Hyksos
dynasty Moses would perhaps not have entered the scene of history, just
as, much later in Babylon, the Jewish people would adapt itself to this
relatively comfortable exile, and only a negligible minority of "Zionists"
would have gone up to the Land promised to the Fathers with the
mummies of Jacob and Joseph, driven more by the urge to make a
pilgrimage than by the desire to build for themselves a homeland.

The pharaohs of the persecution in the land of Goshen were the
immediate and involuntary instruments of the Exodus. Reduced to the level
of slaves, their children being drowned in the Nile, the people of Jacob
suddenly "remembered," but the biblical text does not say that they
remembered God. For after all, when Jacob and his retinue came to Egypt,
it was not to settle there, but to see Joseph. It is understandable that the
children of Israel, who were the guests of honor of their brother the viceroy,
gave in to the temptation of a generous exile. How could they have foreseen
that this new fatherland of which they regarded themselves as the most
faithful subjects, where they were respected and could obtain every post
they desired, and where they could render eminent services, would one day
become a death trap, a country of concentration camps and of a policy of
genocide? It was far away, and not very tempting, the land of Canaan,
where they actually never had felt at home. And far away was He too, the
mysterious God of their Fathers, and his promises had become blurred...

But there in Egypt assimilation already proved to be misleading and
impossible. Whatever they may do, the children of Israel are forever
marked with the indelible seal of the Call and tne Covenant; a bond

stronger than every political treaty, an allurement different from that which the local idols, made by man, could exert, had placed the children of Abraham in this "different" situation, that would henceforth and forever remain their specific situation.

Suffering and martyrdom will bring this people to its God and to the borders of its promised land until, driven to the wall by this policy of genocide, the Return becomes its only alternative and Canaan its only imaginable refuge.

The only comfortable exile that Israel ever was to know, the Babylonian exile, kept the overwhelming majority of the children of Israel in its web. True, a spiritual elite went the way of Return, and devoted itself to the rebuilding of Jerusalem and the Temple, but seen in the perspective of the call of the prophets their number was of no consequence. This return from Babylon, which the theologians of the Church like to regard as the fulfillment of the messianic promises to the Jewish people, was in fact a sad failure, and the prophets were well aware of it.

Which people would have hesitated if it were placed before the choice between the ruins of Judah and the luxury of Babylon? Only when it is threatened with genocide does Israel remember and return only then.

Sometimes it rises up in revolt. That was the case more than once in the time of Roman rule. Revolt is possible when it is kindled by physical contact with the occupied homeland and the threatened Temple. This was also the case when Israel was challenged by the insane policy of Antiochus Epiphanes. But they do not fight for the recovery of their land, they fight to safeguard it, on its own soil.

During the great exile that will last almost nineteen centuries, every revolt seems to be doomed from the outset, Israel knows and understands this. The substitutes for its revolts, the pseudo-messianic adventures led to nothing but the increasing rigidity of the Synagogue, but were nonetheless undeniable attempts of Zionist reconstruction provoked by misery and desperation. In the middle of the pogroms of the Crusades, the Inquisition and the Thirty year war Israel remembered and resisted to the best of its ability. But there was no Moses to defeat the pharaohs of these times. And when under the combined influence of the Encyclopedists, a few "enlightened" princes and, above all, the French Revolution, the exile of the Jewish people began to take a "Babylonian" turn, the hope of Return faded accordingly, to vanish entirely from the soul of the assimilated Jews who had converted for reasons of convenience, and from the heart of part of the Synagogue seduced by the goodwill of some or other monarch...

However, towards the end of the 19th century, the century of the great assimilation, two events intervene in Jewish history, two different aspects of the martyrdom of Israel which in a brutal manner will recall to the Jewish people the forgotten image of the promised land and of desolate Jerusalem: the pogroms and the Dreyfus affair.

The Russian, Polish and Rumanian pogroms were not a new phenomenon. In these countries Israel had always been humiliated, maltreated and massacred. But these sufferings had over the centuries, alas, remained unnoticed, since they were merely an aspect of Jewish martyrdom *on the European scale*. There was nothing special about them for Jews and non-Jews alike. They had their regular place in the general order of the regimes led by princes throughout Europe and encouraged by outrageous Christian teachings, so justly characterized by Jules Isaac as "teachings of contempt." That the pogroms, which began in 1881 and continued practically without interruption for several decades, had the effect of a bolt from the blue, was because the countries of West Europe had almost entirely freed themselves from the double dictatorship of princes who reigned by divine right and of the ecclesiastical regime of the Inquisition. With an amazingly good conscience western Europe cried shame upon the czarist regime and the Holy Synod of the Russian Orthodox Church... Who, indeed, had ever seen such a scandal, such a barbaric act!

A number of Russian Jews found a substitute for revolt and tried to organize emigration to Palestine. The name they gave to their group, as we have related in the previous chapter, and which was itself a program, was 'Friends of Zion." In the crucible of their Russian martyrdom the children of Israel remembered their ancient and remote promised land, as their ancestors had done in the land of Goshen...

Through the detour of suffering God brings the first pioneers of the great Return back to Himself. he prepares the return of others, in the same way...

Among the journalists who attended the trial of an obscure French captain named Dreyfus was an assimilated and rather celebrated Hungarian Jew from Vienna: Theodor Herzl. This rather trite confrontation of two Jews who both had forgotten Jerusalem was to give birth to an unprecedented movement in the history of Israel, a movement which would not only open the gates of the promised land to its persecuted children after a great many difficulties, but, moreover, provoke the establishment of a new State which, before the forum of the astonished nations, assumed the theophorous name of Israel.

Already shaken by the Russian pogroms, Herzl could not escape the trauma of his Parisian experience: in this very city which had restored his peoples dignity and granted them the rights of man and of the citizen, he heard the cry of the mob: "Death to the Jews!" This was enough to bring about a real conversion in the life of this celebrated journalist and man of letters. That the people of Israel is threatened with death in the steppes of the barbaric empire of the Czar, is somehow understandable, but that they are hunted down in the heart of Paris, a hundred years after the famous Revolution, isn't that a sign that the Jewish people have entered the most critical phase of their history, in which all gates will be closed to them, one after the other, and in which every country may turn into a valley of dry bones, which will always be Jewish bones?

Herzl facing the humiliated Dreyfus — isn't that Moses confronted with his murdered Jewish brother in the Egyptian camp? No, we are not mistaken, it is again and again the same history with the same actors, the same agony and the same promise of redemption, the same forgotten Land. This Devil's Island from where Dreyfus protests his innocence with ever increasing vehemence and cogency, isn't it a new Land of Goshen at the beginning of our century? And this changed man with the features of a semitic prince, this trustee of the martyrdom of an entire people, who will meet the crowned heads of his day and even the lord of Palestine whom none of the pseudo-messiahs had been able to approach, isn't he Moses redivivus demanding from the pharaohs of his day: "Let my people go!"?

And Dreyfus, a not very significant man, no more than the Jew who was murdered before Moses's eyes and whose name nobody knows, set the Return and liberation of his people into motion, without knowing it, without even ever thinking about it. The anonymous martyrs of the chosen people did not give their lives in vain. Let no-one ever accuse God, crying out: "If God exists, how can He allow such things to happen?"

For this martyrdom of the Jew is the price he must pay so that Jerusalem will not die on its ruins and the holy land not be smothered forever under the sand of the Arabian deserts and the pestiferous swamps.

The martyrdom of the Jewish nation is the most mysterious and most confusing aspect of the eternal covenant which unites heaven and earth. It is the painful aspect of the Kingdom that will descend from heaven on earth, on the entire earth, to be sure, but centered round a rebuilt, new and cleansed Jerusalem.

This martyrdom, it alone, gave birth to the Zionist revival. But we can no longer evade the most moving, the seemingly most innocent but the most horrible aspect.

When Theodor Herzl offered the Jewish community of the great city of Munich the honor of receiving the delegates to the first Zionist Congress, this community refused and begged Herzl to take his mad adventure elsewhere. The German Jews would not be compromised by a movement which could cause them only harm. Weren't they the best German citizens, the most loyal patriots? Let nobody try to turn their heads with ancient stories about a promised land and about it being a crime to forget Jerusalem. The Jews of Germany had another slogan which was much more sure and reliable: "If I forget you Munich, Berlin, Frankfurt, let my right hand wither away!" And their slogan is echoed everywhere by similar cries which try to outdo each other, in London, Paris, Antwerp and New York...

"This Mr. Herzl, who takes himself for a scion of the House of David, has come to bother us and even, who knows, to provoke a stir and a little antisemitism in our dear fatherlands and our beloved cities!"

Thirty years later this same city of Munich was to become the springboard of the most demoniac pharaoh who has ever stood up to wipe Israel off the face of the earth: Adolf Hitler. When his hordes entered the good city of Vienna, Herzl had been buried there for thirty years, but the

Jews of the German-speaking countries were caught in the death-trap of the nazies...

If I forget thee Jerusalem... I, the Jew of Munich, of Vienna.

It required no less than six million murdered human beings to convince the nations that the promised land must be returned to its children. On their uncountable bones the Zionist State was founded. The world has already forgotten.

PART THREE

THE RESURRECTION OF ISRAEL
or
THE BEGINNING OF THE MESSIANIC ERA

We are witnessing the judgment not merely of a certain period of history, but of history itself...
History has reached the end of its course, a new era opens before us. We must give it a name...

Nicholas Berdiaev,

The fate of man in the modern world
(*The End of Our Time*, p. 11)

I

THE ZIONIST TURNING POINT OF CONTEMPORARY HISTORY

1917: THE BALFOUR DECLARATION

With the end of the Hasmonaean dynasty, which had come into power as the result of the victorious insurrection of the Maccabees, the last semi-independent Jewish state expired in 37 BC. In this year a puppet of the Romans — the Herod of the "Wise men from the East" in the story of Nativity in Matthew 2 — assumed power in Jerusalem.

Palestine remained under Roman and then Byzantine rule until 638 AD, the year that witnessed the conquest of almost the entire mediterranean region, and in the first place of Palestine, by the young Islam.

The two centuries between 1099 and 1291 were the intermediate period of the Crusades and the Frankish kingdom in Jerusalem during which the holy land witnesses the confrontation of knights from the west with Saracenes and other Mamluks.

From 1517 to 1917, exactly four hundred years, Palestine was merely one of the provinces of the vast Ottoman Empire.

1917: in that year a major event took place which its contemporaries could not but regard as one of the many vicissitudes of World War I, but which we will call "the Zionist turning point of history:" the liberation of Jerusalem by a British army unit which included a brigade of Jewish soldiers. But this military operation was accompanied by a political act: almost simultaneously the government in London issued the "Balfour Declaration" which recognized, though in ambiguous terms, the right of the Jewish people to establish a "national home" in Palestine. And when the new League of Nations entrusted Great Britain with the mandate of Palestine, England appointed as its first High Commissioner in Jerusalem a British Jew.

Jerusalem freed from the Turks, the Balfour Declaration, a Jew High Commissioner of Palestine — historical facts of evidently minor importance. But how can a believing Christian forbear to relate them to these words of Jesus (which are echoed by St. Paul in chapters 19 and 21 of his Epistle to the Romans):

> ...they will be carried captive into all countries; and Jerusalem will be trampled down by foreigners *until the end of the time of the nations.*
>
> (Luke 21:24)

The departure of the Turks and the birth of the "Jewish National Home" seem to herald the dawn of the end of this "time of the nations."

In the Bible, history does not revolve around one of the big cities in the world, but around the capital of a very little country: Jerusalem. Herein God, the Lord of history, is consistent, for He has chosen to be in the first place the God of a small people, Israel, whose city *par excellence* is Jerusalem. And Israel, who recognizes the hand of God in the events, alone among all the peoples of Antiquity, therefore became the people which "invented" history in the modern sense, as an irreversible succession of events.

To Israel, it is man who makes history, to be sure, but always in relation to God, with Him or against Him, for it is God who, in the last instance, leads history to the goal He has appointed, and in which His people, their land and their city play a privileged part. In this sense Jerusalem is the center of the world. From its gates and walls, from its Temple, for the first time the message was conveyed to mankind of the truth, justice and brotherhood that are not conceived by philosophical reflection, nor codified by the legislation or morality of the peoples, but that have sprung from the great heart of the Creator and His love for all creatures. This does not detract from the prestige of the other capitals of the world, but in the case of Jerusalem we are placed on a different level.

And he, whom millions of believers worship as their Savior, was from the outset and in the first place a Jewish preacher, whose earthly career ended in Jerusalem. Through him the light of the Bible has penetrated all continents, its text has been translated into thousands of languages and dialects. The Bible, the book which tells us that the last act of history will be performed in the land of Israel! And here Jesus is of one mind with the prophets: he is the guarantee of the truth of their prophecies.

For all these reasons the least one can say is that the return of the Jews to the land of their fathers should give us food for thought.

It is interesting to see how things developed. The Turks did not want the war! Neutrality was much more attractive to them. By participating in the conflict, no matter on which side, they would run an equal chance of losing everything. And the whole world knew that the Ottoman Empire, which for several decades had already been portrayed as "the sick man of Europe," did not need much shaking.

That the Turkish regime was still holding out was only because of the good graces of Great Britain which preferred to see the Straits in the hands of the Turks. To keep Russia outside these waters at any price, that was the aspiration of London which, for that matter, also benefited from the open rivalry between Vienna and St. Petersburg in the Balkan. On the other hand, a new element was undermining the middle eastern balance so desired by England: the German presence in Turkey.

The autumn of 1914 saw the offensive of the Russian armies in the direction of Berlin, while the army of von Kluck was not far from the Eiffel tower. Czar Nicholas II chose this moment to ask England for a free hand with regard to Turkey, in other words for the freedom to occupy the Dardanelles and to lay hands on Constantinople. The German secret service informed the Turks of these dealings, and the latter had no choice but to enter the war on the side of the Central powers. In this way the Czar got "his war," from which he hoped to gain the possession of Constantinople, a traditional Russian dream which the Orthodox Church did certainly not oppose.

While in Flanders its troops were exhausting themselves in fierce battles, the British forces in Egypt were confronted by the Turkish armies in Sinai, which forced them to open a new front, first in Mesopotamia — with disastrous results: an entire army corps was mowed down by the Turks. The British commander Allenby drew the lesson from this defeat, and did not open a new offensive before he had all the trump cards in his hands.

Jerusalem fell without one shot being fired: a flight of aircraft over Jerusalem was enough to cause the Turkish withdrawal. The British Chief of Staff commented: "A true miracle!" And on foot, leading his horse by hand, he entered the holy city.

Without the foolish dreams of Nicholas II Turkey would not have entered the war, but kept its neutrality as it did to its advantage in World War II and Palestine would without any doubt have remained Turkish. The politics of an anti-semitic Czar thus led to the upheaval in the Middle East which, in turn, made it possible for the Balfour Declaration to be issued!

If the birth of the Jewish National Home in Palestine marks the end of the "time of the nations," this obviously does not imply that the nations will no longer play a principal part in the course of history: but he who believes understands that the policy of the small and big powers will eventually lead to the rebirth of the Jewish nation. On the chessboard of history, whose rules are revealed in the Bible and which we may call the "Zionist chessboard" all moves lead to the firm establishment of the New Jerusalem on its hills, and of the children of Jacob in the Negev, so that the "highways of the Lord" be made plain and the promised and recovered land prepare itself for the breakthrough of the messianic times, so that once again this land alone will serve as the base of support of the Lord of History and as the launching site of the new time.

But on the other hand, the nations will make every effort to turn the Zionist epic into a failure, as if they are indeed vaguely aware that their time has been fulfilled and that the return of the Jewish people heralds the era of justice and peace announced by the prophets of Israel, of which the powers of darkness wish no part. In this respect the attempt at total extermination of the Jewish people by the nazis constituted the paroxysm of hatred in the history led by God: the promised land seemed to be doomed to absorb nothing but the ashes of millions of corpses from the crematoria. But to say this would mean to forget the vision of the dry bones of Ezekiel (chapter 37), bones that will regain flesh and life; it would mean to forget that this land, like which there is no other, was called to become a laboratory of life and resurrection in the time of Return.

Let us therefore linger a while on the opposition of the nations and their rejection of history as God as conceived it: through Jerusalem and the Jewish people.

FROM 1917 TO 1919:
THE BALFOUR DECLARATION BETRAYED

Many factors contributed to the birth of this official Charter of Return, the Balfour declaration.

First of all the natural force of Zionist enthusiasm that was triggered by Herzl and snowballed even through the countries where the Jews are freely admitted, such as the United States and England.

The second factor was the man who would become the first president of the State of Israel, Chaim Weizmann, the scientist who made such important contributions to the Allied war efforts with his invention of synthetic explosives, and who could consequently effectively plead the cause of his people before the British leaders.

In the third place, this gesture in favor of Zion doubtless induced the Jewish world, especially in America, to adopt the Allied cause.

Nor should we forget the secret thoughts of the Foreign Office and the Colonial Office who hoped to exploit the Zionist presence in the Middle East for the British interests.

And finally: a perhaps decisive factor which both the Zionists and the "Gentiles" tend to forget, namely the *a priori* favorably inclined frame of mind of a great many British politicians, whose Protestant background and education had imbued them with Biblical notions. Indeed, for many centuries a truly Zionist theology had been developed in Great Britain. We shall return to this. This theology asked for the return of Israel to Palestine, first of all for reasons of justice, but also in order to hasten the second coming of Christ. Lloyd George himself, who can certainly not be considered a mystically inclined man, acknowledged that for electoral reasons it would pay for him to present his own constituency with a policy favoring the return of the Jews to Palestine.

But all these factors which had contributed to the Balfour Declaration could not prevent that even before the peace treaties were signed the situation deteriorated, and a subtle anti-Zionist, not to say anti-Semitic, policy raised its head. For the test of a policy is, after all, its implementation, and the people who were to be in charge of the implementation of the Balfour Declaration, both on the spot and in the ministerial bureaus, did not believe in "the fulfillment of the prophecies," but only in the grandeur of the British Empire. These "imperialistic" officials and functionaries regarded the biblical notions of some of the men in power positions in London not only as subjects for derision, but as a real danger for England's glory.

The officials who had been installed in Palestine even before the Armistice and before the arrival of the first High Commissioner were people who had always reigned over "inferior natives" in India and Africa and elsewhere. They were naturally inclined to racism, and consequently to anti-semitism. The dreams and aspirations of the Jews seemed to them outrageous, and should be smothered at the earliest possible time, not to mention the "bolshevik" danger which these Zionist pioneers introduced in the Middle East.

These people found a favorable political climate. In fact, a myth had been developed in the course of the campaign against the Turks, instigated by the famous Colonel Lawrence and exploited with brio by the British military High Command, the myth of Arab unity and of active Arab participation in the war against the Ottoman regime. Today we know, from the writings of Lawrence himself, that the Arab involvement was strictly limited to skirmishes along the railroad. Mortal feuds between the tribes, thirst for looting, endless palavers in the moonlight with sheikhs bought with English gold — these had been the characteristics of the "Arab campaign" from the outset. Discouraged, Lawrence submitted his resignation and retired to the shade and to humility: a beautiful dream had been proved to be impossible.

But the military and the officials of the Colonial Office continued to buy these rival and corrupt sheikhs at fabulous prices, and when necessary, to offer them crowns and draw kingdoms for them in the sand, to ensure their loyalty to the cause of the British Empire.

Thus appeared on the Palestine chessboard, on the side of His British Majesty, the Arab knight, happy with the bargain and waiting for the support of the infantry of hired assassins of the sinister Mufti of Jerusalem.

But before we go on, let us stress another forgotten truth: until the installation of the provisionary military government (which was to exists till 1920) no Arab voice had been raised in protest against the Balfour Declaration. Emir Feisal declared that he regarded the return of the Jews as a normal and fortunate event, and that the two peoples, both descendants of Abraham, are destined to live in harmony had to work for the prosperity of the entire region which was then still a desert.

It was the British military who turned the two communities against each other, in agreement with the more or less openly admitted wishes of the High Commander in Cairo. As a result, riots would be organized and massacres became the inevitable. And indeed, who became the first military governor of Jerusalem? None other but a fanatical partisan of the Arabs, full of contempt for the Jews and for...the French, whom he regarded as intruders in what should remain an English reserve. And when in 1923 London secretly decided to "liquidate" by political and economic means the Zionist presence, it was this same Ronald Storr who was recalled to Palestine from his proconsulate in North Rhodesia! In a letter of July 25, 1918 he had already summed up the attitude of his staff with regard to the Balfour Declaration:

We preach nationalism in Palestine... We are for the Arabs... We take the Arab tradition seriously, which says that Jerusalem will be returned to the Arabs when a new prophet enters and conquers the city...

Storr even exploits this Arab legend to the extent of using the name of general Allenby for his purpose. This name, when pronounced fast, sounds to Arab ears as "Al-Nebi," the Prophet! By this pun he suggested, of course, that the British army had liberated Jerusalem to offer it the Arabs as a reward for their loyal devotion.

This was the mentality of the men whose task it was, in the words of the Balfour Declaration, "to facilitate the establishment of a national home for the Jewish people in Palestine." "We preach nationalism in Palestine" — under this motto the British military engaged the services of the man who was to become a disciple and friend of Hitler: Husseini. Formally sentenced because he had not hidden well enough the knives of the first pogrom in Jerusalem in 1919, he found in the first High Commissioner, the assimilated British Jew Herbert Samuel, a man who was willing to forgive the murderer and even to install him in the important post of Great Mufti which gave him control over the administration ad finances of the Arab community. By appointing a Jew to the sensitive post of High Commissioner, London had made the right calculations: torn between his loyalty to England and his Jewish conscience, and faced with the hostile attitude of his administrative staff and the military towards the return of the Jews to Palestine, he could not but choose the English camp and, consequently, that of the Mufti and his killers.

Thus, from the very beginning, the Jewish national home was sabotaged by the people on the spot with the heartening consent of a British-Jewish High Commissioner. It is not surprising that the same Herbert Samuel condoned London's decision to detach Trans-Jordan from Palestine and to offer it to Abdallah.

This outrageous amputation already carried the seed of all the conflicts and wars that have poisoned the Judeo-Arab relations until our days.

Several royal commissions of inquiry were to follow each other in the country until 1939. Not international commissions as might have been expected for reasons of logic and honesty since the land promised to the Jews was not dependent on the British crown, but on the Mandate Commission of the League of Nations. A bewildering policy in which London is both judge and party! The reports of these royal commissions usually contained a few hypocritical words in favor of the Zionists and recommendations to restrict Jewish immigration and to aggravate the conditions of its absorption.

1939: THE ABOMINATION OF THE "WHITE PAPER"

When the synagogues were burning in all the towns of Germany, when Jews were openly assaulted in the streets and the first rumors of the concentration camps were heard, when every responsible politician who had read *Mein Kampf* could and should be aware of Hitler's intentions to exterminate the Jews, at that very moment the government of His Gracious Majesty published its White Paper of 1939, which better deserves the name of "blood-red paper."

On May 17, 1939, London announced that Jewish immigration would be restricted to 75,000 persons, that the High Commissioner would be responsible for preventing almost entirely the purchase of land by Jews, and that within ten years an autonomous government would be formed — thus ensuring that the Jewish population remain a permanent minority in its own *national* homeland!

These measures of the British government actually gave Hitler and his henchmen carte blanche to "liquidate" European Jewry in the course of the war that was on the threshold — a terrifying solution to the problem of Jewish immigration to Palestine.

The Jews had no illusions. The Jewish Agency reacted with the following solemn proclamation:

> The new policy in Palestine... intends to deny the right of the Jewish people to rebuild its national homeland in the land of its Fathers, and to transfer power to the current Arab majority thereby placing the population *at the mercy of this majority*... A ghetto is thus being erected for the Jews in their own country... Great Britain delivers its friends to the mercy of those who fight against it... Unlike the Jews the Arabs are not a people without a country, and they are not looking for a country of refuge.
>
> At the darkest hour of the history of the Jewish people, the British government wants to rob the Jews of their last hope and to close the road of return to Palestine...
>
> Three generations of Jewish pioneers have demonstrated their strength by rebuilding an abandoned country. With the same energy they will henceforth defend Jewish immigration, the Jewish national home and Jewish freedom.

Some members of the House of Commons vigorously and with feelings of shame denounced the Palestinian policy of the government. Philip Noel Baker wrote on May 22, 1939:

> The Foreign Minister calmly asks us to surrender to the demands of the Mufti and his gang, and to enact a new Munich of which the Jews will be the victims... What is this terrorism to which the Foreign Minister asks us to surrender?... Its activity started in 1935 at the time of the Abyssinian affair... it was organized by the Mufti who since the 1920s has fought the Mandate and who told the royal Commission that the Jews will be expelled once the Arab state is established... Money, arms, officers, organizers, everything comes from Germany and Italy... According to the Daily Telegraph the Jerusalem police intercepted in 1935 documents which proved that Arab bandits had received 50,000 Pounds Sterling from Germany and 20,000 from Italy to strengthen their resistance...

On one point only the brave Noel Baker was mistaken: it was not in 1935, but rather in 1929 that the troubles had started with pogroms throughout Palestine. How did the British authorities react to these events? Under the eyes of the British police Jews were massacred in Jerusalem, Hebron and Safed, even in their synagogues, by the killers of the Mufti. But on the same day Jews who tried to defend themselves were arrested and sent to jail or expelled!

No serious steps whatsoever were taken to put an end to the agitation of the Mufti and his followers, and until the outbreak of the war the activity of nazi agents was in no way curbed. Can we really be expected to believe that high-placed British mandatory officials were not somehow accessories?

Noel Baker had other revealing things to say:

> Are the Arabs of Palestine really responsible for terrorism? Why do so many assassins and bandits come to Palestine from all over the Middle East? Lord Lytton goes every year to Palestine; he knows the country well. Last week he told me that the Mufti had no more than one thousands followers. *The Arabs who are killed by Arabs outnumber the Jewish victims.*
>
> In spite of this terror, many Arab peasants openly declare their friendship for the Jews. Two weeks ago 1,500 Jews founded a new settlement in Galilee. The Arabs of the region came to welcome them; they stayed for three days and helped them to build a road. They thanked God that He had sent the Jews, for now they would no longer have to fear the armed gangs of the Mufti...
>
> We easily forget what is happening in Germany under the satanic rule of Dr. Goebbels. Half a million maltreated Jews are dying daily from hunger, without a home, without work, without hope. And when they try to escape to Palestine they are treated by our government as "illegal immigrants."
>
> If the policy of the Foreign Minister is adopted, the illegal immigration of these vexed creatures from Germany and elsewhere will increase enormously... The only way to prevent them from entering Palestine is by ordering our brave soldiers to fight them. Does the Foreign Minister believe that he can give such an order?

But the policy denounced by Noel Baker was adopted. A few years later, *after the fall of Hitler*, did the "brave British soldiers" indeed receive the order to fire at these vexed creatures, at the survivors of the concentration camps.

The Jewish population of Palestine gave important support to the British cause during World War II (the country was neutral); but this was never acknowledged, on the contrary, good care was taken that it was not publicized (see: *"The Forgotten Ally"* by Pierre van Paassen).

In 1943, when Rommel's army was pressing onward, and there was no reason to court the Arab leaders who rejoiced in anticipation of the victory of the nazi armies and the massacre of the Palestinian Jews, London convoked in Cairo the delegates of what two years later was to be called, at the initiative of Sir Anthony Eden, the Arab league, "to discuss... the future of Palestine!

How cynical can one get...

At its yearly congresses the Labour Party firmly protested against the policy of the Conservative government and demanded the annulment of the White book of 1939 and the opening of the gates of Palestine for Jewish immigration. But when the Party assumed power in 1945, it informed the Jewish Agency that the White Paper would be maintained.

In fact, the socialist government continued the policy of the White Paper in the most inhuman manner after the fall of the nazis.

It forced the surviving Jews to remain in the camps, it sank the boats which "illegally" reached the coast of Palestine, and put those who had escaped drowning in new concentration camps. Jewish patriots were hanged in Palestine, and terror provoked counter terror. Ernest Bevin, Foreign Minister in his British Majesty's Government, will be remembered in the blood-stained annals of Jewish history side by side with the worst persecutors, from Pharaoh to Hitler.

One thing must be made clear here. It would be simple but unjust to hold Great Britain alone responsible. For all countries, with varying degrees of hypocrisy, closed their gates to the tormented Jews who tried to escape from the nazi hell. We shall yet see how great the Christian responsibility was in this tragedy.

On the other hand, there are a number of questions which never have received a satisfactory answer and some of which were asked during the Eichmann trial:

Why were the gas chambers and other installations in the Camps never bombed by the Allies?

Why was the exchange of Jewish children for trucks rejected by the Allies!

Why were the nazis never warned that they would have to pay for every Jewish life with the life of one of their own?

Why was Germany never informed on the radio that the existence of death camps was known to the Allies?

Why was the nazi policy of extermination of the Jews kept a top secret by the Allies?

Why was Adolf Hitler never excommunicated by the Vatican?

Must we believe that the world did not find it inconvenient that the Jewish people was exterminated in Europe?

The witnesses of a crime are a party to that crime. Does not this blood, which has stained the whole world, demonstrate the active presence in this world of him whom Jesus called "the murderer from the very beginning" — Satan?

During the summer of 1947 the 29th Commission of Inquiry (in 30 years!) arrived in Palestine, this time not appointed by the British government, but by the United Nations.

Its hostile reception by both the British authorities and Arab officialdom was enough to arouse its suspicions. It consisted of 11 members and a secretary, Ralph Bunche the first black functionary in the State Department.

The representatives of India and Persia were from the outside hostile to the Zionist cause, for obvious reasons, whereas those of Uruguay and Guatemala were firmly in favor of the return of the Jews to their land. The representatives of the other seven countries (Australia, Canada, Sweden, Holland, Yugoslavia, Czechoslovakia and Peru) regarded their visit as fact-finding mission. The majority of the Commission soon reached the conclusion that the British Mandate had failed and that the partition of the country into two confederate states was inevitable.

A partition plan was consequently presented to the United Nations. The Zionists who had rightly been allocated the Negev, but saw themselves deprived of Jerusalem and large portions of Galilee, accepted the plan unanimously. The Arab League rejected it and began to move its troops, even entering Galilee and Judea under the indifferent eyes of the British soldiers.

The last days of November 1947 in Lake Success were a particularly eventful period in the backwings of the U.N.

The Arab League had an enormous advantage over Zionist Israel: the Arab delegates used, of course, the weapon of oil boycott and hinted at how they might vote in future debates. Their pressure became so strong that the State Department decided to detach the Negev from the already ludicrous borders of the Jewish part of Palestine. President Truman, who believed in the truth of the biblical prophecies had to intervene personally to prevent this last-minute change of mind.

In the committee ad-hoc which convened on 26 November, the partition plan was accepted with a vote of 25 against 13, with twenty members abstaining. But in the general Assembly a two-third majority was required. All signs seemed to indicate that the Jewish state would not arise, for want of a few votes.

At that moment a sensational development took place: for the first time the Soviet Union and the United States took the same stand and voted against Great Britain! With the communist bloc voting in favor, the Jewish state reappeared on the scene of history *with a majority vote of one!*

That the U.S. abandoned its British ally was, in the first place, because its president had taken up his Bible, in front of his counselors, in front of his own Secretary of State. As to the Soviet Union — that it, too, stood at the cradle of the State of Israel, was, no doubt, due to the fact that it wanted to undermine the British policy and contribute to the eviction of the British troops from the Middle East, but also because it hoped that the Jewish state would one day join its camp.

The joy in Jerusalem, in Tel Aviv, in the kibbutzim, everywhere where the Jews were reviving their land, was beyond description. However, the territory allocated to the Jews by the United Nations was minuscule, the borders indefensible, and Jerusalem, the city of David, was to be internationalized. Moreover, the armies of the Arab League had already penetrated the territory allocated to Israel, equipped with British arms and "miraculously" always finding the road before them free...

The League knew that it had the support of the London government and of its representatives in the land which, in spite of everything, was to remain, until the evening of May 14, 1948, "the Mandate whose task it was to ensure the establishment of a national home for the Jewish people." On May 11 the Egyptian Prime Minister Mokrashy Pasha declared that he relied on the analyses of British military experts who had predicted that the Jews would be defeated within two weeks. And one of the first Egyptian prisoners of war, a pilot who had bombed Tel Aviv, told the journalist Jon Kimche:

> We Egyptians started this war on behalf of the English who wanted us to liquidate Zionism in their place since they had failed to do so; they told us that we would meet no serious resistance and that our army would reach Tel Aviv within a week. I must ask you to warn your English readers that the Egyptians won't fight if they meet strong opposition. The British will have to help us much better, with more aircraft and guns. If they don't, Egypt will lose this war, and that will be a defeat for England as well.

The armies that attacked the State of Israel even before it was born, with the aid of the British military High Command, consisted of the following forces:

— The army of Northern Palestine of Syrians and Iraqis: 4,000 men.

— The army of Eastern Palestine: 4,000 mercenaries and Beduin recruited in Trans-Jordan under the eyes of the British army.

— The army of Western Palestine, 3,000 men, stationed in the suburbs of Tel Aviv and on the road to Jerusalem.

— The Egyptian army in the South, by far the strongest and best equipped, approximately 10,000 men.

Under the eyes of the British soldiers, these armies had, at the time of Israel's birth, already obtained the following advantages:

— they controlled the vital Haifa–Tel Aviv artery.

— they had entirely isolated the Jewish population of Jeruslem and of the agricultural settlements in the Bethlehem region.

— they were a deadly threat to Tel Aviv and also threatened to cut off the roads to Jerusalem and to the settlements in the south.

— they had isolated almost completely the settlements in the Negev from the area bordering on this desert.

The situation of the Jews was thus extremely critical. Field Marshall Montgomery expressed this in the language of the barracks, saying: "The Jews are done for!" To all this we must add that between December 1947 and May 1940 several hundreds of Jews were murdered every month on the roads and in the fields, but the British authorities would not allow them to travel in *armed* convoys.

The situation seemed so hopeless that the American government asked the Security Council on March 30 to order the abrogation of the partition plan and the establishment of a U.N. — sponsored Mandate — in other words: to keep the British army in Palestine and to give the death blow to the Zionist hopes. On April 1 the Council adopted this proposal and called a special meeting of the General Assembly for April 16.

David Ben-Gurion, alone, in defiance of the provisional government which pressed him to abandon the most vulnerable settlements and to concentrate all the Jewish forces, issued the order not to abandon any settlement but to fight to the last man. He probably knew better than anyone else that the only organized military force of the Zionists consisted of the 2,000 men of the Palmah — four battalions of secretly trained men, armed with home-made machine guns, a few mortars and sub-machine guns and hardly any ammunition. Aircraft? A dozen or so "taxis" — one-seaters whose pilots had a machine gun, but had to drop their bombs through the window of their plane at a speed not exceeding 120 km. per hour!

In the beginning of April about four hundred men defending kibbutz Mishmar Ha-Emek won the first battle against the northern army with its guns and tanks. At the same time terrorists of the Irgun and the Stern group launched surprise attacks, sometimes in a brutal manner, and provoked the flight of the Arabs from their quarters in Haifa and Jaffa, thereby accelerating the exodus *that had been ordered by the Arab League.* The League had explained this order with the necessity to enable the Arab soldiers to kill the Jews without harming the Arab population. "You'll be back in two weeks; once the Jews have been killed, all this will be yours," was the slogan. To refuse to leave meant to be sentenced to death.

This state of affairs reduced the anti-Zionist maneuvers in the Security Council and the corridors of the United Nations to naught.

Under unbelievable conditions, recalling some of the military feats at the time of the first conquest under Joshua, the strongholds in Galilee fell one after the other, although the British army, before evacuating them, had delivered them with all the arms and ammunition into the hands of the Arabs. Throughout Galilee the word "miracle" was in everybody's mouth, even of those who were far from religious, and it was even used by the not particularly mystically inclined army commanders!

On April 12 the provisional government addressed the world with a proclamation of which a few extracts follow:

...We inform the civilized nations of the world, the representatives of the United Nations and the Jews dispersed throughout the earth, that it has

151

been decided to establish the supreme body of our national independence...

We declare that we refuse to remain a minority at the mercy of others...

On May 15, His Majesty's government will return to the United Nations the Mandate it received 27 years ago from the Legue of Nations and which it has failed to bring to a good end as it substituted personal interests in the Middle East for the original spirit of this Mandate...

As a result of this policy our refugees were refused admission to Palestine at the hour of their deepest agony... while our frontiers are open to the hordes of invaders in defiance of the United Nations...

At this moment the mandatory power intends to destroy the very foundations of our existence and prepares to leave the country in a state of general chaos. In order to meet this situation we declare today that the end of the Mandate in fact marks the end of every foreign domination in this country...

In this hour we appeal to the Arab citizens of the Jewish state and to our Arab neighbors. We offer them peace and friendship... *Strengthened by faith* we ask all the nations to recognize our right to defend our own security, and we place our hope in *God, the Lord of Israel.*

Thus after so many centuries of shame and contempt, Israel once again addressed the Nations in noble and proud words from its threatened land and with an appeal to the sole Lord of History.

In the beginning of May the opponents of Israel's national resurrection applied to last-minute maneuvers. On the 10th of that month the representative of the Cuban dictator proposed the annulment of the partition of Palestine. England, the Arabs and their friends demanded the appointment of a new (the 23rd!) commission for Palestine. The discussion of these proposals continued throughout the fateful day of May 14 until, towards evening, to the shocked surprise of all the delegates — the American delegation was no less surprised than the others — it was announced that President Truman had just recognized the State of Israel, immediately followed by Guatemala, whose "Zionist" delegate, Garcia Granados, had taken full responsibility for this decision without prior consultation with his government.

May 15 was a Saturday, a Sabbath. It was symbolic that this day should be the day of rest, for Israel could at long last rest from its twenty-centuries long martyrdom, and God was praised in every synagogue. In Rome Jews sang and wept with joy under the Arc of Titus which commemorates the defeat of the Jewish armies and the destruction of Jerusalem in the year 70. David Ben-Gurion, the Joshua redivivus, proclaimed in the Declaration of Independence:

...The State of Israel will open its gates to Jewish immigrants from all the countries of Exile; it will apply itself to the development of the country for the benefit of all its inhabitants; it is founded on the principles of freedom, justice and peace proclaimed by the prophets of Israel... We put our trust in the Rock of Israel...

Faith in the Almighty was certainly not superfluous for a State which at the hour of its birth was faced, in order of urgency, with the following tasks:

to repel several enemy forces — supported by Great Britain — on all its borders.

to organize almost overnight the administraton of a country in chaos.

to absorb hundreds of thousands of refugees divested of everything, and to give them shelter and work.

to fight an economic boycott which left it only one outlet: the sea.

Definitely a special people with a unique destiny and staggering tasks! All this had to be done with a population of a little over 600,000, surrounded by 45 million powerful enemies.

After a few weeks of battles, interrupted by brief periods of truce, the enemy was withdrawing on all fronts, the national territory had been expanded, Jerusalem, with the exception of the Old City, had been recaptured. No military expert can explain what had really happened. "A real miracle," is all one can say, meaning: an inexplicable event.

At this point we wish to make a digression.

In the historical context an objective observer would hardly have noticed the entry of the Jewish people into Canaan. If there had been historical handbooks in the schools of Antiquity, the military campaigns of Moses and Joshua would have received only a few lines in a chapter on the Middle East.

But in the book of history which is called the Bible, this campaign takes a central and unique place, more important than the conquests of the Pharaohs and the Assyrian kings. One may say that this is quite normal, because the Bible deals with national, or even nationalist history. Every people tends to blow up its own history to dimensions of world-wide importance, without fear of appearing ridiculous. That is true, of course.

And nevertheless... The armies of the Pharaohs, of the Assyrians, the Babylonians, the Persians, the Greeks, the Romans — where are they today? On the other hand — the Jewish armies are still and again there, in the same land that was anticipated and conquered by Moses and Joshua. And as to its being "nationalistic" — the biblical view certainly has a point when it insists that the ups-and-downs of Israel and its land have some significance for the history of mankind at large, in the past, the present and the future. And, for that matter, isn't this view shared by millions of Christians, even if they fail to draw the right conclusions with regard to the Jews? The Church actually calls the biblical history of Israel *sacred history*.

It is true that Christian theology finds it difficult to "integrate" the existence of the Jewish people in the history *after* Jesus; but *before* Jesus — in the biblical period — yes, she acknowledges that the people of Israel is the people of God and that its history is "sacred", that is, charged with revealing to mankind the thoughts and feelings of God and, at the same time, with acting in history in accordance with the wish and will of God.

Christian theology is inclined to believe that after Jesus the role formerly entrusted to the Jews was given to the Church while the Jews became merely a relic and a testimony of a past geo-historical era. But in reasoning in this manner Christian theology does not reckon with the views of Jesus himself and of the apostles who never wavered in their belief that the Jewish people, and its land are both decisive elements in all of history and in particulr in its apotheosis.

1956: THE SINAI CAMPAIGN

On the first day of Israeli independence the secretary general of the Arab League, Assam Pasha, said in connection with the general offensive against the Zionist state:

> This war will be a war of extermination and massacres; it will be remembered as the massacres of the Mongols and the Crusades are remembered...

Thanks to God these words merely remained a threatening broadcast; nevertheless all along Israel's existence the Arab leaders continued to threaten the small State, which occupies a territory of 20,500 square kilometers lost in an Arab ocean, with extermination, in spite of their obligations under the armistice agreements, in spite of the duties imposed on every member of the United Nations, in spite of the decisions of the Security Council. On the contrary, precisely from the rostrum of this international organization the most outrageous threats were launched against Israel!

From 1948 Egypt maintained a double maritime blockade against Israel, in violation of the Convention of Constantinople of 1888, of the armistice agreements and of the injunctions of the Security Council, namely in the Suez Canal and in the Gulf of Eilat, thereby making it impossible for Israel to trade with the Far East.

Notwithstanding the signed armistice agreements the Arab countries never ceased to harass Israel, both on the borders and in its own territory. 1,500 dead and injured between 1950 and 1946 alone were the balance of Arab terrorism in general and in particular of the Egyptian death-commandos known as the fedayeen who embarked on their attacks from the Gaza district which never belonged to Egypt, but was illegally torn away from the Palestinian territory. Not to mention the acts of sabotage against railroads, roads, irrigation pipes, and the thousands of cases of infiltration by armed gangs, thefts and damage done to the harvest and livestock of agricultural settlements. Which country would have tolerated this for so many years?

Then came the Suez crisis. Israel, which had kept aloof from this crisis, saw its last hope of removal of the eight-year old blockade vanish.

Nasser never concealed that once he would have settled the Canal affair he intended to turn to the solution, once and for all, of the "Zionist problem," strengthened by the tremendous prestige he was to gain from the capitulation of the Western World. He had already christened the planned campaign "Falastin" and there were several indications that this time he was not bluffing.

These were a indications:

— a large-scale resumption of the operations of the "death commandos", which demanded fifty-four Israeli victims in the last few days before the Sinai campaign.

— a military treaty uniting, evidently under Egyptian command, the armies of Egypt, Syria and Jordan.

— enormous supplies of Soviet war material, and their concentration in the Sinai peninsula.

Israel had no illusions. In the case of an attack the United Nations would, as in 1948, content itself with some words of protest and with an offer of aid for possible Jewish refugees. For the first time Ben-Gurion became afraid, and in this apparently desperate situation he appealed to the only possible ally — France.

The French Left, and in particular the "intellectual" Left, was in the habitude — and unfortunately still is — of regarding the defense of the wolf about to devour the lamb as a sign of nobility of soul. When it protested in 1956 against the French intervention in Egyptian the left was actually giving Nasser and the Arab league carte blanche to liquidate the Zionist state.

France's motives were certainly not absolutely pure: Ben Bella had been kidnapped and it was believed that a decisive action against Nasser might break the Algerian revolt. But it is no less certain that the wish to rescue Israel was genuine and sincere, and it remains to the credit of Frence that it intervened on the side of the Israelis who were threatened with death, and that it succeeded in neutralizing, at least temporarily, London's traditional hostility towards Israel. But why had France's credit of 1956 to be transformed into dishonor in 1967?

Since the Egyptian dictator had just nationalized the Suez Canal Company, the British government agreed to join France in a campaign which also happened to be to the advantage of Israel.

The Soviet Union was at the time neutralized by the revolt in Budapest, while the attention of the United States was engaged by this same event as well as by the forthcoming elections.

Thus the internatonal conjuncture in the last months of 1956 allowed the young nation a week's freedom of action in which it carried the day and thereby rescued itself.

The international conjuncture? To the attentive reader of the Bible it is clear that there is One who in His sovereign way had created such a conjuncture.

The armies of Israel thrust forward into Sinai. Among the baggage of the withdrawing Egyptian army they found boxes with copies of a book that was believed to have been forgotten: Mein Kampf in Arab translation, as well as large supplies of potassium cyanide with instructions for poisoning Israel's water sources.

For a few weeks Israel passed again through Sinai — in the opposite direction, and rediscovered its formidable darkness in which it once had learned, through trial and error, to become a people at the command of the Lord of History, a people and a light unto the nations — the same nations that were soon to be in league against it, in order to deprive it of the two conquered territories — the peninsula of its birth and the Gaza Strip that had been so dear to Samson.

The Soviet Union (the "Gog and Magog" of the prophets, according to rabbinical tradition) brandished its weapons, the U.S.A. ordered a total economic blockade, Britain, Israel's fellow-combatant, had the cheek to send an ultimatum of its own (true, the Israeli paratroopers were at the Suez Canal) and, finally, the General Assembly of the United Nations condemned Israel by a vote of 74 to one, the vote of France.

However, in spite of everything, Ben-Gurion succeeded in achieving, in compensation for the evacuation of Sinai and the Gaza Strip, the termination of the blockade in the Gulf of Aqaba, and the stationing of a U.N. contingent in the territory that once belonged to the Philistines. Indeed until 1967 Nasser's death commandos were to leave Israel in peace and the port of Eilat became Israel's gateway to the Far East and Africa. A road was built which linked the Mediterranean with the Red Sea for the first time in history. At the opening ceremony the Israeli prime minister called this road "our Suez Canal."

We conclude this chapter with an anecdote. One of our friends from Tel Aviv, a young, very observant artillery officer, told us the following story:

> I was with my battery at the foot of Mount Zion, opposite the Jordanian positions. Our orders were not to attack under any conditions, but to go into action at the first shot, with the river Jordan as our target!
>
> Jordan was Nasser's ally, their armies were under a united command: it was therefore committed to helping the dictator on the Judean front. We were waiting for its attack, but nothing happened...
>
> Then, during the night I prayed: "O Lord, let them attack us, let them open fire at us!" But nothing happened...
>
> One night, I wanted to take it upon myself to give the order to open fire and thereby to provoke the capture of Jerusalem and the recovery of our biblical borders, but a strange power withheld me, and I did nothing...

"Nothing happened" then, but in 1967 the Jordanians did open fire, Jerusalem was captured and the Jordan was reached.

1967: THE SIX-DAY WAR

Since the end of 1966 Syria had adopted the same policy the Egyptians had conducted in the year preceding the Sinai campaign: terrorism continued, entailing violent Israeli retaliation (Migs were shot down, and the reader perhaps remembers the Iraqi pilot who "offered" his Mig to Israel and asked for political asylum).

Towards the end of April 1967, Moscow warned Nasser of alleged Israeli troop concentrations on the Syrian border. Levy Eshkol, the Israeli prime minister, suggested in an official audience that the Soviet ambassador come with him by plane to this border, but the diplomat dryly refused.

About two weeks later, exactly on the 19th anniversary of Israel's independence, Nasser brought his tanks into Sinai and subsequently achieved in a remarkably easy manner (that is the least one can say) the evacuation of the U.N. troops. And finally he took the measure which rendered an armed conflict inevitable: Egypt closed the Gulf of Aqaba.

The diplomatic palavers and juridical quibblings began. From the outset it was clear that none of the big powers was willing to compromise itself for Israel's sake. The French government made its notorious turn-about and abandoned Israel. Jordan's King Hussein lost his head and joined Nasser in Cairo where he signed an alliance with him, returning to Amman accompanied by the man who had demanded his death on the radio: Ahmed Shukeiry, the since then discredited leader of the Palestinian nationalists.

And the Israeli reactions: Moshe Dayan, the hero of the Sinai campaign, and Menahem Begin, the former leader of the Irgun, joined the government, and everyone understood that war was on the threshold.

Egyptian pilots could reach the three main Israeli cities, Haifa, Tel Aviv and Jerusalem, in three minutes. The problem was how to prevent the destruction of these towns. In the early morning of June 5 Israeli fighter planes liquidated in a surprise attack practically all of Nasser's air force.

The latter, without knowing that his air force no longer existed, conducted a telephone conversation with the King in Amman. Nasser assured Hussein that the Egyptian tanks were thrusting forward to Tel Aviv, and thereby induced the Jordanians to actively enter the war before the Egyptians would gain their victory! The Hashemite King ordered his troops to open fire on the Jerusalem front, and the Jordanian radio called on them to be merciless and to kill and destroy all Jews by all possible means.

It was King Hussein's bad luck that other tanks — those of the Israelis — were at that time on their way to the Suez Canal through the Sinai peninsula! Within three days he lost all of Cisjordan (which had been annexed by his grandfather in 1950), including the Old City of Jerusalem, Hebron, where David was annointed king, and Sichem, where Joseph, once the viceroy of Egypt, was buried...

Before these six days, when the lots had not yet been cast, western conscience was shocked by the television and radio newsreels which showed the Arab masses giving vent to their hatred of the Jews and their thirst for an overall massacre of the Israeli population. The world had been accustomed to regarding the Jews as poor, unfortunate people (true, it had done its bit to render them unfortunate...), persecuted, expelled, robbed, murdered, burnt to death. Until the six days everything had thus been normal, in accordance with the rules, and the world could in good conscience feel sorry for the Jews of Israel.

But then came the outrage of the Six-Day War: this time the Jews did not conform to the traditional scheme, they had the cheek to be the victors in a war they had not sought, while the world had charitably occupied itself with plans for their possible escape from the genocide of which the incited masses in the Arab world dreamt. Yes, the outrage of this victory! Soon it was said that these Jews were warmongers, who had taken no risk whatsoever, that the Pentagon had calculated with electronic means the Israeli victory to the day, take or leave twelve hours, and that, consequently, the pity one had felt for the unfortunate Jews should now be directed to the real victims, the poor Arabs.

The Jews throughout the world, and the Jews in Israel in particular were forced to reach the conclusion which their ancestors had reached before them, almost everywhere and at all times: "Whatever we do, we are wrong; whatever our situation, we are to blame."

Israel had the gall to talk about negotiations, about a solution of the Israeli-Arab drama! And the height of impudence, it adopted an attitude never before encountered in the world: it refused to evacuate the conquered territories before having obtained serious guarantees for the security of its citizens.

And there was more! When the Israeli parliament decided on the reunification of Jerusalem, it caused general and almost holy indignation, first of all of the Vatican which was horrified at the thought that the Christian "holy places" were now under Jewish jurisdiction. For nineteen years it had not been troubled by the fact that these holy places were under Arab jurisdiction, and nobody had deemed it outrageous that during these same years the Jews had not been granted access to *their* holy place — the Western Wall, which had now witnessed the tears of joy of Israeli paratroopers and pious Jews with sidelocks immediately after the last exchange of fire in the Old City.

It is not difficult to compare ironically the attitude of the Israeli soldiers with that of the noble Crusaders of the West, who burnt alive the Jews and Moslems who had sought refuge in their respective sanctuaries... Why was the Church so touchy as far as Israel was concerned, whereas it had not hesitated to sign concordats with Mussolini and Hitler?

But not only the Church of Rome: all the Christian denominations have demonstrated a strangely biased attitude towards Israel. One example among many: the Jordanian army had stationed batteries and dug trenches on the premises of the German Lutheran hospital on the top of Mount Scopus. The Israeli army therefore occupied these positions and in particular the barracks belonging to the hospital. The Lutheran World Federation, whose seat is in Geneva, submitted a strongly worded complaint to the Israeli government and to the President of the State...

The situation has not improved since then, and it would be rash to predict future developments. But we will nevertheless conclude this chapter with the words of the Chief Rabbi of Israel at the Western Wall immediately after the victory: "Now we are only waiting for the Messiah!"

THE YOM KIPPUR WAR OF 1973
AND ITS CONSEQUENCES

A great number of books have been written on the Yom Kippur War, and many more will probably be written. These works have said everything there is to say about the war itself and about the astonishing and seemingly miraculous way in which the Israelis changed the situation by turning the defeat of the first days into an brilliant victory.

As an Israeli I have nothing to add to what has been written, to what history has said. It is certain that the responsible Israeli leaders were caught by surprise, and lacked foresight as well as resoluteness and audacity. For this reason none of them should have remained in a position of power, certainly not general Bar-Lev, and most certainly not Golda Meir who on the third day of the war, towards the end of the morning could only react to the anguished exhortations of the Chief of Staff to preempt the shock by attacking the Syrian and Egyptian positions with the words: "No, for what will they say in Washington!" But it was Elazar who was dismissed...

Her words were, alas, a classic manifestation of the ghetto mentality. As if we in Israel do not know "what people will say" — the same they always say, whatever Israel does. As if Israel had not been regularly judged and censored. As if we had not been blackmailed, even before the end of the war, from the day that Sharon made his counter-attack and crossed the Suez Canal, by the amiable Kissinger who in an amiable manner threatened us with the suspension of economic and military support.

But we shall add a few thoughts that were not offered by these many works, thoughts of a spiritual nature with which neither the war correspondents nor the other journalists of name have ever bothered themselves...

To begin with: for the first time in its long and painful history, in the long history of wars waged against Israel in order to deprive it of its Land, or to exterminate it on the spot — for the first time Israel was attacked on this Special Day, when the overwhelming majority of the people was engaged in prayers of repentance and in day-long fasting. The day that Israel withdraws from the world in moving nearness to God, wrapped in its traditional prayer shawl. The prayer shawl, the tallith, that was also worn by Jesus!

In spiritual, biblical perspective this unprecedented attack has a formidable, hidden significance. The attempt, after Auschwitz, to exterminate Israel, to exterminate the generation of Auschwitz in its own promised land on the day of their encounter with God, has set a dramatic process in motion which has spread from the Middle East throughout the world. A process which, for Israel and the Nations alike, is the beginning of a major crisis whose consequences and outcome were described by the prophets of the Bible.

In Israel the shock of the war proved to be too hard, too cruel. This little nation was brutally confronted with too many dead, too many wounded and disabled, too many people in trauma. Something broke in the metabolism of fragile Israeli society.

All the more so since very soon it became clear that once again the enemy had merely withdrawn to prepare himself for the next attempt, that a new conflict would have to be faced, without doubt with Egypt and, in the north with unrelenting Syria. The nation had to be rearmed with unequaled intensity at a time that the state of the national economy was at a depth. The victory of Yom Kippur, crippled by Kissinger's pressure, increased the thirty-year old drama instead of solving it. Gradually a mood of being under siege took hold of the Israelis, taxes became increasingly heavy, internal conflicts and strikes frequent. The Zionist ideal seriously wavered. We are confronted with the flood, but know that it is impossible to shrug our shoulders and say just that: After us the Flood. We in Israel, are the generation of the Flood...

In order to survive Israel should direct the lion's share of its national budget to education, social affairs, health care, housing. But there is no choice, most of the money goes to defense, to the arms industry, and the budgets of the other departments must be drastically cut...

More and more Israeli experts begin to say: the country is running towards its ruin. The enemies of Israel know it, so why should they make peace with us? Don't they hold all the trump cards in the United Nations, in the Security Council and in every international assembly? Don't they have a hold on the countries of the west and elsewhere with their simple blackmail: No more oil if you won't help us liquidate Zionism!?

But there is a factor of which the world is not aware, for it does not recognize its existence. Since 1933, since the beginning of much of the nazi cancer, the so-called Christian world has abandoned the Jewish people to its trials, to its camps, to its gas chambers. It is true, many Christians, even in Germany, risked their life to save the honor of the Jew Jesus, but on an individual level alone. On the official, hierarchic, political and humanitarian levels the Christian world remained silent, in so far it did not sign a treaty with Hitler...

In the promised land Israel is even more abandoned, and London sends its ships of war, *after the fall of the nazis*, to "intercept" the survivors of the death camps in their striped garments of the condemned to death, and wearing the yellow badge, the yellow badge of the Council of 1215! Until today the Christian Vatican refuses to salute Israel, to recognize it! Is a greater outrage thinkable? This attitude reaches its ignoble highpoint during the Yom Kippur War: none of the dignitaries of the Churches on the spot, in Jerusalem, raises his voice, and only very few outside Israel.

We must be just and say: the churches of Holland and Scandinavia and the reformed churches of the Swiss cantons Berne and Zurich did protest. But in the city of Calvin, the Consistory not only remained silent, but it refused, without discussion, to extend its sympathy to... the Jewish community of Geneva!

And since then, in unison with the nations and the Arab League, the vaticans of Rome and Geneva have regularly directed their hypocritical moral sermons at Israel, judged and censored it...

In spiritual, biblical perspective, the attitude of some of these institutions arouse the ire and indignation of God and Christ, who, let us not forget it, will judge them all *in Jerusalem*. The drama of Yom Kippur was needed to understand why!

Finally, a new and major phenomenon is that this conflict of Yom Kippur has introduced in the world the worst economic crisis of modern times, because of the Arab oil boycott, a boycott orchestrated from behind the scenes by Moscow. If we recall the crisis of 1929, which was a sudden as it was brutal, we know that the nations will yet witness the deterioration of the catastrophe from which no-one will be able to escape, not even the American giant!

Isn't it incomprehensible and utterly insane that such a crisis should expand throughout the world because of a local conflict? Isn't this hatred of the nations for the Jewish people, even for the generation of Auschwitz, utterly insane? Because this little nation refuses to come down upon its knees before those who were unable to carry out their murderous designs, the entire world, from Tokyo to Los Angeles, from Helsinki to Cape Town, should shake on its foundations?

How can we not distinguish behind this enigma the spiritual meaning of this drama which has placed Israel opposite three quarters of the world?!

General Elazar, whom we have already quoted, called this war, in the middle of the battles, "the great War of Judgement." In Israel it is the curious privilege of the people that even generals can, unknowingly, prophesy...

The apocalyptical biblical literature, of both the Hebrew Bible and the New Testament, predict a moment in history when the nations will break down under God's judgement. Not only because the sum total of their crimes and wars has reached its paroxysm — 'pleroma,' the greek text says — but because it is the period in which *their hate of Israel in the*

Land of Israel has reached its zenith. That is why the royal Messiah, the Prince of the Universe, judges the nations *in Jerusalem,* in His capacity of King of Israel!

We know that this will provoke the derisive laughter of some people. But this has been the case since the day God chose this people, forever, to be the geo-political pivot of the messianic Kingdom *on earth.* We are writing these lines on the day after the U.N. condemned Zionism. Let no nation doubt for one moment that by its vote it has sealed its own destiny in the scales of Divine justice...

Some of the prophetical texts become glaringly clear if we read them in the context of our modern world. From among these we choose the one which is probably the most dramatic and instructive for the understanding of our epoch: chapter 34 of the book of Isaiah.

But who among the powerful and the "wise" reads Isaiah? They only read their own specialized reports, their scientific literature and, in addition and for their recreation, as they say, works of science fiction, crime stories or simply the horoscope in their morning paper. They read everything, they know everything, these poor men, everything except Isaiah!

Here are the principal passages from this chapter:

> Approach, you nations, to listen! let the earth listen and everything in it, the world and all that it yields... for the anger of YHVH is turned against all the nations and his wrath against all the hosts of them!
>
> (1 and 2)

> For the sword of the Lord appears in heaven. See how it descends in judgement on Edom... (5)

> For the Lord has a day of vengeance, a year to requite for the controversy of Zion (8)

> Edom's torrents shall be turned into pitch and its soil into brimstone, and the land shall become lazing pitch which night and day shall never be quenched and its smoke shall go up for ever, from generation to generation...
>
> (9 and 10)

Three truths, three Divine judgments are pronounced here. They do not only relate to our time as well, but can be understood properly only in our time!

First: God's anger and wrath explode at the nations and peoples at a certain, very exact moment in history. The whole universe is taken as a witness, thus lending to this drama of cosmic dimension. The bellicose policy of the nations and their foolish and satanic arms races clearly provoke the Divine ire. But there is yet another, more precise and, let us say it, more frightening motivation.

Secondly, and this is God's deepest motivation as the Lord of history, history has reached a crisis which the Bible calls "the controversy of Zion."

True, the conflict between Israel and the nations has existed since the first appearance of the Jewish people on the middle eastern scene, but it was not until the last decades of the 20th century that this conflict expanded throughout the world, even involving the Chinese and the Russians and their allies on four continents! So that the General Assembly of the United Nations and its Council, which is euphemistically called "Security Council," may officially outlaw the State of Israel and Zionism.

Isaiah tells us in this chapter that there is *a Zionism of God* linked to the salvation of the world.

Thirdly, a conflict breaks out in the land of Edom whose pitch will burn from generation to generation. Let us not blame Isaiah that he did not use the word oil! But let us read this unique prophecy, uttered 26 centuries ago, with respect, for it predicts what many specialists, politicians and strategists foresee in the near future: war in the Persian Gulf and the collapse of the trade in oil.

The visionary of the book of Revelations supplies more precise information about this conflict. In the two chapters devoted to "the fall of Babylon" (17 and 18) he introduces the two categories of people who will be hit hardest: the great businessmen and the ship owners! Which modern industry can operate without the energy derived from oil? Which giant ships are today crossing the oceans and the seas if not the oil tankers?

Is all this sufficiently clear?

For a few decades Lebanon was the middle-eastern center of several branches of world trade: Arab oil banks, casinos, white slavery and drugs traffic. What does it tell us about a country, what does it tell us about the city of Beirut, when they are presented as the bastions of christian civilization...?

And what about the right-wing extremists of the Phalange mowing down their neighbors in defense of a well-fed bourgeoisie living in the midst of a poor people, in the midst of hundreds of thousands of refugees who are deliberately left to their misery and their hate?

It is from Beirut that in since years the most perfidy attacks have been launched against Israel and Zionism. An the Lebanese Christians were in the first ranks of these perpetrators, because of their pathetique and vain desire to appear to the Muslims as more a royalist than the king, as more filled with hatred towards Israel than the Saudis and the Kadhafis. We see where this has led them.

The Divine judgment, set in motion by the Yom Kippur War, has come down on Beirut in view of the whole world. The others will follow. And the only prayer of all of them in this time of apocalyptic insanity should be that God may cut short that time, cut short the trials and catastrophes, as Jesus himself has promised:

> If that time of tribulations were not cut short, no living thing could survive, but for the sake of God's chosen it will be cut short!

THE HARD WAY
TOWARDS REDEMPTION

Menachem Begin came to power less than 4 years after the shock of the Yom Kippur War, and after 30 years spent in fierce opposition, except for the brief euphoric period that followed the fantastic victory of June 1967.

For the Israeli socialist politicians, this amazing rise to power was a complete surprise. Begin's support came mostly from the underprivileged strata of the population, the vast majority of whom were Sephardim who were encouraged to "raise their standard of living". The new government did little to conceal its intentions to unsettle, as much as possible, the socialist structures that that nation had known since 1948.

Sadat's arrival in Israel came like a thunderbolt, followed by the dramatic and difficult meetings which culminated in the Camp David Accord. What a remarkable achievement for the former leader of the Irgun, who suddenly found himself in front of the world television screens, flanked by Sadat on one side and the President of the USA on the other!

It was not known at the time (indeed, to this day a large section of the Israeli population still does not know) that in September 1977, two months before the "fairy-tale visit" of the Egyptian leader, Moshe Dayan had been sent to Morocco where, in the King's presence, he met one of Sadat's right-hand men. And there and then the whole of Sinai peninsula was offered to Egypt. Without the agreement of either the government or of parliament! So that when Sadat arrived in Israel, he already knew that he had won the Sinai!

The Begin government went still further: unhappy Israeli soldiers were sent to destroy the little town of Yamit, and a horrified nation sat watching a Jewish struggle between the army and ardent settlers on their television screens at home. Yamit, a magnificent town wrested out of the harsh desert of the Sinai, was just below the border between Israel and the area which was to be given to Egypt in settlement of the negotiation. Could Sadat not have been generous enough to allow Israel to retain just that little portion of desert sand with its town of Yamit? But the Egyptian answer was, "No". Yamit had to be destroyed. It was traumatic for the Israelis. There is little doubt that this drama had the same deadly effect on the morale of the Israeli population as that other drama of October 1973. For thus was born the Gush Emunim settlement movement in Israel's administered territories.

Never in the history of international negotiations and peace treaties had such a crushing price been paid by the one who — after all — was the victor! And this in exchange for nothing more than a simple promise to refrain from another war. It would not be hard to imagine the angry reactions of Begin and his colleagues, had a socialist government returned the Sinai and destroyed Yamit, pulling up and bulldozing entire orchards that had been reclaimed from the desert.

No effort was made to sign a peace agreement based on a just compromise, which could have kept the magnificent road from Eilat to Sharm-El-Sheikh for Israel. As these pages are being written, the Egyptian government is putting pressure on Jerusalem over the tiny enclave of Taba, a suburb of Eilat, which will doubtless finally be given back under that other, "friendly pressure" from Washington. Truly a strange and fragile peace, indeed.

In the face of such surrenders by the Begin government, it is easy to understand how Egyptian ministers, following on from Sadat, can use terms as surprising as the one now being heard in connection with the enclave of Taba: "The sacred earth of the Arab and Moslem Sinai!" But one knows that the Sinai peninsula was never part of Egypt (except by permission of the British occupants); and as for the "sacred" element, it was neither to a pharaoh nor to Mohammed that God gave his holy Torah, but to all the people of Israel through the hands of Moses. It was on this peninsula that the Jewish nation of the Bible was formed through a period of 40 years, and not some Arab nation. This new and surprising idea of the holiness of the Sinai for Islam, took root in Sadat's terminology under the sole impulse of Begin's government, abandoning this "sacred" land of Israel.

A fragile peace, as we said. Yet there is also a prophetical dimension to it. The great prophecies of Ezekiel refering to the plotting of Gog and his allies, make no mention of *Mizraim* — Egypt — amongst these allies, even though Gadaffi's Libya and ancient Persia — of the present-day Ayatollahs — both have a place there.

This new evidence that today's events are unwinding in accordance with the biblical messianic scenario, stigmatizes all the more the scandalous surrender of the Sinai. The end of Begin's life, cloistered in his Jerusalem apartment, forgotten as much by the world as by his own nation, takes on the appearance of a Greek tragedy. And likewise with Sadat's assassination at the hands of his own people, while celebrating the 8th anniversary of what he called his "victory" over Israel: ...providence with merciful to him but seven times only...

The Israeli intervention in Lebanon in June 1982 marks yet another period of tragedy. Whereas it had been agreed that the army would not go further than the northern 40 km limit in protecting the bombarded areas of Upper Galilee, General Sharon took it upon himself to present his government and nation with a brutal *fait accompli* and for the first time in Israeli history the civilian population of Beirut was bombed. It was to the credit of many officers and Israeli soldiers that they said 'no' to this!

Even if it is true that Israel liquidated the terrorist centres of Arafat and his companions, their recovery when the Israeli army began to withdraw from Lebanon was better than ever before. Not only did they reappear but the Lebanon war led to the birth of a new Shi'ite Lebanese terrorism.

As for the massacres in the camps of Sabra and Shatilla, the world information networks were only too happy to be able, once again, to accuse the Jewish conscience, even when only the Phalangist Christians were guilty. It is to Israel's credit that a commission of enquiry was called amid strong public pressure.

The present so-called National Unity Government would more appropriately be called a government of "national paralysis": for every twelve votes in favor, there are twelve against on most major issues.

Crushed under these burdens, prey to deadly inflation, and dependent more and more upon American "generosity", what fate is the nation of Israel now drifting towards?

A biblical prophecy, much ignored until the present, now comes into its own for the attentive reader, sensitive to the maturing apocalyptic significance of the end of this century. In the last chapter of the book of Daniel, verse 7 shows Israel's situation, standing on the threshold of the Parousia. The visionary asks the heavenly messenger for an irrefutable sign, to which he replies:

When the power of the holy people (Israel) has been finally broken...

It is undeniable that since the terrible shock of Kippur 1973, the Israeli nation has been living this ultimate crisis, in company moreover, with the rest of the world. And such, paradoxically, is the source of hope and secret joy: the worse the situation becomes, the closer her salvation draws...

II

THE SPIRITUAL CRISIS IN ISRAEL

Paradoxicaly, it is the rebirth of Jewish independence in the Holy Land, which has caused a grave spiritual crisis within Judaism.

During twenty centuries of dispersion the Jewish people had the choice between two alternatives: assimilation or stubborn adherence to its traditional positions (which was stimulated by life in the ghetto). The existence of a state with a Jewish majority eliminates to a certain extent the assimilatory tendencies, since being a Jew is the normal situation, while life in the ghetto has become futile, not to say ridiculous. For every human community it is a difficult test to abruptly pass from a state of permanent persecution to sovereignty. The Church itself went through this experience at the time of Constantine, when it suddenly found itself, after life in the catacombs, on the side of the Emperor!

Notwithstanding Ben-Gurion's repeated statements the State of Israel is in no way the direct successor of the Maccabean kingdom. It is impossible to simply ignore the developments, crises and sufferings of so many centuries. Even if it were true that the Jewish patriots who contributed so much to the creation of the new state are in the line of the glorious Maccabean family, it is certainly not true of the totality of its citizens who came from so different backgrounds and were not prepared for such an abrupt metamorphosis. The "dry bones" are certainly not being revived without a crisis... It is therefore imperative to examine the various aspects of this spiritual crisis, of which the following are the outstanding characteristics.

First of all, this Jewish crisis is part of a world-wide religious crisis and it must be viewed in this context.

Secondly, the unity of the Synagogue is merely a surface-unity behind which several rather conflicting trends are hidden.

Moreover, the orthodox rabbinate, which prevails in the State of Israel, confronts the nation with extremely grave problems and places it — and in particular the younger generation — in a conflict situation. Let us make this aspect of the crisis clear in the following manner: for the first time in modern history the rabbinate has been forced to face, in the promised land itself, the challenge of an epoch dominated by technology. How can the thirty-centuries-old commandments be reconciled with the development of a modern state which, moreover, aspires to be among the leading scientific conquerors of the world?

Finally — and this is doubtless the most dramatic aspect of this spiritual crisis — to the extent that the State of Israel represents the fulfillment of the Zionist dream — what is the role of the religious ideal in this achievement? Will not independence and recovered human dignity suppress in the soul of the nation the pursuit of another independence which must still be conquered — that of the spirit? Doesn't the tremendous danger exist that the prophetical writings will be "nationalized?" In the tense relationship of secular socialism and the ideal of the Prophets which of the two will prevail?

The next question that must be asked in order to broaden the discussion and continue (and conclude) our research is: has this spiritual crisis in Israel made its appearance with the rise of the State of Israel, or rather much earlier, namely with the dramatic events that led to the destruction of the Temple of Jerusalem?

If this is the case, and if, moreover, the religious crisis in Israel must be placed in an "ecumenical" context, will it be possible for this crisis to be solved without a reform or revolution on a global scale affecting all believers?

In other words, is not the resurrection of the Jewish state and the concomitant spiritual crisis of eminently prophetical significance for the entire world and thus for the Christian world?

This is what we shall try to discover.

World War I marked the beginning of a major spiritual crisis, in particular in the western world, a crisis which was amplified to world-wide proportions in the wake of World War II and its horrible after effects.

What an enormous stumbling block for the African and Asian world that Christianity not only failed to prevent such slaughter, but even greatly contributed to it! The deplorable failure of the League of Nations, which boasted to represent a biblical ideal, and the support of so many statesmen and industrialists (not to mention the Vatican) for gangster regimes such as those in Italy, Germany and Spain greatly assisted in plunging the young generations into a mood of cynicism and desperation.

The Africans and Asians who served in the colonial troops discovered to their stupefaction that the whites — i.e. the Christians — did not shun from internecine, ferocious and organized massacres. In Japan the people can't forget the atom bomb, the Christian bomb...

The Jewish people, doubtless the greatest victim of World War II, having lost one third of its members (mainly from observant communities, as in Poland), has not overcome its trauma and cries to heaven: "O God, if Thou existest, why hast Thou allowed this?"

Before Hitler it was possible to be an idealist or a humanist, to have faith in man. But after Hitler, after Auschwitz?

Before Hiroshima the scientists and scholars were genuinely optimistic, having taken over, in a way, the banner of a Christian world in full flight, and declared: the peace and justice which the religions have not been able to install upon earth, will be inaugurated by us, through our discoveries. We shall render war ludicrous and defeat misery and disease...

Since the death of Einstein every honest scientist rings the alarm, knowing that he is caught in the inexorable machine of science-without-conscience delivered into the hands of men of war and politicians.

How many of the younger generations of this century will be able to escape cynicism and desperation, caught as they are between two nuclear bombs? How will they be able to rediscover some ideal? Through the prospect of the conquest of the Universe? But don't we know that man will recommence his bloody history on other planets bringing with him his hatred, his weapons and his seeds of death?

Has the western, Christian world still a chance of regaining the trust and hope of the world? Will the world of Faith be able to offer a satisfactory answer now that the scientists have admitted, for the first time in history, that they too are in a terrible impasse? It is no longer the time for half-hearted measures and beautiful slogans, nor for calls for peace and justice. It is a time for radical and heroic positions.

It is time for the Christian world to take at last the words of Christ seriously.

We know that it is senseless to ask questions about the past and speculate what would have happened if... But such naive questions can nevertheless help us put our finger on the source of the disease which in our century may certainly be called "Legion" — it is called Treblinka and Guernica, Hiroshima and Nagasaki, Vietnam, Biafra and Sudan.

If in 1914 all the Christian leaders in all the involved countries had forestalled the Socialist International and had said "No" to the planned slaughter — what would then have happened? The armed conflict would certainly not have taken place, and, consequently, the Nazis would not have been able to install themselves in a Germany disintegrated by the first World War.

We are well aware that many will evoke in this context Christ's famous saying: "Pay Caesar what is due to Caesar."

But this text has been misunderstood for many centuries. The first Christians understood Christ better. It was, once again, the upheaval during Constantine's reign which confused everything.

So long as the Christian world does not understand that Christ proclaimed in this simple formula, *that everything belongs to God*, it will not be able to offer mankind a solution for its problems and its conflicts. All things belong to God and nothing belongs to Caesar, least of all silver and gold! Everything Caesar possesses, has been *borrowed*, and whenever he wants to exploit his powers for wicked purposes, it is the duty of the believers to call him to order in the name of Christ, and to oppose him.

Because the Christian world has regularly assumed the role of courtier of the Caesars, instead of that of their judges (as the prophets of Israel did towards their own rulers) it has failed and been irreparably compromised in the eyes of the non-Christian world, whose masses have become increasingly numerous. It is because of this failure that a substitute religion, a substitute messianism arose in Russia in 1917 which subsequently spread throughout the greatest part of the world. It is because of this failure that

169

men have built gas chambers and crematoria in which they burnt children.

Without any doubt it is now too late. Without any doubt we have entered the era of which Christ said that "if it were not cut short (by the Parousia) *even the chosen would perish.*" Without any doubt we are living in a time in which the Church should wear sack and ashes...

In this context of a world-wide spiritual crisis the jewish, Israeli crisis must be seen.

Convinced that henceforward it can rely upon itself alone and certainly not on the "Christian" world, the People of Israel can only harden its positions, forgetting that it should place its faith not in its own forces, but in the Holy Spirit. Not recovered from the trauma of its recent martyrdom, it has lost this faith and trust and increasingly engages in a dangerous "realpolitik" (such as was castigated by the prophets).

It is certainly not the Israeli Ministry of Religious Affairs nor the religious parties which will emerge from the bosom of the nation to take upon themselves the prophetical ministry... That is the tragedy.

We believe that Israel, after having witnessed the realization of part of its Zionist dream (since 1948) has entered the period announced by the prophets: the time of hunger and thirst for God. But nobody arises and there are no longer prophets... Instead there is the agitation of the religious parties which are caricatures of the religious ideal, increasingly loathsome to the younger generation. Instead of a cry and an appeal to return to the Lord, ritual prayers are said on the occasion of some or other religious or national holiday.

But happy, happy are they who still feel hunger and thirst for the word of the living God!

Arthur Koestler, in his analysis of the nation engaged in building itself in the Land of Israel in spite of great difficulties, speaks of a "microcosmos of humanity" in this small strip of land on the Mediterranean shores — a most appropriate expression.

To gather people - from every human and sociological background, people who speak more than 50 different languages, does not easily further national unity, but rather recalls the adventure of the people of the Tower of Babel...

What can a lawyer from Berlin have in common with a petty craftsman from Iraq? Or a physician from Budapest with a merchant from Kabylie? Nothing but their mysterious belonging to this equally mysterious people named Israel.

If we deliberately oppose here the Jews from the West to those from the oriental countries, it is because their cultures and *weltanschauung* are so different. This is an extreme case, but there are hundreds and thousands of other examples.

The first pioneers came to revive a desert, from Dan to Beersheba, to use the biblical expression. Although they had no deep religious faith, they were nevertheless motivated by a great and pure ideal enabling them to overcome the terrible conditions which greeted them when they landed in Jaffa. Today, for an encounter with the desert one has to leave Beersheba behind; everywhere else there is vibrating life, and the sprawling town of Tel Aviv attracts the majority of new-comers who are no longer tempted by the desert.

Everybody has already forgotten the difficulties and disappointments of those who made the country, in the literal sense of the word, in a time when there was no Jewish Agency to pay for their passage and — partly — for their absorption, a time when the government did not install new immigrants in new houses. Nowadays, everybody complains that this Jewish Agency does not do enough...

The human being is not fit to live with his fellow-men. In every country rivalries set colleague against colleague, neighbor against neighbor, even though they speak the same language. In Israel this tendency is aggravated by the fact that one's neighbor is nearly always a "stranger." He does not speak your language, he often looks "oriental" and his manners are repulsive.

As the country is ridiculously small everybody seems to know everybody, and people soon begin to feel that they are living "in each other's backyard." How can one speak of unity in such a situation? Is there one other nation in the world for whom it is more difficult to realize its national unity? What other legacy have the children of Israel of our days in common *except the Bible* and — often — their martyrdom?

We believe that the constant danger on the borders is one of the most striking elements of what a believing person would call "the Divine pedagogy." If the Bible is not enough, the Arab League is always present at the borders to remind the Israeli people that in spite of everything it must close its ranks.

This constant danger also greatly restrains the mutual struggle of the many political parties. Nobody can tell how fierce this struggle will be in a time of peace...

There is a popular ironical saying to the effect that the Jewish people had for twenty centuries no opportunity to engage in political brawls and is now making up for the lost time! They are certainly doing their best...

Speaking of political brawls, it is time to deal with the most negative element of the religious crisis in Israel: the existence of religious political parties.

Thus far nobody has been able to give a satisfactory definition of the term "Israeli". And it would, without doubt, be rather rash to attempt to define the character of the State of Israel in political terms. Is it a democracy of the classical or rather of the socialist type? Is it a phenomenon closely resembling a theocracy? Is it a little of all this? Without any doubt. But the theocratic element is the most baffling, and perhaps the most conspicuous, at least for one who lives in Israel...

However this may be, Israel is also a human community linked to a monotheistic religion which has generated other religions. To be a Jew certainly means in the first place to attend synagogue services regularly. How much more so, if one is a Jew in the holy land!

To be a Jew also means to observe the commandments and rituals of both the biblical *and* rabbinical tradition. How much more so in Israel!

On the other hand, Israel wants to be a state of the twentieth century, and in the merciless economic competition of our epoch it has to be this, in order to survive. It is evident, however, that large parts of the biblical tradition — we recall the Laws of Leviticus — as well as the entire rabbinical tradition are rooted in a sociological context which is in radical contradiction to that of our time. Israel has no other choice: either it will be a levitical state, and will consequently live on the margins of the time (this may be respectable, but will it be liveable?) or it must break with this levitical and rabbinical law. To eat the pudding and keep it, as is now constantly being tried, does not satisfy anybody, least of all the defenders of the religious tradition.

A few examples.

There is still no religious freedom *for Jews* in Israel. In fact, the supreme rabbinical Court (which would like to be regarded as a revived Sanhedrin), only recognizes rabbis belonging to the orthodox, strictly observant synagogue. The Conservative and Reform synagogues are merely beginning to gain a timid foothold in Israel, but their live is made very difficult.

What is called the unity of the synagogue, is nothing but a myth, recalling that other myth, of the unity of the Church.

The dietary laws are highly respectable as such, even though today's hygienic conditions (not to mention refrigerators and modern packaging) greatly differ from those of Antiquity and the Middle Ages. But they are all applied in Israel, many have access only to *kosher* products, which often increases prices, in particular of meat.

There is no civil marriage in Israel. This makes it necessary for a non-observant, or even atheist Israeli, to apply to the rabbinate in order to have his union legalized. Partly because of this situation, the Parliament has thus far been unable to draw up a Constitution. How can such a state of affairs be reconciled with the demands of modern times?

From the rabbinical viewpoint, women play a highly subordinate part. They are required to be good housewives, good mothers. During the first years of Israeli statehood the bloc of religious parties launched a campaign against women's suffrage.

And nevertheless one of Israel's Prime Ministers was a woman and the role of women in public life and in the army is well known (Orthodox girls can receive dispensation from army service).

The strict observance of Sabbath rest causes insoluble problems when tradition makes its demands beyond the sphere of individual life and interferes in public services. The religious bloc holds that nobody should work in these services, including water and electricity supply, during the Sabbath, but it nonetheless uses water and electricity, thus exploiting the work of non-observant Jews and thereby violating its own religious precepts.

Public transport totally ceases on Sabbath, except in Haifa. As a result, only car owners can enjoy a little fresh air on the beach or in the woods. In Jerusalem brawls between "Sabbath violators" and observant "stone throwers" are a regular occurrence!

Again we ask: How can the religious elements not understand that imposing religious precepts on the population cannot but alienate this population from religion itself? The overwhelming majority of the younger generation has become extremely critical not only of this religious tradition, but of Faith itself, thereby throwing away the baby with the bath water.

Finally, we must ask whether a *religious* party is at all conceivable, either in Israel or anywhere else in the world. Being a political party, it will always be committed to a certain policy, to a coalition, to economic interests which are just as evident as they are particularistic; it will therefore soon be doomed to become in the eyes of the people and of God a *caricature* of a religious community. A religious party is the very contradiction of prophetical behavior in the political sphere, of that political activity of which the prophets were the driving force, frequently in fierce opposition to the parties. Isn't a religious party a community of believers who have sold their freedom, if not their soul, to Caesar?

This is what the confused young generation of Israel resents. This generation is healthy enough, close enough to the biblical sources to realize that the existence of religious parties is in fact a betrayal of the prophetical message, and that these parties, rather than making themselves the champions of truth and justice in the biblical sense, must reckon in the first place with the realities of the ballot and with their own prestige.

What the young generation and the majority of the Israeli population deeply resents is that tradition has become the contradiction of religion. This, at least, is one of the major problems of the phenomenon called "the State of Israel."

Not by forcefully imposing — by parliamentary votes — on an entire people the observance of commandments which are only vaguely related to the biblical text itself, can this people be brought back to the faith of their fathers. On the contrary, they will be alienated and even become disgusted...

What the Lord has always demanded from Israel is not the observance of a ritual which does not come from the heart, but living faith, in joy and hope.

By saying this haven't we put the finger on the ancient controversy between the Sadducees and most of the Pharisees on the one hand, and the prophets and the little people on the other...?

Isn't it a noteworthy fact that the two great religious crises which the Jewish people has experienced were both connected with revolutions in the political sphere? The first of them occurred towards the end of Jewish independence with the fall of Jerusalem under the assault of the Roman general Titus, and the second in the mid-twentieth century with the restoration of this independence.

It is true that when the Temple was about to be definitely destroyed the Jewish religion was alive in the many synagogues in both the promised land and the centers of the Diaspora. But this religion derived its inspiration from Jerusalem, from the Temple. The daily sacrifices and the yearly pilgrimages were the heart of this Jewish faith. It was in Jerusalem that God dwelt (even though He was present wherever His name was invoked); it was from Jerusalem that the Word of God and the commandments of life went out. It was from Jerusalem that Salvation came. It was from Jerusalem that the Redeemer was to come. And finally, it was Jerusalem to which all the nations of the world were to go up in the time that the will of the God of Israel would be honored and fulfilled "on earth as in Heaven." The prophets had proclaimed it with great force: this Jerusalem was not only to be the heart of the Jewish nation and the source of its Faith, it was destined that from here the Messiah will reign in justice and peace over the entire world.

Thus when the messianic city fell and the Temple collapsed in the Roman flames, the messianic hope and faith collapsed with them.

Isn't it therefore equally surprising that at this very moment of history a community of God (not Israel, but springing forth from Israel) arose in the world to announce to the nations the Word of God contained in the Hebrew Bible and condensed in this new book with the prophetical title (announced by Jeremiah) *Berith hahadash,* the new covenant, the New Testament?

From the hands of the dying Temple the young Church took the torch of "light unto the nations" and embarked with unprecedented enthusiasm on the conquest of the entire Meditteranean region. Let us merely recall the accomplishment of one man, one servant of this new covenant with the Gentiles: Rabbi Saul of Tarsus!

As in the parable of "the wicked husbandmen" the vineyard was taken away from the unworthy hands of the Temple chiefs and entrusted to other hands.

But what became of Judaism? Did it die? Did it become lethargic? Or, to use the terminology of the Church fathers, of St. Augustin in particular, was it reduced to the secondary and rather contemptible task of being "book carriers"? Had it lost its mission in the world for always?

Before answering these formidable questions let us simply say that Judaism went through a crisis that was unique in its history and much more serious than that of the brief period before the short Babylonian Captivity which the prophet Hosea had announced in these words:

> For the Children of Israel shall live many a long day without king or prince, without sacrifice.
>
> (3:4)

Even during the Babylonian Captivity Israel had centered around its Royal dynasty, around its priests, and it returned with its princes and Levites at the end of this brief Exile.

But now the Jewish People was to live almost twenty centuries without a King, without princes and without a Temple...

The revival of the Jewish State in Israel has not brought the solution of this two-fold — political and priestly — mutilation. Nobody in contemporary Israel can claim the throne of David. And how would it be possible to rebuild the Temple on the site of the Dome of the Rock?

True, the vast talmudic tradition has taken the place of the daily Temple worship. True, the State of Israel has its President and its ministers. It is equally true that in modern Hebrew the words used for president and minister are the same as those for "prince" in biblical Hebrew. But can all this satisfy the profound nostalgic yearnings of the burning Jewish soul? Can it content itself with such surrogate solutions? Can the numerous talmudic institutions ever make it forget the spendor of the Temple? Or can the Labor Party and its ministers wipe out the remembrance of the greatness of David's House? Obviously not.

Thus we see that the year 70 of our era marked the beginning of a spiritual crisis in Judaism which has not been solved by the restoration of Israeli independence. Since that most fateful date Israel has been passing through a transitory period which may be characterized as a period of spiritual Exile. Isn't this precisely what the prophet Ezekiel predicted in his "Zionist Charter," in his vision of the resurrection of the Jewish skeletons "in those days"? Certainly, these skeletons have survived, put on their new members, they walk, speak, build. But "the Spirit is not in them."

What does this mean?

Must we regard this as a grave judgment of the Zionist venture of this century? Must we join the Christian theologians and proclaim, like the good Anglican bishop of Jerusalem to the United Nations Commission of Enquiry: "God counts here for nothing!"

However, it is at God's command that these skeletons have revived. God has time, He does not put the carriage before the horses. To begin with, He uses the Knesset which is far from an assembly of prophets! But this assembly, together with others, was ordered to rebuild the desolate land. And this is has done with admirable zeal. One does not have to be a prophet to revive a desert, one does not have to be a prophet to build Tel Aviv. but one can be placed in the prophetical stream without knowing it, and this is what is called the sovereignty of God.

When the desert will be revived, the cities that for so long have been sand-covered ruins will be rebuilt and the ancient language of the prophets be spoken again, then the nation and the parties will reach the "crest of the wave" and may make way for prophets. When the Zionist dream will be firmly rooted in the soil of this holy land (that is a land set apart, not a land of little saints...) then the politicians and party officials, together with the entire nation, will realize that the corner stone of their beautiful building is

175

missing, and that man shall not live by bread alone.

Then the second stage of this resurrection, foreseen by the prophet Hosea long before Ezekiel, begins:

> But after that they *will return* and seek the Lord their God and David their King and turn anxiously to the Lord for his bounty *in days to come.*

(3 : 5)

A few remarks:

According to the prophetical point of view the great spiritual crisis of Israel will not be solved in a relatively near future, nor will it be solved by measures of "this world," by they of an economic, political or "religious" nature.

The Jewish people *will return* "in days to come,' that is at the hour known to God alone which marks "the end of the time of the Nations."

It will not come about through a simple revolution caused by some or other coalition government, or by some or other prince heading the re-assembled nation in the promised land, but by the second David — a perfect David, the Messiah Himself.

Nor will it be some religious reform that Israel will experience "in the days to come", not even a restoration of the priesthood of a new Temple, but the presence of the Lord Himself...

Thus we see that this great Zionist venture, even in the depth of the great crisis through which it passes, heralds the new time. No less certain than in Ezekiel's vision, does the resurrection of the skeleton announce and *entail* the resurrection of the spirit and the heart.

Let us now, in order to see all this clearer, turn to certain aspects of Israeli reality which we do not hesitate to call prophetical, since they herald the new time for which Israel is preparing itself before any other nation, because it remains the nation set "apart."

As the laboratory of that time the State of Israel is characterized by "experiences" which are unique in this century and which, notwithstanding their imperfections, open a path to all nations, a path leading to the messianic kingdom.

Once again the Jewish people, gathered in the Holy Land, represents for all of mankind a condensed picture of history, of civilization, of humanity. Even though the nations are blind, the diplomats conceited and the politicians the toys of their own game, let the believing world at least recognize in this unique land among this for ever chosen people, the signs of a coming mankind finally reconciled with itself and with its Creator.

Let us say it once again: what we have called Zionist theology is in fact nothing but a theology of history which appeals to all men of every race, language and confession. From Jerusalem God appeals incessantly to all men, not to the people of Israel alone. From Jerusalem the Lord of History has always called upon the princes of this world, rendering this city into the potter's wheel of his salutary policy for the world, not for Israel alone.

It is in Jerusalem that He, who was truly the light of the nations, appeared, spoke, gave His life and arose to eternal life, first-born among all beings.

And it is in Jerusalem that God has laid the foundations of a new world in which justice is not a farce, peace not an infernal arms race and brotherhood not a caricature.

Let us, like unusual archaeologists, discover in the physically revived soil of Israel the prophetical and messianic foundations; let us clear the thick layers of debris and millenia-old clay, which belong to this aeon, to mankind erring in darkness, and seek for a glimpse of the dwellings of God.

III

PROPHETICAL ASPECTS OF THE
STATE OF ISRAEL

*Today we witness the marvellous phenomenon of the ingathering
of the tribes of Israel, bone by bone, member by member, into one
single nation... I pray that the Redeemer of Israel bless us and
that in our days Judah be saved and Israel dwell in peace.*

Yitzhak Ben-Zvi, second President of Israel
Inaugural address, 1952

*In our days, now that we are restoring our independence, our first
goal is to build the country, its economy, security and
internatonal position. But that is not our final goal. The final goal
is a State which fulfills the prophecy, heralds salvation and is a
guide and example for all men.*

David Ben-Gurion, *Rebirth and Destiny of Israel*,
p. 437

On the soil of its recovered promised land the young Jewish nation has
addressed itself to a number of experiments which are amazing and
revolutionary to sociologists, linguists and agronomists alike. Experiments
of which we have said that they are laboratory tests for a new society, for a
new mankind. What is merely an interesting experiment to the objective
scientists, the amazed technologists or the sceptical sociologists, should
assume entirely different dimensions for the believers and theologians. For
the touchstone of these experiments in the Holy Land remains, far beyond
scientific standards or philosophical premises, the old Hebrew Bible and, in
particular, the prophetical message.

On example: to the average tourists the rebirth of the Philistine city of
Ashkelon is not more interesting than the reconstruction of any other city
of Antiquity. But to the believer who opens his Bible while wandering
among the inhabitants of this new Ashkelon and reads the following verses
from the little book of Zephaniah, interest and surprise make place for
religious awe:

And the coastland of Philistia shall belong to the survivors of Judah...

178

They shall lie down at evening in the houses of Ashkelon, for the Lord
their God will turn to them and restore their fortunes.

(2 : 7)

He is all the more overwhelmed since this ancient city never belonged to
Judah, and the fulfilment of this prophecy from the Scriptures had to wait
for the rise of the State of Israel in our time! It is true that the "Zionists"
who returned from the Babylonian Captivity had applied Zephania's
prophecy to themselves, but Ashkelon remained in the hands of the
Gentiles and the returning Jewish settlers did not lie down at evening
within its walls. This prophecy was not fulfilled until 1948. This is a fact
which cannot be undone by consigning the Hebrew Bible and the message
of the prophets to the bulk of writings from Antiquity, by stiffling the
breath of the Holy Spirit in these pages (as has been done by the
theologians throughout the centuries until our day...).

Let nobody misunderstand us. We do not say that the Jews of our
century who have come from the four corners of the earth, and often from
the nazi camps, and who are now living in the attractive dwellings of
ancient Ashkelon, constitute the Israel of God and are singing the Lord's
praise from morning to night. What we are saying, again referring to the
"Zionist Charter" of Ezekiel 37, is that God begins at the beginning. He
gathers His Jewish children in from their millenia-long exile, places them in
their new dwellings and makes them and their children read the prophecy
of Zephaniah. And He waits for the outcome. But whatever will happen,
Israel is involved in what we have called "the mechanism of salvation," on
the road to its massive return to its God, and this can only be a messianic
road.

"If you keep silence, the stones will shout aloud," Jesus said. Wherever
the biblical ruins revive under the hands of the zionist pioneers and
builders, the stones shout out at them. One may regret that these pioneers
do not hear it, but it is distressing that the Church, too, remains deaf and
blind in Israel, to Israel.

Let us therefore now consider the following aspects of the zionist venture
which we have called prophetical: the ingathering of the exiles, the
renaissance of the Hebrew language, the communal life, the resurrection of
the arid regions, the biblical revival and the aid to new nations.

All these six "experiments" are integrated parts of the zionist venture.
They arise from the fact that for the first time in twenty centuries a specific
people which the Bible (and St. Paul) call the Chosen People, has recovered
a specific land which that same Bible calls the (for ever) promised land.
These are in the first place Zionist experiments and must be rightly placed
to the credit of the Movement. It is dangerous to regard Zionism as merely
a political movement of "the return of the Jews to Palestine." This would be
like looking at events through a reducing glass during the night. Zionism is
also the movement which gathers men, women and children from the four
corners of the earth, whatever their conditions, in order to make them into

one nation. It is the movement which has given to this ancient nation a new language, the language of the Bible! It is the movement which goes down to the very root of the crucial problem of human relations and proposes to install a communal life based on individual freedom. It is the movement which — a novum in history — has begun the struggle with the deserts of its homeland under extremely precarious security conditions. And finally, it is the movement which has placed the Holy Scriptures in the center of its educative system.

A heavy program for a nation which at its birth numbered only six hundred thousand souls and was, moreover, attacked on all its borders... But a program which may be truly called *messianic* since in every respect it is an attempt at physical and spiritual *resurrection*. An attempt to create a new life, a state "that will not be like the others."

One last remark before we address ourselves to these prophetical experiments: what is the West (which likes to call itself Christian) doing, and what is the world (which likes to call itself free) doing for the realization of the ancient dream of a new mankind? What are they doing to instill the biblical demands of justice and freedom into the conscience of mankind? What are they doing to conquer the desert, to overcome famine, ignorance and fear?

To conquer other planets while our own earth experiences the horrors of an imminent war, of famine and fear — isn't that tragic and ridiculous? And it is certainly not enough to inscribe on the dollar: "In God we trust..."

THE INGATHERING OF THE EXILES

These are the words of the Lord God: O, my people, I will open your graves and bring you up from them, and restore you to the land of Israel.

Prophecy by Ezekiel at God's command,
chapter 37:12

In Chapter IV of the First Part of this book, The Dialectics of Exile and Return in the Prophetical Writings, we quoted the writings of these Jewish visionaries at length. Perhaps it would suffice to simply read these verses again and meditate on them, if possible in the land of Israel on its way to resurrection...

Let us nonetheless recall some of our conclusions. It is evident (though often forgotten) that the announcement of Return was never realized after the return from the Babylonian Captivity. We have seen that only a small part of the Jewish people returned to Jerusalem. We have seen that only a small minority came back from Exile (it was a good life in Babylon...). We have seen that the Jewish people was uprooted from its land for a second time and dispersed throughout the earth notwithstanding the frequently repeated declaration of the Holy Writ: *I shall lead you back for ever.*

Finally, it must be admitted that the return from Babylon did not lead to the beginning of the messianic reign of peace and justice, neither for Israel nor for the Nations. And this is exactly what the final Return must entail.

Although it had happened before that Jews left one specific country of Exile, the modern Zionist venture was the first occurrence of Jews returning to Zion from all countries. Thus this venture for the first time affirmed the words of Isaiah:

> I will bring your children from the *east* and gather you all from the *west*.
> I will say to the north: Give them up! and to the south: Do not hold them back! Bring my sons and daughters from afar, bring them from the ends of the earth.
>
> (43:5, 6)

One must have stood on the quay of Haifa with the book of Isaiah, open on this extraordinary page, in one's hand, and seen them come ashore from the end of the earth and the sea, all these children of Israel, overwhelmed, battered, awed and often in tears.

It is certainly the East which brought them home: they came not only from middle-eastern Mesopotamia, but from China and India. And Israel was so amazed to discover them that it could hardly recognize them as fellow-Jews.[1] But this amazement was also foresaid by Isaiah:

> You will say to yourself: All these children, how did I come by them...?
> *Who reared them...?* I was left alone, exiled, *where did I get them all...?*

It is certainly the West which set them free, not only the Mediterranean countries of the ancient Exile. They return from the two Americas, the offspring of the western world, more tolerant than their aged mother, the "faraway Islands" (far away in relation to Jerusalem) to use a favored expression of the prophets. Nor has the South held them back, in spite of some reserve and hatred. They have come from Ethiopia, from South Africa. They will continue to come from North Africa, from where many have already arrived during the last decades. They escaped illegally from Morocco, from Tunis... And Egypt — the South *par excellence* in the prophetical writings — expelled them after having ruined them...

As to the North — the first heroic pioneers came from the countries of the cold, refugees from the pogroms. But the North is also the Kingdom of Gog and Magog! And it is not a coincidence that at the time of the great messianic Return millions of Jews are held there in relative captivity since

---

1 Since the return of Indian jews to Israel, the rabbis have discussed and questioned the Jewish "purity" of this oriental community, which was deeply hurt by this attitude. We were acquainted with some of these young Indian Jews at the time that this painful, but, as we have seen, "prophetical" discussion began...

the gates of emigration are hermetically closed until the present day.

But this world, too, will eventually have to obey the voice of the Lord of History, the God of Israel, who day after day cries unto it: Give them up! We must doubtless wait for the final struggle and the great judgement of Gog and Magog! And it is not a coincidence that at the time of the great strongest Jewish communities in the world have not responded to the prophetical call: that of the United States, for life is comfortable in Babylon, and that of the Soviet Union, for the gates are firmly closed. However, let us not fail to discern the hand of Providence in both these cases, for the Jewish state is not ready to absorb the enormous influx of Russian Jews, nor to integrate the even greater influx of American Jews. It might easily have perished during the first years of its existence when it had to absorb, *while engaged in war*, the refugees of the nazi camps (and of the English camps!) as well as the masses of deprived, ruined and suffering Jews from the Arab countries...

Much has been said about the return of the Yemenite Jews. Books have been written on the subject, and everybody has doubtless heard of this Exodus which may be compared with that of the Bible. We shall nevertheless recall it, for it remains the most "messianic" element in the movement of massive return to Zion.

The Jews of Yemen were not expelled from their country, even though it was already at war with Israel. They simple rose up, leaving their meagre possessions behind, and crossed a desert, like their fathers, on the way to the new Jerusalem. They were not afraid to board a plane (which they had not even heard of), for the Lord had sent them "His great eagles" in the hour of Redemption! Nothing could surprise them, *for the Messiah had called them...*

Indeed, who but the Messiah could have ended in such a miraculous way their millenia-long Exile? Who but the Messiah could have sent them these great and formidable eagles?

Great was therefore their disappointment when they realized that they had preceded the coming of the Messiah (in order to level his messianic roads and to revive his future gardens). This Yemenite aspect alone of the final Return of the Jews in this century suffices, we believe, to demonstrate the full prophetical meaning of Zionism. In the persons of these Yemenites biblical figures presented themselves at the gates of the promised land, authentic witnesses of the prophetical era, untainted by the influence of the machine, by the progress of cynicism and the cruelty of our age. Their only wealth, their only knowledge was the biblical text which they knew by heart. Their ears had heard the message from the mouth of the prophets themselves, nothing had changed during their life in Exile, and the Word of God had remained the same, yesterday, today and tomorrow.

Thus they alone realized that they had preceded the coming of the Messiah, and perhaps they alone truly learned from this realization...

Neither the cruelty of the centuries, nor the weariness of the long wait, nor the Crusades and the Inquisition, nor the pogroms since Titus and

Nebuchadnezzar before him, have thus been able to erase from the face of the earth, nor from amidst hostile nations, this people which was promised to Abraham, born with Isaac and marked with Jacob.

How remote, fragile and insignificant seems the return from Babylon, in spite of the insistence of so many Christian theologians, compared with this continuous flow from the four corners of the earth!

After Hitler and his gas chambers, after so many "Exoduses", and at a time that Nasser of Egypt was surrounded by nazi advisors — how miraculous is this Return of the new Israel!

THE RENAISSANCE OF THE HEBREW LANGUAGE

Hebrew does not know the concept of matter. The susceptible therefore assumes a significance and plays a role which is unknown to Greek thought... Hebrew has a liking for the susceptible, because it is not dualistic; it has a feeling for, and understanding of the elementary because it does not condemn the susceptible to being irreducibly separated and remote from the intelligible... To have a sense of the carnal, a taste for the elementary, and to have a sense of contemplation, of spiritual values — it is all one from the biblical point of view, because the susceptible world is language, it was created by the Word... Hebrew has a sense of the carnal because it recognizes the spiritual essence in it.

Claude Tresmontant, *Essai sur la pensee hebraique*,
pp. 56–57

In his remarkable vision of the Jewish State in his book *Altneuland* Theodor Herzl already asked the question of which national language should be employed after the realization of his vision. This was one of the few instances in which he erred. Not only did he believe that the Jewish people would continue to speak their many languages, but he even deemed it entirely impossible for the Hebrew language to be revived.

This makes the revival of Hebrew even more remarkable.

It would, however, be false to assume, as some people do, that Hebrew had ceased to be spoken after the destruction of Jerusalem by the Romans. Although the two Talmuds, those vast summaries of rabbinical wisdom, law and theology, confined to writing after this drama, are entirely written in Aramaic, the rabbis and leading spirits of the synagogue never abandoned Hebrew. A rich Hebrew literature, mainly poetical, flourished until the dawn of modern times.

The Jewish people in exile had not ceased to speak the biblical language in order to adopt the languages of this Exile, but had rather adopted two dialects of their own: Yiddish and Ladino.

Hebrew was reborn at the very moment that Russian Jews, faced with pogroms, arose to embark on the long march to Jerusalem, calling themselves *Hovevei Zion* — the Lovers of Zion. At that moment Hebrew was reborn as a national language without the Jewish people themselves being aware of it.

What Herzl was for the Jewish State, Eliezer Ben-Yehuda (1858–1922) became for the renaissance of the Hebrew language.

The spark needed by this visionary, who went to the promised land in 1880, to lighten the torch of Hebrew was the contact with the land of the Hebrew ancestors itself. The people will rediscover their ancient mother tongue by returning to their fatherland — a holy and indissoluble trilogy. From the moment he arrived in Jaffa he made a pledge to his wife to speak henceforth only Hebrew. He kept his word, and his son, who was born two years later became the first Jewish child in modern times to speak this language from his first children mumblings.

He met with the fierce opposition of the Jerusalem rabbis who regarded the profane, daily use of Hebrew as no less than a sacrilege. Eliezer Ben-Yehuda became a true martyr for the cause and his family with him, but he persevered and worked until his death on a dictionary which, when it was recently published, consisted of 17 volumes and more than eight thousand pages.

In 1921 the British mandatory government recognized Hebrew as one of the official languages of Palestine, together with Arabic and English. In 1904 a Hebrew Language Committee had been founded to determine the correct orthography of new words and to solve the grammatical and syntactical problems presented by the requirements of the 20th century. The Committee also published technical lexicons, such as a list of musical terms, one for road users and one for postal engineers.

One of the basic rules of the Committee was to remain close to the roots of the biblical language. This is relatively easy since Hebrew, like all semitic languages, is an "extendible" language.

Thus the concept "electricity" was discovered in one of the most obscure words in the Ezekiel theophanic vision! (The least one can say is that there is electricity in the air when God interferes...).

It will now be understood why we regard the rebirth of the Hebrew language as a phenomenon which surpasses by far any other linguistic experiment. In their effort to reconstruct their ancient language, the people of Israel were incessantly confronted with the books of the Bible. Nobody in Israel can claim to have a good command of Hebrew if he does not have an equally good command of the ancient biblical text...

This is doubtless still an additional aspect of the Divine pedagogy which is at work in Israel and which we will meet again and again in our discussion of the problem of the Bible itself.

In the remote past, a past of which the archeologists still hesitate to determine the precise date, a remarkable civilization, that of Sumer, had perished in the wake of events which the writer of Genesis sums up in the story of the Tower of Babel.

The unity of mankind was broken up at that time and men, swarming out into the then known world (and maybe beyond it, who knows?) entered into the era of division and distrust which was the consequence of the multiplication of languages.

Several millennia later men, women, and children coming from the four corners of the earth and speaking the languages of "the sixty-six nations," have gathered in the land of the Bible to speak there only one language: the language of the prophets, of Christ...

One must have participated in this fascinating experiment, in a language course in a kibbutz, to realize its prophetical implications. What do they have in common at the outset, these Jews from the United States, Romania, India, Argentine, Kabylie, to mention only a few? Very little, nothing but the mysterious and baffling fact that they all belong to the same people. They don't understand each other, their sociological and religious horizons have drifted apart during the centuries, if not the millenia.

They all find themselves together on the benches of the Hebrew school, studying the Hebrew alphabet. The Italian journalist with the elderly man from India, the French theologian with the young Jew from Kabylie. Where else on earth can one have such an experience? Or at what other time of history? This is truly a "Tower of Babel," not "inverted," in a different sense, a return to the sources from beyond the seas, from beyond civilizations, patterns of thought and ways of life, to become, once again, little children... a biblical virtue, an evangelical blessing.

And how many times does one or other child of Israel in these schools in a kibbutz, or in a seminary in the towns, on these school benches which are unlike any others, meet for the first time the Bible? The holy Book of his fathers, the Book so often forgotten and sometimes even forbidden...

Thus we have the following situation: grown-up people from every state of life, from all origins, are deciphering, in a democratic country, for the first time in their life the chapters about Creation and the visions of the prophets in which they may find and recognize themselves... And theirs is work of deciphering *par excellence,* for this is the original text!

Israel is the only country in the world where a whole generation of children is able to decipher *at first glance* the famous Dead Sea Scrolls...

Whoever can read the original text of the Hebrew Bible, even if it is only a little, whether he is a theologian or not, experiences the same emotion. Much more than from the Greek or Latin text, a strange power makes itself felt, the power, it seems, of *origin.*

If it is true that every human language is imbued with a spirit of its own, a breath which belongs to it alone, do we not feel behind the Hebrew letter a Spirit and a breath which come from elsewhere, which are part of Eternity?

This is what may furnish an explanation for this mystery of the Return from so many Babylons, of the assembly around a language which the Lord of History used to address His servants the Prophets...

KIBBUTZIM
(THE COMMUNAL LIFE)

The attempt at a communal life in the Land of Israel is an avant-garde experiment for all of mankind.

Martin Buber, *Zion als Ziel und Aufgabe*

When the first pioneers from Russia arrived in the promised land, it seemed as if the land had been promised to the desert, to swamps and malaria. Their spirit of sacrifice was not sufficient to counter-balance their lack of experience in agriculture and neither was the generous but ill-managed aid of Baron Edmond de Rothschild. Almost all of the first settlements ended in echec.

Under this system, farming for immediate profit had the advantage over farming for elementary subsistence. In most of the wine-growing centers the farmers had to buy vegetables for their daily living, and were entirely dependent on their harvest which was far in excess of the local needs.

The decisive turning point can be traced back to the first years of this century when the young pioneers ranked around the man who has remained the secular prophet of Israel's return to an entirely new type of agriculture based on solidly equalitarian principles. This secular saint was Gordon, who was already 50 years old when he settled in the country in 1904.

Subconsciously influneced by the teachings of Israel's prophets and their passionate call for social justice, and deeply affected by the doctrines of Rousseau, Dostoyevsky and, above all, Tolstoi. This is why this new form of communal life which suddenly sprang up in the promised land can appeal to the faith of Isaiah, the noble philosophy of "return to nature", to the two giants of Russian thought all in one breath. Unusual companions, as we see. But obviously nothing less would have been able to see of a moment which was to defeat malaria, the swamps and even the Negev...

Gordon incessantly repeated the same slogan: "Only cultivation of the land will bring about the regeneration of the Jewish people!" This work of cultivation, more than any law, more than any other duty, is the essence of the mysticism which unites man with the universe, a mysticism which guided the life of the people when it still lived in the land in biblical times. Gordon was wary of both the Marxist ideal and the classical socialist doctrines. The former had been corrupted by the concept of class struggle, the latter by party interests.

On the soil of their recovered, tormented land the Jews should build a new mankind, a new society whose members live from the work of their hands, a society without party interests, without class struggle, because the entire nation will live from the land and all classes will be united in the same cooperative village. A new class must be created.

Thus the first kibbutzim were born, and first among them Gordon's own kibbutz: Degania on the banks of the Jordan, where it leaves the Lake of Galilee.

Considering the fundamental selfishness of human nature, one can imagine the difficulties which Gordon and the other Kibbutz founders encountered. When people of common origin, of the same social background decide to live together in complete equality, the problems will be enormous. But when groups of people of all origins and all classes join together, it becomes an almost utopian venture.

It is certainly appropriate that the Jewish people, which for thousands of years was compelled by laws of the empire and the Church to become usurers and peddlers, should have given the world a lesson in humanity, brotherhood and equality at the beginning of the 20th century, the century of the machine, of sprawling towns and world wars...

Thus they rediscovered their original vocation, the vocation of the Patriarch, of the King-shepherd. If there is a science without conscience, it brings forth criminal industrialization. Against this soulless society the Jewish founders of communal life arose; in order to escape from the barbarity of our civilization they united and laid the foundations of a new mankind.

Let us ask this question: is such ambition, such a program, not clearly a reflextion of the messianic message of the prophets?

What the Bible calls the Kingdom of God, what is it, if not a civilization freed from the curse of money, from envy and hatred? Sure, we know — although Gordon's heroic pioneers certainly doubted it — that the Kingdom of God will not come through human hands alone. But it is man's task to prepare this Advent, this real Revolution. In this sense we agree that "God needs man."

It is also not by chance that the first foundations of this new life were laid in the land of Israel and not elsewhere. Since the moment that a man named Abraham took possession of it, this land, that was "set apart," witnessed a long range of rather unusual events and revolutionary experiments. On this soil God entered into a dialogue with His creation as once in the vanished Garden of Eden. Here the battles were waged in which the feeble forces of light defeated the strong powers of darkness. From this land went out to all men messages, calls and promises which are unlike any others. Here they were born whom popular tradition has always called "the giants of faith." Here, finally, appeared He who will be a light for all nations, and here a Kingdom will be established which will extend over the entire world, a Kingdom freed from the power of arms, from pride and Mammon...

Why does the Christian world not more clearly perceive that the Israeli experiment of communal life heralds with such power the coming of new, messianic times? Why does it not recognize that here is a promise for all men, for all nations which are engaged in discussions on the horrors of underdevelopment and famine?

One speaks of the crisis of the kibbutz, and it is true, there is a crisis. A crisis which is in the first place part of the Zionist crisis itself whose nature we have tried to define.

We are well aware of the fact that is not the social foundations, but the human heart that must be changed, if we eventually want to create a new mankind. That is why the kibbutz has experienced this crisis, this tension from the moment that the first kibbutz was founded.

During the last few years, as many kibbutzim began to prosper, this crisis has aggravated. Mammon, having invaded every domain of human life, is now threatening to seduce and poison the Israeli pioneers. But this is what may be expected in our human economy.

However, as long as there remains a stretch of desert that asks to be revived new kibbutzim will be established in the sand and on the rocks, to prepare the green paths of the Messiah.

Every human experiment is corrupted and fades in the course of time. The Zionist experiment and its noblest aspect, the new communal life, seem to become corrupted and to fade. But Israel is the people that cannot be suppressed, all the less when it is gathered in its own land. The Jewish people, even though it is going through a particularly dramatic spiritual crisis, has been promised that it shall be healed and finally reconciled; at the zenith of its daring venture and the zenith of this century and its conquests.

If Israel has suffered and hoped for the sake of all nations, in preparation of the first stages of the messianic times, in our days, at the hour of final Return and life in the kibbutz, Israel is still suffering and hoping in its threatened land for the sake of all nations, on its way to resurrection which leads it through the agonies that Christ himself has called the agonies of *confinement*.

The first Christians, almost all of them Jews, also tried to live a communal life, as we are told in the Acts of the Apostles.

Their experiment lasted only a few years. It failed for many reasons of which the most important seems to have been that the time was not yet ripe.

The laboratory test in the promised, recovered land which is called "kibbutz" has already lasted eighty years. New settlements are still being founded in the desert, young people are again abandoning a life of comfort in order to fulfill the ancient prophecies.

One marginal remark: the first kibbutzim were founded before the Russian revolution. They do not owe a thing to the Soviet kolkhoz in which membership is not voluntary and from which one can leave only with difficulty.

But it is an old story, the story of Goliath who would not accept David's lesson…

THE REVIVAL OF THE NEGEV

In the election of Israel the desert is the moment of purification the place of asceticism and recognition. In the desert Israel frees itself of the customs of the nations and becomes totally dependent on its God... Before its entry into the Holy Land this mystical renouncement prepares it for the knowledge of God which is preceded by God's knowledge of Israel: "I did know thee in the wilderness, in the land of great drought..." The silence of the desert is the condition for understanding which consists of listening...

Claude Tresmontant, *Essai sur la pensee hebraique*,

The barren triangle which constitutes more than half of the territory of the State of Israel was alive in the patriarchal epoch: Beersheva was an important oasis which Abraham had chosen as his dwelling place. The territory was alloted to one of the twelve tribes, the tribe of Simeon. Solomon, who operated the port of Eilat for his trade with the East, certainly developed this region with a network of roads, just as one of his successors, King Uzzia, did.

During the first centuries of the Christian era, the Nabataeans turned the Negev into an international link of communication, of which the impressive ruins of such cities as Shivta and Avdat are the silent witnesses.

It was only with the Arab conquest that the desert swept down upon this region to remain its master for more than a thousand years. At this point of time human life vanished from this vast region, so that the first Zionist pioneers were confronted with an extremely difficult task: they had to begin here from scratch.

We know that the small number of "Zionists" — a few tens of thousands — who returned from the Babylonian Captivity, was not sufficient to revive even the small territory of Judah alone, and that they had great difficulties in rebuilding Jerusalem and the Temple...

That is why the prophetical annunciation of the resurrection of the Negev waited in vain for its fulfilment. If there is one message in the Scriptures which is still awaiting its fulfilment it is this annunciation of a blossoming Negev!

The year 1943 marked the beginning of the fulfilment. Three advanced posts were then established by the Jewish Agency, in fact, three small laboratories to prove that in spite of the general scepticism it is possible to revive the desert, to demonstrate once again that the Bible "does not lie." Soundings were taken and water was discovered, too salty for drinking water, but suitable for irrigation. It was noticed that heavy rains fell in the desert and that it would be worthwhile to collect this water in a cistern and other reservoirs. The experiment promised to be exciting...

At this juncture the British authorities forbade the development of the Negev, which they wanted to render into a military base. Moreover, they were not very eager to see the Jewish pioneers install themselves there under their eyes, and thus enabling them to eventually claim that the Negev is part of the Israeli homeland...

Then, one night in 1946, eleven agricultural settlements were established on the sands. A 170-kilometer long pipe-line (consisting of pipes that had been used for fire extinction in London during the Blitz) carried water to these kibbutzim.

During the War of Independence in 1948, the 27 settlements in the Negev were turned into fortresses and helped save the new-born nation. A second pipe-line was installed in 1955 through which yearly 45 million cubic meters of water were conducted.

Beersheva, which had a few hundred inhabitants at the time of its liberation, has just passed the one hundred thousand and serves as the capital of the Negev.

Nowhere does one understand better why water is the symbol of life in the Bible than in the Negev. On it everything depends; on its inrush into the gates of the desert depends the conquest of this region which will make it possible for hundreds of thousands, if not millions, of immigrants to be absorbed. That is the future Israel is trying to build in this desolate land.

In 1953 the personal representative of President Eisenhower, Eric Johnson, submitted to the countries bordering on the Jordan a plan for development and irrigation with financial aid of the United States. After a long period of study, research and negotiations Lebanon, Syria, Jordan and Israel finally agreed. This was a spectacular event in the Middle East which might have led to a peaceful solution of the conflict between Israel and at least some of its Arab neighbors. However, at the conference of the Arab League in Cairo in October 1955, Nasser and his nazi advisors, who could not stand the idea of cooperation with Israel and of contributing to its prosperity, succeeded in convincing these Arab nations to withdraw their agreement...

Let the Arab countries themselves remain desolate deserts, if only Israel is destroyed.

Israel then announced that it, for one, would continue the work as if nothing had happened and made it a point of honor to declare that it would not use more than the quantity allotted it by the Johnson plan. Huge conducts, with tunnels and open canals were constructed. But it is certainly not merely good luck that water, such a highly valued element in the Bible and in particular in the Gospels, should be the reward for the resurrection of an entire desert which, as we have been, covers more than half of Israel's surface.[1]

Nobody who, with the books of the Prophets in his hand, has witnessed this, or has driven on the new roads through the Negev, the road to Sodom and that from Beersheva to the Red Sea (which Ben-Gurion in his inauguration speech called "our Suez Canal"), can have the slightest doubt.

1 We like to recall that it is the water of the Lake of the Gospels which revives the desert.

These are not merely human goals, but all these leveled hills, these roads breaking through the mountains, these hundreds of kilometers of water conducts are the tokens of another resurrection, of other harvests and other victories over human hunger and thirst which only the Messiah can allay.

One of the remarkable photos in Izis' photo book of Israel, namely that of the Sodom road under construction, has as its caption two quotations from the prophet Isaiah, which we deem it fit to reproduce here, because they show the fantastic efforts of the new Israel in their proper light:

> The Negev and the parched land shall be glad; And the desert shall rejoice and blossom as the rose. It shall blossom abundantly and rejoice, Even with joy and singing... For in the wilderness shall waters break out, and streams in the desert. And the parched land shall become a pool, and the thirsty grounds springs of water... And a highway shall be there, and a way, And it shall be called 'The way of holiness... And the ransomed of the Lord shall return, and come with singing unto Zion... Clear ye the way of the people! Cast up, cast up the highway, Gather out the stones! Lift up an ensign over the peoples... Say ye to the daughter of Zion: 'Behold, thy salvation cometh'
>
> (35:1, 2, 6,7, 8, 10 and 62:10–11)

It is just that not only man's heart of stone participates in the messianic venture, but the stones of Israel's desolate roads as well. Someone else said it in Jerusalem — it seems as if it were yesterday: "If you keep silent, the stones will shout aloud."

Together with the entire Creation, the burnt and cursed land of Sodom cries in great anguish for its redemption, in this hour of the H bomb (and others that are being prepared), which is, however, also the hour in which the children of Israel of our days are on their way from Sodom to Jerusalem, in spite of all the obstacles.

THE BIBLICAL REVIVAL

> *And as for me, this is My covenant with them, Saith the Lord; My Spirit that is upon thee, and My words which I have out in thy mouth, shall not depart out of thy mouth, nor out of the mouth of thy seed...*
>
> (Isaiah 59:21)

The links uniting Israel with the Bible can perhaps offer us the key to understanding what is conveniently called "the mystery of Israel."

The Christian world has too often been inclined to forget that the Hebrew Bible is not only the Holy Writ of the Jewish people, but also its *handbook of history.*

One may push aside a holy book (as the so-called Christian world has done with the Gospels) but it is impossible for a people to ignore its own history. Indeed, in this handbook of history, unlike in any other, Israel is incessantly confronted with the Lord of History. It is difficult to expurgate this text, as certain extreme leftists in Israel have realized. The books of Genesis or Exodus become entirely illegible and incomprehensible if the Divine presence is expurgated.

One has either to cling to this mysterious God, who is so near and at the same time so far, or turn the entire (biblical) past into a tabula rasa, which, of course, no people can do. A similar discovery can be made with every Jewish intellectual and scholar who is alienated from his Jewish sources. Through the Bible God holds on to His people.

In the course of the long centuries of Exile, the Bible was often forsaken and its place taken by science and talmudic tradition. What tradition has become for the Roman Catholic Church, the Talmud has become for the Synagogue.

Originally the Talmud was essentially a defense against a triumphant Christian society which had "annexed" the holy books of the Jewish people. According to the words of the great rabbis of the period, the building of the Talmud had to be erected on the ramparts of the Torah, as a protective fortress for the biblical text. The latter, however, "protected" by such an impressive building, became to a certain degree a dead letter in both the life of the people and the synagogue. Since the treasure itself was so well guarded, the most important thing was to ensure that the ramparts remained firm.

This is doubtless the reason that Israel has not experienced a Reform, that is, a rediscovery of the text, such as it had done to its benefit during the reign of its exemplary king Josiah. Continuously on the defense, the Synagogue could not but regard every movement of Reform as a lethal danger, a fatal breach in the talmudic walls.

This also explains why the Reform movement which sprang up in Germany and the United States in the previous century, have produced effects which are diametrically opposed to those of a genuine Reform. Whereas the Reformation was justified in defining itself as a return to the biblical sources, as a sudden rediscovery of the biblical text itself by the minor clergy and the people, the "reform" movements in the Synagogue became movements of *alienation* from these sources, not unlike Liberal Protestantism.

That was why the core of Jewish faith — messianic hope — was adulterated and reduced to mere humanism (of a very anglo-saxon type), which is obviously no longer relevant in this century of nuclear conflicts and gas chambers. One has to be an American to still believe that man is good by nature and that with his own hands he will establish the kingdom of peace and justice on earth...

This is not the kind of reform which the Israeli nation so badly needs;

what it needs is a true pilgrimage to its sources, and in its own way it is indeed making this pilgrimage.

Through their renewed contact with the land of the Bible, the Jews of Israel are beginning to rediscover the natural, physical and geographical sources of their faith. Sources which are incessantly being confirmed by archeological finds throughout the country, from the north to the south, from Dan to Eilat.

Let us recall the astonishing event which occurred when the State of Israel was born: almost simultaneously with the Proclamation of Independence, Professor Sukenik presented the Dead Sea Scrolls to his people. Scrolls which not only cast a bright light on the life of one specific, vital Jewish community, but also remind us — and how forcefully — of the physical and spiritual Jewish roots of the Church.

In Israel the Jewish religion has freed itself of its millenia-long defensive attitude. It has suddenly become the religion of state, although the ground had not been properly prepared. For the first time in 20 centuries *not to be a Jew* has become the abnormal situation.

At the same time, and as the result of an equally sudden metamorphosis after a long period of recession, everything not essential to this religion is threatened. Everything which is not the text itself, which does not belong to the time of the prophets, has become superfluous or simply outdated. This is what the overwhelming majority of the Israeli nation, and first and foremost the young generation, feels.

On the soil of Israel, the cradle of the Bible, it is inevitable that an extraordinary revival of this Book is taking place. We have already mentioned the three-fold thread Land-People-Book. This thread has its dangers, especially the danger of "nationalization" of the biblical writings to which certain politicians seem to be inclined.

But no-one can deny this reality: through its contact with the ancient fatherland the Jewish people is on its way to recovering the characteristics of its profound nature and to losing in the course of the same process the traits and qualities of exile and captivity. A new generation has arisen in Israel, very close to the generaton of the Maccabees and of David the shepherd. Through this same physical contact with the land the Bible has suddenly become more familiar, more alive, more a book for every day. As the preeminent Manual of History it has a central place in the country's schools. All the children of this nation not only read as a matter of course the biblical books in the original text, but learn entire chapters by heart. Indeed, this is playing with fire, the fire of Sinai...

For this is not a text like others. This history is not a history like others. The Spirit of One who is hidden breathes behind the ancient Hebrew characters, the Spirit of the God who has an appointment with this people in a land which is also not entirely like others...

It is quite natural that this nation organizes national and international Bible quizzes. It is quite natural that its chief builder, David Ben-Gurion, presided over a Bible-study group. It is quite natural that this Bible is taught at the new universities not in a theological faculty, but in the literary faculty... And it is equally natural that the prophets are being quoted daily, even in government reports and official leaflets, or that Israel reminds the nations of the world through its stamps that it is the people of the Bible and is well-aware and proud of it.

To our knowledge the prophets have been cited only once in the United Nations, namely when the Israeli representative took the chair in the debate on disarmament to declare that "the time will come when the nations shall turn their arms into instruments of peace..."

Thus the entire people, without being aware of it, prepares itself for the final Reform of Judaism. The religious parties and their sordid deals in the

Israel is a country where hunger and thirst for the Word of God are tremendous. but there are no prophets, neither in the parliament, nor in the government to proclaim the will of God.

But the old Book is there, in the heart of the people, in the schools and in the mouth of the children. This is a unique phenomenon among the nations, certainly among the nations which call themselves "Christian..."

Blessed the people whose children know the prophecies of Isaiah, Jeremiah, Amos and all the others by heart.

Blessed the people which assembles round the Word which is not a human, vain, ephemeral and misleading word.

It is on the straight way towards its spiritual renaissance, it has turned — without knowing it, and that is the wonder of Grace — towards the desert where the bush is still burning...

THE AID TO THE NEW NATIONS

In that day shall there be a highway out of Egypt to Assyria, and the Assyrian shall come into Egypt, and the Egyptian into Assyria; and the Egyptians shall worship with the Assyrians. In that day shall Israel be the third with Egypt and with Assyria, a blessing in the midst of the earth...

Isaiah 19:23–24

If one thinks of the small size and the vulnerability of the State of Israel, not to mention the many tremendous problems it has to face, its influence in Africa, Asia, the Pacific and Latin America becomes truly amazing.

In less than five years almost a thousand specialists were sent to some forty developing countries, Agronomists, doctors, educators, trade-union officials, technicians, economists, and businessmen brought practically overnight the name (and repute) of Israel to the Third World, whereas it had hitherto merely evoked biblical reminiscences...

When the new Israeli nation was born in 1948, it was one of the first in the Afro-Asian world to be confronted with the difficult problems presented by independence. Unlike its sisters which followed suit at an increasingly fast pace, it had been able to prepare itself for this confrontation during several decades. The Jewish population had actually not been submitted to long and cruel colonial exploitation, nor been systematically kept at the lowest possible intellectual level. Despite the inclinations of certain high-ranked officials and officers of the British Mandate, it had never been really possible to regard these Zionists as "natives."

In fact, since the last decade of the 19th century when the first Zionist pioneers arrived, an experiment had been in process in the midst of an Afro-Asian world which was left to itself, exploited, betrayed and abused. Without knowing it themselves, these first pioneers, the refugees of tsarist pogroms, had brought with them in their poor luggage a weak ray of light which was destined to become a great light for many nations that were not yet born...

This is probably why all the powers which were somehow interested in imposing the heavy weight of their wordly domination on this Afro-Asian world — in particular in the Middle East — joined hands to fight with every means at their disposal this Zionist penetration of their fiefdoms of exploitation, slavery and obscurantism. From this angle and in this perspective one may say that the officials and pashas of the Sultan linked up with the nazi advisors in Cairo via the functionaries of the War Office and the Colonial Office during the period of British rule over Palestine...

Only a few honest men, like Emir Feisal, understood and proclaimed that Zionism offered to the Arab world a unique chance of progress, sanity and recovered dignity. But alas, the voice of such genuine a statesman was not heeded and they were forced to surrender their command into the hands of corrupt adventures.

Notwithstanding the hostility of its Arab neighbors, the State of Israel started a laudible aid program in the hope that its closest neighbors would one day realize their short-sightedness and be cured of their hatred.

The following are only a few examples of such projects:

In the semi-arid region of Namsang in Burma Israeli experts laid the foundations for its conversion into agricultural land, and the results are already very encouraging. On land where rice culture is impossible because of the lack of water, sisal, sorghum and peanuts have been introduced, as well as dairy cattle breeding.

In Liberia an Israeli team of ophtalmologists has opened a clinic in Monrovia which has treated thirteen thousand patients within eighteen months. Other, similar clinics have already been opened in the country.

A similar project has already started in Tanganyka.

In the Republic of Central Africa, in other African countries and in Burma nuclei of kibbutzim have been established, an experiment which in the near future may offer an unequalled solution to the problem of agricultural and human development.

In Ghana the Israeli shipping company, in cooperation with the local government, has founded the "Black Star Line" and a nautical school in Accra to ensure the Line's future. After sufficient Ghanese sailors and officers have been trained, the Israeli teams (and their funds) will be withdrawn to avoid all suspicion that Israel wants to benefit from investments in a foreign country.

In Niger an Israeli building company is opening the country's roads, constructing public buildings and training personnel and cadre until it can withdraw and deliver the project into the hands of the Nigerian government.

This Israeli aid-programme does not operate in one direction alone: yearly impressive numbers of African and other trainees come to Israel for training and refresher courses. In 1958 the number of trainees was 137 from 26 countries, in 1962 1547 students from 77 countries participated in agricultural courses, courses for youth leaders, vocational training, administration, communal and cooperative settlements and academic courses.

In all the rapidly developing countries the role of women is of tremendous importance. Israel therefore organized in 1961 and experimental seminar for the promotion of the interests of women. Soon afterwards a permanent International Institute was founded.

An Afro-Asian Institute for vocational training and the training of trade-union leaders, sponsored by the Histadruth, the Israeli federation of trade unions, has been operating in Tel Aviv for several years. The far-sighted leading team of this Institute uses Arabic as its language.

Whereas the big powers — the United States and the Soviet Union — run the risk of being accused that they are trying to win over the young nations, to which they too extend aid, to one of the two rival camps and their ideologies, Israel's aid can in no way be qualified as "imperialism", not even in disguise. Three and a half million Israelis at the service of hundreds of millions Africans and Asians — the numbers speak for themselves.

Well aware that the world, in particular the western world, is inclined to make much of the infamous legend of "international Jewish finance," Israel, as we have seen, withdraws its funds as soon as the projects to which it gave its support can be handled by the country in question itself.

The Israeli aid is, of course, not entirely unselfish: the vote of so many young nations in the U.N. is needed from time to time to support Israel's case against the unbridled hostility of the Arab League and the veiled enmity of the community bloc. But why should the Israeli nation deprive itself of this help and not expect some form of recognition, which, moreover, does not cost these nations one single dollar.

Nasser also extended his aid to the Afro-Asian world, mainly in the form of arms, armed conspirators against his close or far neighbors and propaganda which can only be qualified as subversive.[1]

It can do no harm that this same Nasser encountered on his way a different kind of aid: of doctors, agronomists, masons and kindergarten teachers. Nor can it do harm that he hears in the United Nations the young and strong voice of Africa in support of Israel.

We have not forgotten that we call this chapter "The prophetical aspects of Israel," and we are well aware that some people may raise objections and say: "We don't see why Israel's aid to the developing world is so remarkable and more important than the aid extended by any other country; and we certainly don't see what is so prophetical about the Israeli trade union opening roads in Nigeria.

To this argument we would answer: "Don't you regard it as extraordinary that such a small country with a population of hardly more than three and a half million, which is threatened on all its borders, which faces enormous problems of human integration, which has to conquer a desert, has nevertheless decided to send hundreds of experts — whom it badly needs itself — to so many young nations in distress?"

"Allright," one might retort, "but what about these famous votes in the United Nations, which you have just mentioned? Don't they make up for such sacrifices and audacity?"

The answer to this aspect of the problem was already given at the beginning of this century, long before the existence of the Arab League, the United Nations or even the State of Israel, by a man named Herzl in his book "Altneuland", a book which we don't hesitate to qualify as prophetical:

> An additional problem of racial discrimination has not yet found its solution: a problem of which only a Jew can grasp the depth and horror. I refer to the African problem... After we have restored the dignity of our own people, we shall help Africa to restore its dignity.

Israel of our days tries to live up to these proud words, for it knows that few people used such language in 1902... Resounding from a period in which colonial exploitation was at its height, they have become hallowed marching orders for Israel now that the Third World has arisen as a giant on clay feet...

But there is even a more mystical element. For isn't Israel the people of the Patriarchs and Prophets? The world did not have to wait until the beginning of the twentieth century to hear a Jew give such marching orders. Was it not Jews who were the first in history to call for peace *and justice* more than 2500 years ago?

Don't we hear behind these six aspects the voice of these prophets and their eternal message?

We have seen, and we know, that God did not choose Israel from among

---

1 Egyptian pilots (flying Soviet Migs) bombed schools, hospitals and markets in Biafra.

all nations at a time in which the latter were the prey of their tyrants and the victims of regimes of servitude, merely for its own sake. No, Israel was chosen to be a light unto all nations. And until its fall at the hands of the Roman Colossus, Israel was indeed to a large extent such a light. Has not Israel during the centuries of Christian history which so painfully correspond with the centuries of Jewish suffering, in its own and profound way remained a light unto the nations? How many doctors, scholars, artists, poets, musicians, good and righteous men has it given to the world? How many has it given to Germany alone, even in the period that the abominable Hitler seized power in that country?

And how much light doesn't it radiate in our own days from the torn Middle East which is entirely in the hands of the powers of war and hate?

In this light every believer should see and comprehend the aid Israel extends to the young nations of the Third World, which are going up to Jerusalem, learning the Hebrew language and rediscovering the Bible at the source...

In this light every believer should see the revival of the Negev after so many centuries of negligence and death, for doesn't this Negev herald the time when all the deserts will blossom for the happiness of all men?

In this light every believer should study the Bible and its central place in the heart of the Israeli people and in the mouth of all its children. For is it not these children who herald the time in which the World of God shall be abundant on the entire earth as the water in the ocean and no-one shall teach his neighbor, for "all shall know the Lord?"

And should not every believer see in this light the communal life in Israel, in the kibbutz?

For does not the kibbutz herald the time in which all men shall live in equality and harmony, "every man under his vine and fig-trees?"

In this light every believer should regard the astonishing revival of the Hebrew language. For does not this language, spoken again by Jews from the four corners of the earth, herald the time in which men, all men, shall again understand each other because they speak the same language of the heart and the spirit?

And finally, it is in this light that every believer should see the Return of the exiles of Israel from the midst of so many nations. Indeed, from the midst of all the nations among whom Jews are living and have lived (and not merely the children of Judah and Benjamin, returning from Babylon alone in small numbers...). And does this final Return not herald the time of return of all mankind to the "House of the Father" where they shall all take an equal part in the blessings of the eternal Kingdom?

This (threatened) laboratory presented by the State of Israel is preparing in the land of the Prophets and of Christ the ways of the Messiah on which all nations will walk one day.

IV

THE CHURCH
IN THE ISRAELI NATION

It is the homeland of divine Oneness, of human Oneness. Its people have loved it as no other people have loved their country. They have carried it with them from place to place during twenty-five centuries, and then, breaking through the barrier between the impossible and the possible, they have brought it back today to the very place where it had been waiting for them wasting away in the clutches of death to be revived together with it. And just as multitudes once left it multitudes must now again go up to it.

Edmond Fleg, *Vers le monde qui vient*
p. 268

Isn't it remarkable that Zionism, the revivalist movement, the ecumenical movement and the charismatic movement in the churches are parallel developments? Is this not evidence that we are nearing "the end of days," the point which Christ has called "the times of the nations (Gentiles)"?

And doesn't the end of World War II in particular mark a decisive turning point in the long history of the Christian western world, and above all the beginning of an unprecedented crisis in the shadow of the gas chambers and the atom bombs...?

One may even discern in this movement the evangelical desire to gather the scattered herds into one flock which will be entrusted to the hands of the only Shepherd, on His return...

After so many centuries of ignorance, of rivalry and sometimes overt conflicts — *a period coinciding with the centuries of Israel's Exile* — it is one of the most gratifying facts — that the Christians are coming closer to each other.

The Church must now rediscover the Jewish people, and also the land of its origins. The Church feels that it is involved in a pilgrimage to the sources, that it is on the road to Damascus. It also feels that in its contact with Jerusalem and the new Israel the revival of the Hebrew language in its own midst, represents a salutary and invigorating Reform.

Paradoxically, in this era of rapprochement the Christians are nowhere more divided than in Jerusalem, nowhere is the competition of the church bells so scandalous as there. The "policy" with regard to the holy places has a great deal to do with it... Nothing is more disappointing than these basilics, churches and buildings whose ownership is contested by several denominations. Nothing is less encouraging for meditation, retreat and prayer. Not to mention the uncertain authenticity of these places most of which were arbitrarily identified by the mother of Constantine the Great, some three hundred years after the events related in the Gospels...

To complicate the situation even more, all the Churches have been amazingly hesitant with regard to the resurrection of the Jewish State, and the moves of the Vatican in many of the world's capitals in the years 1947–48 against the creation of a Jewish State are well known. Until this very day this oldest institution in the western world with its long political and diplomatic tradition has not recognized the state with its biblical name...

The lament of so many Christian dignitaries on the spot just before the birth of Israel, that the holy places had fallen "into Jewish hands", would have been comical, if it had not been so saddening, if we recall that it was not until June 1967 that every child of Abraham had free access to all these places, for the first time in history...

Indeed, one wonders what this policy (or rather this "business") of the holy places has to do with Christ and the Gospels. It is admittedly an instance of superstition and exploitation which are found in every religion, but this admission can hardly console the Christian...

It is a narrow and rocky road, this road on which the churches have begun to embark. A pilgrims' road towards the sources, in search of our roots of the first days of the Church.

One never forgets entirely the place of one's birth. The Church has never completely forgotten its place of birth. It has never entirely forgotten earthly Jerusalem.

It is always a serious matter for a community of God, as the old Psalm reminds us, to forget Jerusalem, the old Jewish mother of the Synagogue, but not of it alone...

If Christendom's right hand has withered away so often during the centuries, it was because the Church had broken its links with its matrix, because it had long neglected to nurture and cultivate its spiritual life from the Hebrew sources. For a too long time the Church has neglected the Prophets, the Book of Deuteronomy, and lost the prophetical concept of History of which Jerusalem will for ever remain the fulcrum.

For a long time the Church has courted the Caesars of this world and forgotten the sacred demands of Justice of which the people of Israel was the first trustee in History and which it continues to proclaim in the face of an indifferent world, even through the mouth of Anne Frank...

Isn't there a place in the world where the Christians can rediscover (not

1 ...or Moscow?

only meet) each other on common terrain, where nobody is the more or less patronizing host and nobody the more or less humble guest? A neutral place where all feel that they are summoned by a different Power...?

True, after so many centuries of a "policy of the holy places" there is little hope that the various churches and their "vaticans" will gracefully accept the amazing upheaval of the Six Day War.

During the twenty years of Jordanian desecration of synagogues, religious institutions and cemeteries of the Jewish religion in the Old City, none of the Christian dignitaries in Jerusalem raised his voice. On the other hand, we have all heard the cries of indignation at the slightest mistake of the Israeli regime.

Christ's prophecy of the return of ancient Jerusalem to the bossom of Israel was fulfilled in 1967. We might have expected that even these Christian dignitaries would greet this event with emotion and draw their healthy and necessary conclusions from it...

As long as the churches are indifferent to the sufferings of Jerusalem they will remain shamefully divided in this biblical, prophetical and messianic capital. Their testimony will be without effect, sterile — as it already is — to a degree that has never been reached yet. And let nobody here evoke the churches of silence, for these so-called churches of silence are the most courageous and vital of all.

There is only one real Church of silence in the world, a Church that is afraid to speak out: that of Jerusalem. And precisely this Church of united Jerusalem should have spoken and acted for the reconciliation of all the children of Abraham.

Every Reform is a new discovery of the origins, the sources, the texts, beyond tradition and dogmatics. The sources, origins and texts of the Church are Hebrew, beyond the domain of Graeco-Latin philosophy. It is precisely the rebirth of the State of Israel which has shown this clearly, if only through the renaissance of the Hebrew language.

The Gospels are themselves Greek "translations" of Jewish and Hebrew thought and theology; perhaps they are even translations in the literal sense of lost Aramaic and Hebrew texts. Israel reminds us of all this, sometimes forcefully, after so many centuries in which it was ignored.

The Church's wish to unite in order to be stronger, in order to be a more powerful voice in a world threatened by so many lethal perils is understandable. It seems wise to affirm the unity of faith and action in a world facing the colossus of communism and a Third World rather disgusted by Christianity. But if Christian unity is not in the first place inspired by the hope for a new aeon the work of the builders is in vain. If it is not inspired by the wish to entrust a brotherly flock to the hands of the Lord, and by the passionate expectation of the Parousia, the entire ecumenical edifice is built on sand.

A Christian world only apparently united has no message of hope for this century of agony and dispair. It will continue to sing the praise of Caesar, to bless all his conquests and acts of hubris, just as it has done since an artful Caesar gave it a place on the throne next to him. It will continue to regard itself as Caesar's permanent "train-bearer" rather than placing itself in front of him to show him the only way of the Lord, and, if necessary, to block his road!

In this era of the A bomb, at the dawn of the conquest of space, a conquest for conquest's sake alone inspired by human pride, at this juncture when two thirds of mankind are starving, the Church, like a foolish maiden erring in the darkness, preaches the Return of its Lord in places where the message is not heard.

In Rome, in Constantinople and in Geneva the Church is firmly established, rich and confident of its power. In Jerusalem, as in the time which the visionary of the Apocalyps has called the "time of His first love," the Church will feel again that it is poor and weak. Only there will it realize its false richess, its false security, its false hopes, and — let us say it — its errors.

In the heart of this world which belongs to the children of Abraham, in the midst of these divided and torn nations, the Church will be able to shake off its gilded mitres, the crucifixes which it has turned into jewels and the sonorous and idle titles which are just as many insults to Him who came to be the servant of all, even unto His death on a Roman cross. It will repent and humbly devote itself to the task of healing Jerusalem for the sake of all of Abraham's children.

Thus, in this new perspective, Jerusalem, too, will serve as a laboratory. The old Jewish mother is calling all her children.

The Church should not be surprised that Jerusalem is the capital of Israel, and least of all should it be irritated. It should rather rejoice and offer thanks to Heaven. The old Jewish mother, so long forgotten and so often betrayed, is calling her children from the four corners of the earth and in her call, let us not doubt it for one moment, is the breath of the Holy Spirit.

She gathers her children "as a hen gathered her chickens." She shows them the desert whose revival was foresaid by the prophets; she places the Bible in their hands. She has laid the foundations of a new way of life.

She calls her Christian children and is bewildered by their silence and indifference. Once again, as in the days of the apostolic origins, she speaks to them in Hebrew, for the cycle is closed and they must rediscover each other and themselves at the place where they were born, the place of their first unity. She offers them true holy places which were dead and are alive again; the ancient Scriptures, from Genesis to the vision on Patmos, in the letter and spirit of their origin, and, above all, the ancient messianic hope which had dramatically run dry in the course of the centuries.

She also calls her Arab children, for she knows that the day will come when the children of Jacob and the children of Esau will find each other in repentance and tears in the heart of this royal capital with which she has such mysterious ties.

This city which has heard and seen within its walls so many messages of justice and hope, so many prophets and finally Him who remains "the Light of the Nations," calls on all men, on all nations to go up to it in brotherly pilgrimage.

But isn't this voice calling from Jerusalem, the battered city, once again a voice calling in the desert?

Who among the mighty of this world is worried about the peace of this city whose name — sad irony — means "city of peace?"

How many among the dignitaries of the Church pray for Jerusalem and realize that only here men will rediscover each other, naked and humble?

Yes, isn't this voice of the old Jewish mother, surrounded by the remnant of her children after the murder of the six million in the heart of so-called christian Europe, the voice calling in the desert, the voice of the wounded man on the road from Jerusalem to Jericho which was ignored by the priests and the scholars...?

THE ESCHATOLOGICAL SIGNIFICANCE
OF ISRAEL

Behold, I will make Jerusalem a cup of staggering unto all the peoples round about... a stone of burden for all the peoples; All that burden themselves with it shall be sore wounded; And all the nations of the earth shall be gathered together against ... In that day shall the Lord defend the inhabitants of Jerusalem; And he that stubbleth among them at that day shall be as David; And the House of David shall be as a godlike being, as the Angel of the Lord before them... I will seek to destroy all the nations that come against Jerusalem

Zechariah 12

When the Son of Man comes in his glory and all the angels with him, he will sit in state on his throne, with all the nations gathered before him.

Jesus, in Matthew 25:31

From the first pages of this book we have seen that Zionism when seen from a biblical angle is obviously a theology of history. .

We have seen that the first promises of the Lord to his "friend" Abraham, linking the Jewish people forever to the promised land, derived their profound significance from a universal perspective in which all nations recognize that their own salvation is connected with this people and this land.

History is not the (Greek) succession of wars and civilizations in a continuous. monotonous and pessimistic cycle. Nor is it the tragic and inexorable process of estrangement from the Golden Age that was lost for ever.

The biblical vision is the only one that offers a satisfactory response to the enigma of human destiny. It offers us a concept of human history which pursues its course through a succession of horrible crimes, conflicts and cataclysms.

But this history is a process of *ripening* towards a point of such decay that it must be abruptly interrupted in order to prevent the total destruction of our planet.

The first Hebrew prophets already developed, in their own terminology, this concept of decay and in their writings the last phase of this process will invariably take place within the walls of Jerusalem. Not a celestial, but an entirely terrestrial Jerusalem with its stains and its sins, but heavy with messianic hope and ripe for repentance and the Return to its God.

As a reminder and illustration of the "atmosphere" of this vision of the last of days some of these prophetical texts follow here:

Joel:

> For behold, in those days, and in that time, When I shall bring back the captivity of Judah and Jerusalem, I will gather all nations, and will bring them down into the valley of Jehoshaphat; And I will enter into judgment with them where for My people and for My heritage Israel, whom they have scattered among the nations, AND DIVIDED MY LAND...

Micah: (4:1-3)

> And now many nations are assembled against thee, that say: "Let her be defiled, and let our eye gaze upon Zion." BUT THEY KNOW NOT THE THOUGHTS OF THE LORD, NEITHER UNDERSTAND THEY HIS COUNSEL...

> (4:11-12)

Zephania:

> Therefore wait ye for Me, saith the Lord, until the day that I rise up to the prey; For my determination is to gather the nations, that I may assemble the kingdoms, to pour upon them Mine indignation...

> (3:8)

Isaiah:

> They shall be ashamed, yea, confounded, all of them; They shall go in confusion together that are makers of idols. ISRAEL SHALL BE SAVED BY THE LORD WITH AN EVERLASTING SALVATION.

> (45:16-17)

Jeremiah:

> At that time they shall call Jerusalem The throne of the Lord; AND ALL THE NATIONS SHALL BE GATHERED UNTO IT, to the name of the Lord, to Jerusalem; neither shall they walk anymore after the stubborness of their evil heart.

> (3:17)

Ezekiel:

> Behold, I have spoken in My jealousy and in My fury, *because ye have borne the shame of the nations*; therefore thus saith the Lord God: "I have lifted up My hand: *Surely the nations that are round about you,* they shall bear their shame...

> (36:6-7)

Zechariah:

> Behold, I will make Jerusalem A CUP OF STAGGERING UNTO ALL THE PEOPLES ROUND ABOUT, and it shall come to pass in that day, that I will make Jerusalem a stone of burden for all the peoples; All that burden themselves with it shall be sore wounded; AND ALL THE NATIONS OF THE EARTH SHALL BE GATHERED TOGETHER AGAINST IT...
>
> (12:2–3)

It follows from these texts from the prophetical books that "in that day" a particularly explosive situation will prevail in the Middle East (all the exegetes agree that the expression "in that day" invariably refers to the end of days and the Parousia). On the one hand the promised land, promised to the children of Abraham for ever, will be divided and Jerusalem will be in mortal danger. On the other hand — and it is Micah to whom we owe this biblical truth — the nations will not understand at all the prophetical implications of this explosive situation. They cannot recognize in this ingathering of the Jews from all the countries of the world and in the division of the holy land the hand and judgment of God.

The best example of this blindness of the nations — apart from the confusion prevailing in the United Nations — is the leading contemporary historian Arnold Toynbee who dares to compare Zionism with nazism. How insulting can one get in one's blindness...

Zecharia casts an amazingly bright light on the efforts of the United Nations to find a solution of what they call in not very biblical terms "the Palestinian question." Because the nations are motivated by their own interests, because they are pawns in the hands of powers which will eventually crush them, and above all because they do not want to accept the biblical vision of History, they cannot but admit that they are powerless and confused in face of the Zionist venture which itself is the key to the divine mystery of History. To the nations Jerusalem is merely a capital city like many others (but they refuse nevertheless to recognize it *as the capital of Israel*, a strange attitude which needs no commentary if we confront it with these texts from the prophets!).

But it is incredible that the christian theologians themselves have fallen victim to this same blindness. What a cruel demonstration of their alienation from both the letter and the spirit of the Hebrew Bible, that they don't know anymore how to read the prophets, that they assign to these words of life a place in the remote past and condemn Israel to eternal exile, hypnotized as they are by the very partial return from Babylon in long past centuries!

They are there for them to see, these texts by which Christ himself was so deeply inspired, of which He was the very incarnation, texts which announce the division of the holy land, the agony of Jerusalem, the ingathering of all the children of Israel, the resurrection of the Negev, the rise of the Arab League and its nazi advisors, "in that day" — and they do not believe them...

They could come and witness the drama unfold itself *on the spot*, but they do not leave their academic chairs, at least not often enough...

They hear the stones of Judea cry out, they see Jerusalem being revived, but they remain doubtful and silent...

We know that there are many among them who accord to what they call "The Old Testament" a purely archaeological and philological significance. Let us therefore meet them on their own territory and open the New Testament again.

Christ, placing himself in the line of his predecessors the prophets with an appeal to some of Daniel's visions, and in the stream of apocalyptic literature, develops his own vision of History. It is easy to understand that this vision embarrasses the theologian Bultmann and the entire school of biblical criticism with him. The Jew Jesus of the Gospels is, after all, extremely embarrassing to some learned spirits... It is more dignified to sit at the feet of a Greek philosopher! Let us therefore leave these dissectors of the Bible to their "scientific" task, and return to our Hebrew Gospels and to the *"Eschatological discourse"* of the Jew Jesus, as the Jerusalem Bible calls it.

This sermon of Christ, which appears, with certain variations, in all the synoptic Gospels, contains the following themes:

I The beginning of suffering.

II The preaching of the Gospel to the world.

III The threat to Jerusalem and the defilement of the Sanctuary.

IV Cosmic troubles and the Parousia.

V The judgment of the nations (only in Matthew).

Let us analyse these successive phases of what we may call "the apocalyptic scenario."

THE BEGINNING OF SUFFERING

Let us begin with the remark that Jesus holds this speech in response to the question of the disciples, as related by Matthew: "What will be the signal for your coming and the end of the age?" This question immediately follows the announcement of the destruction of the Temple, and we may therefore assume that to the apostles' mind such an unprecedented tragedy could only be followed by the Parousia itself. History seems to them inconceivable if the Temple and Jerusalem are destroyed...

That is doubtless the reason for Jesus' warning against such a vision of History. The destruction of Jerusalem and the Temple heralds the beginning of a new era which before long will be revealed, because it is the era in which the Good Tidings will be announced to all nations.

In other words, the "missionary" era. But from a characteristically Hebrew angle it may also be called the time of birth pangs, *the time of Jacob's suffering.*

Since the sacrifice of Isaac, Jewish tradition had developed the concept of the birth pangs of the Redeemer. Had not the entire history of Israel, and in particular the period of captivity in Egypt, demonstrated that salvation and liberation are born in agony? Soon a new concept was grafted on this early notion, the concept of Jewish suffering for the sake of the nations. True, Israel itself is also a people of sinners — the Prophets leave no doubt about it — but at the same time its long martyrium assumes a mysteriously redeeming quality in that it will bring forth the Messiah.

In Jesus' days the suffering of the Jews had worsened considerably during the previous decennia and reached an almost unbearable degree which brought the messianic hope of the people to a paroxysm.

In spite of this extremely dramatic situation Jesus remained a realist with regard to his own time: he knew that a Jewish revolt against the Romans was doomed to end in a bloodbath. His prophesy of the coming of false messiahs is clearly an allusion to the heroic attempt of Bar-Kochba, exactly a hundred years later.

The Hebrew Good Tidings will not only be brought to Judea, Samaria and Galilee, but "to the end of the earth," and he had therefore no illusions.

THE GOSPEL PREACHED TO THE WORLD

With regard to this phase as well, things proved to be difficult and dramatic. Jesus does not conceal from his disciples that preaching the Gospel will entail suffering and blood, first of all in Jerusalem and the Promised Land. Those who plotted against the prophets — the scribes and the priests — will always be there and drag the first missionaries of the Gospel before their tribunals.

From the beginning of their ministry the Apostles knew that the early Church, if it remained true to its vocation of being a community of "the first love," would be remembered by history as the Church of Martyrs.

> Men of all nations will hate you for your allegiance to me.
>
> (Matthew 24 : 9)

We note that Jesus himself had no illusions about the conversion of the nations. Moreover, he did not give them an order to convert the whole world, but rather to preach and to serve. It was only with the rise of Constantine that that most fatal era for the Church was to begin, with its conversions by coercion and its persecution of the recalcitrant (in the first place the Jews, of course...).

It was good and natural that the Church wanted to convert the entire world, but this desire entirely spoiled the quality of its hope. It put itself in the place of the Holy Spirit and made conditions for the Parousia. Jesus, who had already asked the immensely sad question: "When the Son of Man comes, will he find faith on earth?" now makes this somber prophecy:

> ...and as lawlessness spreads men's love for one another will grow cold.
>
> (Matthew 24 : 12)

But his following statement which defines the exact limit of this time of the Church is not less categorical

> and then the End will come.

When all the nations have heard the Gospel, when they all have been confronted with its demands and no people on this earth can faithfully say: "We have never heard of this Jesus!" then the Parousia will take place. In other words, then the time of the nations will be fulfilled.

We know from Christ himself that there is another event which will mark the end of the time of the nations, in a manner that is very evident in History.

It is surprising that it is Luke and not Matthew, the most "Hebrew" evangelist, who mentions this extraordinary prophecy:

> And they shall fall by the edge of the sword, and shall be led captive into all nations: and Jerusalem shall be trodden down of the Gentiles, until the times of the Gentiles be fulfilled.
>
> (Luke 21:24)

Thus two parallel histories enfold in the course of the centuries: the history of the Jewish people dispersed among all nations, and the history of the Church propagating for better or for worse, often for worse, its faith. As long as the time of the Christian Missions last, the "captivity" of Israel will last as well, and its biblical capital Jerusalem will remain in the hands of the nations. But, to return again to this extraordinary prophecy of

Christ as reported by Luke: when the captivity of Israel among the nations has ended, when Jerusalem has again become the capital of the restored Jewish state, than will the time of the Nations, *the time of the Missions*, be fulfilled. That will be the sign that the Gospel has been *heard* (not accepted...) by all nations.

THE ABOMINATION IN THE SANCTUARY

Many exegetes and the majority of the theologians of the Church, misled by certain expressions in this eschatological discourse of Christ, regard the tragedy of the year 70 as the fulfilment of these prophecies. But in doing so they forget several important points.

Their mistake — among others — is that they fail to recognize Christ's vision of history. The same exegetes who attach an absolutely prophetical significance to the year 70, carry the fulfilment of what Jesus called "the abomination of desolation *of which Daniel spoke*" even further back into the past. These dissectors of the Holy Writ hold that the Book of Daniel has had no meaning for the Church (and consequently for Israel) since the reign of the Graeco-Syrian King Antiochus-Epiphanes — some 170 years *before Christ*!

Jesus however, in the three synoptic Gospels, and in particular in the Gospel according to Matthew (24:15) places this "defilation of the Sanctuary" in the future...

It is evident that the fall of Jerusalem and the Temple was such a tragic event in the history of the Jewish people that it has not entirely recovered from it till the present day. but this drama marked *the beginning*, not the end of the time of the Nations! That is why Jesus placed this mysterious sacreligious act and the unprecedented dangers that will threaten Jerusalem, the people of Israel and doubtless the entire world with them, in the far future. What happened in the terrible year 70 in the heart of David's city was but the general rehearsal of a much greater drama which will take place in the future. If this were not true why would Jesus have given this terrible warning:

> It will be a time of great distress; there has never been such a time from the beginning of the world until now, *and there will never be again...* And if that time were not cut short, no living thing could survive.
>
> (Matthew 24:21–22)

And the version of the Gospel according to Luke is even stronger:

> ...men will faint with terror *at the thought of all that is coming upon the world*; for the celestial powers will be shaken.
>
> (21:26)

Let us remember that the Roman armies which burnt Jerusalem never caused the Empire to suffer such horrors, but rather led to the malicious joy of Titus's trimphal procession and to the erection of the triumphal Arch which is still standing!

No abomination was introduced into the Sanctuary in the year 70 for the simple reason that the Temple was immediately set to fire and destroyed, and the vessels and other sacred objects — among them the great golden Menorah, the symbol of Divine Presence — were dragged through the streets of Rome... Nothing similar to the deed of Antiochus-Epiphanes who ordered to sacrifice a swine and thus provoked the heroic revolt of the Maccabee family, happened in 70.

At what then does Christ allude?

Obviously at the brief reign of him whom St. Paul called the Anti-Christ and whom he described as follows in the Second Epistle to the Thessalonians:

> That day cannot come before the final rebellion against God, when wickedness will be revealed in human form, the man doomed to perdition. He is the Enemy. He rises in his pride against all who bear the name of God, *and even taken his seat in the temple of God* claiming to be like God... but the Lord will destroy him with the breath of His mouth *and annihilate him by the radiance of His coming*
>
> (2:3, 8)

In other words: a man will one day enter the Temple compound and even the Holy of Holies, proclaim himself the master of all, the enemy of all "who bear the name of God."

We have said it earlier in this book: the Temple compound is actually in the hands of Islam, and the Dome of the Rock, a Sanctuary for the entire Islamic world, rises on the place of the Holy of Holies.

During the twenty years before the Six Day War it was from this same Dome of the Rock that regular calls for a holy war, for the destruction Israel were launched. And even today, after Jerusalem has witnessed the demolishing of the walls of shame, the same call is still launched in the sermons in this Mosque. Thus, from the very site of Israel's destroyed Sanctuary people are being incited to genocide. Isn't this a foreshadowing of the ultimate future abomination foretold by the prophets and by Christ Himself, that from the dwelling place of the God of Israel the preachers of the man of sin would urge the destruction of Israel?

A further precision: anti-Christ means anti-messianic as well as "anti-Jesus." If this man is hostile to the Christian world, he is just as hostile to Israel whose place is still, through the grace of God, at the heart of the messianic drama. It is because of this unique situation that Israel has so often been confronted with the threat of extermination. Satan has an interest in the destruction of this people which will bring forth the messianic times. That is why he has incited all the empires of antiquity agianst Israel. Everything was set into motion to prevent the Jewish people from giving birth to Jesus, including even the order of Herod to massacre the infants of Bethlehem...

211

Similarly, everything must be set in motion to prevent this people from gathering in the promised land (Hitler and Bevin in our days!), to prevent it from bringing forth the time of the Parousia.

One of the most unsettling verses from the Gospel of Matthew is the following:

> Wherever the corpse is, there the vultures will gather.
>
> (24:28)

Perhaps it is appropriate to recall here also Jesus' parable of the budding fig tree in which he referred, not to the exact day, but to the time of the Parousia.

We know that the fig tree is one of the biblical symbols of the Jewish people in its land. Like the vine which had been uprooted from its original soil for so many centuries but is flourishing again in the Holy Land, the budding fig tree in the parable of the Lord of the Church, heralds the ultimate and final Return of Israel.

And what a wretched corpse was this biblical land, so long abandoned and left to the beasts of the desert, the sands and the pestilent swamps! But as soon as this dried out skeleton showed the first signs of revival, as soon as the desert began to withdraw and the swamps to disappear the birds of prey of all around gathered as if they had been given the word: the killers of Mufti Husseini, the men of the Colonial office, the Imperial Bureau in Cairo, Rommel's Afrika Korps, the fleets and armies of Bevin, the politicians of the Arab League with their nazi advisors, and lately the Soviet power which has installed itself in Damascus and Tripoli. So many predators who all, each in his own way, have plotted and fought to destroy Zionism, to prevent for ever the revival of Israeli Jerusalem...

Another verse is sometimes quoted and much is made of it to minimize the significance of Jesus' eschatological discourse, or in other words to demonstrate that He erred, "a victim of Jewish myths" as Bultmann puts it. This is a dishonest interpretation of the Greek text of Matthew 24:34, which reads:

> Truly, I tell you this: *This people will not pass away* until all this happens...
>
> Heaven and earth will pass away; my words will never pass away.
>
> (24:35)

This would have been a bold expression in the mouth of any prophet, and only the Messiah Himself, who was from the Beginning, could allow Himself to use it. Thus the two realities which nothing can erase are united: the people of Israel and the Word of God...

Is it really coincidence that the resurrection of Israel exactly coincides with the tremendous scientific accomplishments in the field of nuclear research? It was not until the mid-twentieth century that the word of Christ which we have already quoted and which is reported by Luke alone, assumed its full significance:

> ...men will faint with terror at the thought of all that is coming upon the world; *for the celestial powers will be shaken.*

> (21:26)

This text speaks doubtless of a wave of suicides, or at least of unprecedented horror. Some people in the Christian world begin to have their doubts about man's encroachment on the terrain that is reserved to Divine authority alone, by his conquests of space, his nuclear experiments and his poisoning of the genetic roots of life. For never before Creation has so "groaned in all its parts as if in the pangs of childbirth," to use the words of Paul (Romans 8:22).

It is undeniable that man has begun to "shake the celestial powers." Nor can it be denied that a terrible agony is rapidly spreading throughout the world. When will the Church at last take to heart the words and warnings of its Master, launched more than nineteen hundred years ago?

Throughout the centuries many of the Bible have poked fun at the apocalyptic sections of the Prophets and the New Testament. The world had to wait until Hiroshima before the full meaning of these grave warnings was realized. Now that we are at last surrounded by this new terror every nation knows "what is threatening the world."

Within a few years man has become used to the revolutionary developments in space research. Henceforth nothing but the conquest of a new planet will excite him. We are talking of landing a man on Mars (the moon has already become a "suburb...") just as only a few decades ago people discussed the exploration of the earth.

Shouldn't we regard this fantastic development as a sign of the Lord's pedagogy, as His way to familiarize the human being with the world of "the celestial powers?"

The idea of Parousia about which so many refined spirits used to smile indulgently can no longer be regarded as part of "some biblical, Hebrew mythology." If man has only a few decades ago embarked on a conquest of the universe, why should the *opposite* movement be so chimerical? When Gagarin was sent into space for the first time a leading personality in the French Communist Party permitted herself to speak ironically about "the legend of that little Jew who ascended to heaven and whom nobody has ever seen again." With all due deference to Mrs. Thorez, this "little Jew" has made a much deeper impression than our cosmonauts imprisoned in the little cells of their monstrous space ships. He is of quite a different stature!

This conquest of space which has just begun has plunged our century into an orgy of pride, but we do not realize how limited man's movements still are, how unfree he is in his new space suit, how strongly he is still tried to the earth and its laws. And what is he going to do, this man in space? To try to create a new mankind, a new society? Or rather, driven by insane desire to arrive there before the competition of the other clan, to take a hold in space in order to dominate, to rule, to threaten and to fight? What are we going to bring to that world which the Bible calls "the dwellings of God," except our batteries, our weapons and hate? What will we accomplish there, except the expansion of our barbary and pride?

That is why we believe that the celestial powers are "shaken" by this intrusion of sinful men into a virginal world which has not been entrusted to their authority and genius, as the earth has been. The era of the sorcerer's apprentice which started with Hiroshima, and which is the time in which man can no longer control the results of his sorcery, will end, *exactly as in the days of the Tower of Babel* in the desire to 'take the place of God' in the entire universe.

For we do not sufficiently realize how monstrous this just begun conquest is in view of the fact that none of the acute problems of our own little planet have been solved. In view of the fact that bombs and guerillas still have the last word, that hunger and hatred prevail in two-thirds of the world. In view of the fact that within a few years China will be able to draw us into an apocalyptic conflict.

On the verge of the abyss, the nuclear sword over his head, man of the space age has found a fascinating, explosive toy and he is delirious with pride.

Because so many problems are unsolved, human foolishness is so great and the sorcerers' apprentices have caused such anarchy, the Lord has decided to return, for only He knows the antidote against the deadly poison which for first time has penetrated the vital parts of Creation.

The Prophet Daniel contemplated and announced, long ago, the Coming *on earth*, from the right hand of God, of this heavenly cosmonaut, unimpeded by monstruous, inhuman machines. Alas, it is not faith the Son of Man will find on our planet when He comes in power and glory, but a kingdom of pride in the clutches of fear. A world about to jump in the abyss, a society based on demonic arms, while hundreds of millions of poor slaves are hungry for bread and justice, in body and soul.

That is why it is not coincidence that the world of Hiroshima, of gas chambers and satanic forces is also the world of this little State of Israel which has embarked on the conquest of the desert, the search for a just society and whose children speak the language of the prophets.

Without really knowing it — and that is the wonder of Grace — it is preparing the paths and gardens of our Messiah. In the desert of the Nations it is the voice which, like that of the Baptist, calls for repentance, forgiveness and brotherhood. It continues to be the voice which cries out in the name of the innocent Martyrs who were burnt in the gas chambers of the "very-Christian" western world...

Its neighbors, supported by the great and mighty of this world, respond by piling up these same demonic weapons and by talking daily of wiping it from the face of the earth...

And that is why the Messiah, coming in glory, will not set foot in one of the boastful capitals of the "great", but rather on that hill he knows so well, where he so often prayed under peaceful olive trees.

To the world which refuses to greet Jerusalem as the capital of the new Israel, and to the Church which also does not recognize it as such, *the King of the Jews* shows that it is *his capital*, and the capital of the Kingdom of justice he will establish and impose on all nations, as both the Prophets and the Apostle have announced:

> And His feet shall stand in that day upon the mount of Olives, which is before Jerusalem on the east...
>
> (Zechariah 14:4)

> Men of Galilee, why stand there looking up into the sky? This Jesus, who has been taken away from you up to heaven, will come in the same way as you have seen him to.
>
> (Act 1:11)

This time of the Church, the time of the Missions which began with the Ascension and the descent of the Holy Spirit, is reaching its end. Notwithstanding the cruelty of men and the hostility of the Nations, Israel has rebuilt Jerusalem, opposite the City of David and the Wailing Wall, which has been recovered and transformed into a place of joy, for the time of wailing, which coincided exactly with the time of the Nations, has ended for Israel.

Men are looking up into the sky, not because they await their Redeemer, but to watch the passage of their metal capsules or the radiance of their nuclear conflicts; they are trembling and start hiding in their laughable subterranean shelters.

But another light will go up, not to exterminate them, but to save them. is the light of which Christ spoke in the Gospel according to Matthew, the light heralding his Return:

> Like lighting *from the East*, flashing as far as the west, will be the coming of the Son of Man.
>
> (24:27)

VI

A DEFINITION OF ZIONIST THEOLOGY

Both Christ and his servant Saul of Tarsus, the outstanding interpreter of the theology of the Church, link the destiny of the Christian community to that of Israel.

The history of the Jewish people is consequently part and parcel of the Church's doctrine and the key to its theology. Born in the land of Israel, forged in the Temple compound and developed in the synagogues of the Roman empire, the Church of Jesus of Nazareth marches side by side with the Synagogue throughout the centuries. At the end of this long march, as at its beginning, it encounters on this Jewish soil the children of Israel who have returned from the midst of the nations, and are facing Zion, facing the mount of Olives whose tremendous messianic and eschatological significance we know.

The theology of the Church is essentially a theology of Divine grace. Whenever the Church ceased to be anchored on the rock of this grace, its doctrine became a rigid dogmatic system which invariably led to such excesses as the trial of Jeanne d'Arc, the Inquisition and religious wars.

Since the days of the "first love" of the apostolic period the Church, instead of cultivating a theology of grace, has confronted its Jewish mother with a rigid dogmatic doctrine of contempt, of which some of the poisonous fruits are called auto-da-fe, yellow badge, ghetto and organized pogroms.

Instead of preaching that the death of Christ is also for Israel, the Church had preached that "the Jews killed Jesus" as if they were solely responsible, when actually God predetermined the death of His son to provide redemption for all. Instead of preaching that the blood of Christ can bring forgiveness to the Synagogue, by their actions Christians have excluded the Jewish people from salvation of the One who shed His blood for the redemption of all. Instead of preaching, like Paul, that God will forever keep His promises to His people it has taught throughout the centuries that God has rejected His people.

Instead of loving Israel, it has despised it.

Instead of showing to Israel the face of its King radiating love, the Church has shown it the horrible crucifixes on the stake and at the head of pogroms.

Through the gross and merciless judgments without appeal of the Church fathers, Luther and many, many theologians until our own days, the Church has paved, doubtless without intending to, the road towards the nazi persecutions.

Finally, when the Land of Israel and Jerusalem its capital were revived the Christian world and the Church refused to acknowledge the hand of God in these events, refused to recognize Jerusalem as the capital of the

State of Israel, the only state in the world which bears the Holy Name of God in its name...

All this was possible because the Church has forgotten that the Jewish people remains the focal point of the grace of God, that the whole bewildering and bloody history of Israel is no less than a theology of History itself. Zionism is nothing but *the passionate love of Zion*, from the Exile of Ezekiel until Herzl and Ben-Gurion.

The Church has too long been indifferent to peace and justice *on earth* as in heaven, concentrating on eternal, celestial salvation alone. But this is a Greek view of human life, not the biblical theology of the Kingdom. The commandment to fight for just peace is not only a commandment given by Moses and the Prophets, but it is the heart of Christ's prayer: "Thy Kingdom come on earth as in heaven!"

Entirely turned towards heaven — although its feet were firmly planted on earth and its worldy power — the Church has forgotten Jerusalem, which will remain the corner stone of the Divine policy until the coming of the messianic Kingdom on earth. In other words, the Church has forgotten Zion and, as the Psalm had predicted, "its right hand withered away", its hope ran dry. It does no longer await its Lord, it has become like the foolish maidens who did not find their way to the Bridegroom, because they had not taken with them sufficient oil for their lamps. It howls with the wolves of the century, it flatters Caesar and, too often, blesses his crusades and arms.

Consequently it no longer understands the destiny of Israel, is bewildered by the resurrection of Zion and shocked by the term "Zionist theology," although this ought to be its own theology, because it is the theology of Christ and St. Paul and not our personal invention.

On which foundations is this theology built?

On God's eternal faithfulness and His promises to the Patriarchs, to the Prophets, to King David *and to the Apostles.*

We have mentioned the Divine promises to the Patriarchs more than once and there is no need to do so again. We merely recall that these promises have nothing in common with those of politicians in an election campaign, but that this "treaty of Alliance" (for the covenant with Abraham is such a treaty) was signed for ever, unlike so many treaties in human history. When the nations sign a treaty or a pact of alliance they are always motivated by economic, military or political interests, which in turn are the products of either pride or fear. The fact that every treaty between nations includes military clauses condemns it to failure, sooner or later.

The Alliances God concludes with men do not include military clauses but are inspired by His love for all creatures. There are no "reservations" in His treaties.

God has chosen a certain people called Israel and a land called the Land of Israel for ever. No transgression by this people, no catastrophe in this land can nullify the Covenant. Let us listen to Isaiah:

Zion said: "The Lord hath forsaken me, And the Lord hath forgotten

me." Can a woman forget her sucking child, That she should not have
compassion on the son of her womb? yea, these may forget, *Yet will not
I forget thee*! Behold, I have graven thee upon the palms of My hands;
Thy walls are continually before me.

(49:14–16)

We are well aware that the traditional theology of the Church will
probably come with its sledgehammer argument: all these promises lost
their significance and validity with the coming of Christ whom Israel has
not recognized...

We shall ignore the fact that this way of thinking restricts God's love
and faithfulness, making them provisional on Israel's faithfulness.

Let us rather see whether there has been a moment in history in which
Israel presented the image of a community of "converted people!" We
would have to look a long time... Sacred History is a long succession of
human apostasy and revolt and of Divine forgivingness. Hardly liberated
from Egyptian bondage in a miraculous way, the people already grumbled
and complained to Moses. Hardly arrived in the promised land, the young
nation fell prey to Canaanite idolatry and to fraternal quarrels. Before long
they demanded a king of their own, so that they would be like the other
nations, a desire which is the preeminent sin. David became a tireless
warrior, Solomon a corrupt monarch and after him the schism became
inevitable.

At the depth of one of Israel's most serious crises the Prophet Elijah
believed to be alone and wished to be dead, not knowing that a faithful
remnant, known to God alone, had not bent its knees before the Baal...

Even if this remnant were to vanish, God would not revoke His
covenant of love, for He is like the mother who never ceases to love her
child. Such is the grace of the God of Israel. This is the cornerstone of
biblical theology.

Shouldn't we draw a profound lesson from the famous battle of Jacob in
that night at the ford of the Jabbok, the night in which his name was
changed into Israel...?

Was it merely for his own sake, or for his merits that he was allowed to
prevail and even blessed with an unprecedented blessing? Or are we rather
confronted with what is doubtless the most striking example of God's grace
in the entire history of Israel?

One may be surprised and even shocked by the manner in which this
strange battle is concluded, just as one may be shocked by the strange
judgment of God in the matter of the lentil broth. But if we are indeed
shocked it is only because our human nature — and perhaps our
theological inclinations — do not recognize the grace of God. For our
reason and God's grace are fundamentally opposed. We always expect
and demand that virtue be rewarded and vice punished, taking it for
granted that we belong to the virtuous and are entitled to determine who is
not...

And doesn't the history of the Church teach us the same lesson?

Where do we find the pure Church without sin? Isn't the history of the

Church, like that of Israel, one continuous manifestation of God's grace which persists notwithstanding the transgressions of His children?

How outrageous is this habit of the Church, itself so guilty, of judging other human communities! How distressing is this Christian insistence on the Israel's exclusion from the continued purposes of God!

Thus what we call Zionist theology is but one of the possible names for God's love of Israel. Since Zionism is linked to this people and its martyrdom and to the resurrection of the promised land, it must be seen in the context of Grace. In this blood-stained 20th century it demonstrates that God has not abandoned His Jewish children. It is the answer of the Lord of History to the gas chambers of the nations. Of course, we have said it before Zionism is also a matter of political implications and diplomatic games — but since when has God been afraid to associate Himself with human politics? If God does not hesitate to use men of flesh and blood like Samson and Gideon and even *to take their side,* why should He hesitate to use men like Herzl, Weizmann, Ben-Gurion and Dayan whose character and education are certainly superior to those of Delilah's partner?

If God guides history, it is inevitable that He mixes His own policy of love is "tarnished" by the interests and stratagems of the petty lords of the nations. Is this not the astonishing lesson of the Incarnation?

We see it: a theology of Love. But also a theology of History. And it is clear that from the moment that a certain tyrant named Constantine raised Christianity to the rank of religion of state (and instrument of his imperialist policy), the Church ceased to understand History and in particular its own role in History.

Once hunted and persecuted, maltreated by history, the Church now became itself the servant of history. The same Church which once had been an outcast, now found itself next to the throne of Caesar, the *maker* of history! It was inevitable that it, too, began to seek ways of making and guiding history, through laws and arms...

Installed in the seats of power, loaded with honors and wealth, what else would it hope for than the continuation of the status quo? Soon it got into the habit of choosing and crowning kings, abandoning its own King on the Roman cross and forgetting, or trying to forget, that He will come again one day to judge and to call the Church to account!

Soon it began to believe that everything is possible, and that it is its right to forcibly "convert" the nations. Thus it confused the outrageous justice of men with the justice of God, turning the peace of the Kingdom into the armed and shameful peace of the nations. At the height of the era of nuclear threats and ideological struggles which divide the nations, confronted with a wounded, divided and misunderstood Jerusalem, the Church no longer knows exactly to whom it should pledge allegiance. Caught in the trap of its flirting with Caesar it has payed for this insane alliance the price of its Hope. Neither its popes, nor its princes, bishops and Councils proclaim to the world that only the Parousia will cure mankind of its diseases.

It is true that God's sovereign rule of History is manifest in mysterious ways which can be seen by Faith alone. This mystery of the policy of God is nowhere in the Bible better expressed than in the renewed and precise Divine promises which the Prophet Nathan conveys to King David:

> I will make thee a great name, like unto the name of the great ones that are on earth. And I will appoint a place for My people Israel, and will plant them, that they may dwell in their own place, and be disquieted no more; neither shall the children of wickedness afflict them any more... I will set up thy seed after thee, that shall proceed out of thy body, and I will establish his kingdom... *And thy House and thy kingdom shall be made sure for ever before thee*; thy throne shall be established for ever.
>
> (2 Samuel 7:9, 10, 12, 16)

If we remember that after the death of David's son Solomon Israel was split up into two kingdoms, that the northern kingdom of Israel ceased to exist in 722 B.C., and the kingdom of Judah less than two centuries later, these promises to the House of David sound rather cynical!

At the time that Jesus appeared among his people, the throne of David was occupied by a cruel Idumean named Herod who had no relation whatsoever with the house of David! Rome was already the real master of the country...

But the Church believes that the authentic royal title was vested in this Jesus, *and that it is vested in him for ever*, beyond the great Exile and the great martyrdom of Israel... That is why Jesus, confronted with Caesar's representative Pilate, places His Kingdom in another dimension, *beyond time.*

In Jesus, and in Him alone, this extraordinary and bewildering promise to David, obtains its real meaning. A meaning which has *not yet* become manifest in History, but remains of a prophetical and messianic nature.

The powers that be do not recognize this Kingdom, and the Church has often made it into a caricature by assuming itself the role of Christ.

But other powers, which are not of this world, and beyond our understanding, have recognized it from the Beginning. This crucified Jew whom the Churches continue to crucify in their sanctuaries, remains the Prince of the House of David. The hour of his reign on earth has not yet struck, and His Kingship is still hidden, *but it does exist.*

It is not merely a Liberator who will be given to the Synagogue at the time of the Parousia, but a King, its own King. Listen to the words of the prophet Ezekiel in the rebuilt and dedicated Temple:

> Afterward he brought me to the gate that looketh toward the east. And behold, the glory of the God of Israel came from the way of the east... And the glory of the Lord came into the House by the way of the gate whose prospect is toward the east... And I heard one speaking unto me out of the House: Son of Man, this is the place of My throne, *and the place of the soles of My feet*, where I will dwell in the midst of the children of Israel for ever...
>
> (43:1, 4, 7)

With the arrival of the first Zionist pioneers a movement started which no power in the world can halt, which nothing can destroy, we are certain of that while we are writing these lines in new Jerusalem, in the midst of this people which is returning from the four corners of the world...

During the centuries of the great Exile the Jewish people remained the focal point of History, though in a hidden manner. But since the days of their Return, and in particular since the day of their recovered independence they have presented themselves to the nations and the Christian world under conditions which are exactly the same as those that prevailed in the biblical period of independence.

Indeed, they have experienced a second Exodus, they have escaped the web of their torturers, they are rebuilding the ruins and the biblical cities. They have reassembled around a common language and a rediscovered Bible in the land of their origin. They are still being threatened on all their borders, caught between two rival ideologies. A new pharaoh has appeared on their way threatening their final extermination (once again!).

Isn't this the same Sacred History, the same history *set apart?* This history which no classical handbook has yet analysed, and which laughs at the professors of history!

Isn't this the same Divine pedagogy which compels Israel, surrounded by enemies, to close its ranks with one hand on the load and a weapon in the other...?

Isn't this the same faithfulness of God who does not forget one of His children, let alone His first-born who bears the name Israel?

A theology of Grace and a theology of History, but also and finally, a theology of the Incarnation.

This is a truth which the Church can understand and accept, because it has sprung from Incarnation, but which is outrageous and foolish to the learned and the philosophers.

Through the Incarnation God has joined men on their own level, in their humility and misery. he has entered History personally, physically as it were. But wasn't this Incarnation, which became manifest in a Christmas night in Bethlehem, the town of David, always latently present in the Hebrew Bible, from its first pages, from the moment in which the Lord engaged in a dialogue with His creation, a dialogue of love and forgivingness? Was it not manifest in His pact of friendship with Abraham and his descendants? And did it not always remain latently present from this crucial moment is Sacred History onward — in the cloud and the pillar of fire of the first Exodus, in the simple Tabernacle in the desert and then in the sanctuary in Jerusalem? And not less mysteriously, did it not even remain present "in spirit and truth" in the lands of exile, without Temple, priests and sacrifices...?

The Church was in fact already presented and alive when the Apostle Paul, in his Epistle to the Romans, wrote the following remarkable words, of which the Church has forgotten the real significance:

221

I am speaking the truth in Christ... for I could even pray to be outcast...
for the sake of my brothers, my natural kinsfold who are Israelites: *they
were made God's sons*; theirs is the splendour of the divine presence,
theirs the covenants, the Torah, the worship and the promises. Theirs
are the Patriarchs, and from them, in natural descent, sprang the
Messiah.

(9:1–5)

Israel evidently is and will remain for ever the people of the Incarnation.
For ever elected (an election which has brought it more suffering than
happiness...) it is the trustee of Divine Presence. It is bound up with God
through the threefold thread of the promises, the Scriptures and the
Messiah Himself. Nothing that happens to it in its history can be detached
from this policy of salvation, which is the policy of the Kingdom. The
Divine promises and covenants link it forever to this land of which
Jerusalem is the capital; how can we then fail to understand that the
Zionist epic is at the center of this policy of the Kingdom of peace and
justice on earth as in heaven?

Through the Bible Israel remains forever linked with the will of God;
how can we then exclude it from His grace?

Through the Messiah it will always be at the center of every movement
yearning for temporal and spiritual redemption; how can we then fail to see
that its place is at the center of the stream which leads to the Parousia, to
acknowledge its pivotal in the world? How can we disbelieve St. Paul when
he sums up this series of extraordinary privileges in these words:

and from their midst the Lord will appear in His glory!

After Titus and his legions of destruction, after the edicts of contempt
and hate of a "Christian" empire, after the autos-da-fe and the pogroms,
after Auschwitz and the miraculous rebirth in 1948 — is there a better and
clearer manifestation of the grace of God than this Zionist epic which is
still in progress?

*   *   *

Has there ever been a more convincing proof of God's sovereign reign of
history?

*   *   *

Has there ever been a clearer announcement of the Parousia (The
Second Coming)?

*   *   *

A theology of Grace, of guided history, of the Kingdom that will come
— this, it seems to us, is what Zionism stands for if we see it in the light of
the Holy Scriptures.

To show this was the aim of our work, out of love for Israel, in the service of the Church, for the passion of Christ and the glory of God alone.

This then should be the only prayer of the two chosen communities: Israel and the Community of Jesus.

If they will lift up this supplication to our common God, I am certain, by the turn of our century with the spread of terrible catalysm, God will have mercy on us all.

For it is not only the fact that the nations do not repent which is an obstacle on the path towards immediate salvation, but also the torpor of Christendom gone astray. For aren't so many Christians gratifying themselves with the pious certitude of their "personal salvation" while the world may rush to its destruction? The main thing to them is that they, they alone, be saved...

The time has come to take to heart the fate and the temporal salvation of the millions on earth who live in misery and desperation without a shepherd. The time has come for us to cry out to our common God, in communion with the Psalmist:

Rend the heavens, O our God and give us Thy salvation!

BIBLIOGRAPHY

BAECK, LEO	The Essence of Judaism. Shocken, New York, 1984.
BEN-GURION, D.	Rebirth and Destiny of Israel, New York, 1954.
BERDIAEV	The End of Our Time, Sheed & Ward, New York 1933; The Fate of man in the Modern World, Morehouse, 1935; Toward a New Epoch, Geoffrey Bles, London, 1949; The Meaning of History, Scribner, New York, 1936.
BUBER, MARTIN	Israel and Palestine, East and West Library, 1952; Zion als Ziel und Aufgabe, Berlin, 1936; Toward Union in Palestine, Jerusalem, 1947; Das Kommende, Berlin, 1932.
CHASLES, R.	Israel et les nations. Edition Patmos, 1960.
CHOURAQUI, A.	Herzl. Seuil, Paris, 1960; L'Etat d'Israel. P.U.F. (Que sais-je?).
COHEN, A.	Everyman's Talmud. Dent & Sons, London, 1932.
COHEN, I.	History of Zionism. Miller, London, 1951.
CRUM, BARTLEY	Behind the Silken Curtain. Simon & Schuster, 1947.
DAVIES, W.-D.	Paul and Rabbinic Judaism. Lutterworth Press, 1949.
DENTON R.-C.	The Idea of History in the Ancient Near-East, Yale 5.
EDERSHEIM	The Laws and Polity of the Jews. London.
EINSTEIN A.	About Zionism, Speeches and Letters, 1931.
FINKELSTEIN L.	The Pharisees. J.P.S.A. Philadelphia, 1946.
FLEG EDMOND	Vers le monde qui vient. Albin Michel, 1960; Jésus raconté par le Juif-errant. Albin Michel, 1953; Anthologie juive. Sulliver, Paris, 1951.
GILBERT G.-M.	Nuremberg Diary. London, 1948.
GILLET, LEV.	Communion in the Messiah. Lutterworth Press, 1942.
GUINESS Gr.	The Divine Program of the World History. Hodder & Stoughton, 1889.
HAY, MALCOLM	Europe and the Jews. Beacon Press, 1960.
HERTZBERG, A.	The Zionist Idea. Doubleday, New York, 1959.
HERZL TH.	The Jewish State. 1896; Altneuland. Haifa Publishing Co., 1960; Tagebuecher. Juedischer Verlag, Berlin, 1922.
HESS MOSES	Rome and Jerusalem. Bloch, New York, 1918.
HUDGINGS, FR.	Zionism and Prophecy, New York, 1936.
ISAAC JULES	Jésus et Israel. Fasquelle, 1959; Genèse de l'antisémitisme. Calman-Levy, 1956; L'enseignement du mépris. Fasquelle, 1962.